GLOBAL INFORMATION SOCIETY

Human Geography in the Twenty-First Century

Issues and Applications

Series Editor
Barney Warf, University of Kansas

Human geography is increasingly focused on real-world problems. Applying geographic concepts to current global concerns, this series focuses on the urgent issues confronting us as we move into the new century. Designed for university-level geography and related multidisciplinary courses such as area studies, global issues, and development, these textbooks are richly illustrated and include suggestions for linking to related Internet resources. The series aims to help students to better understand, integrate, and apply common themes and linkages in the social and physical sciences and in the humanities, and, by doing so, to become more effective problem solvers in the challenging world they will face.

Titles in the Series

GLOBAL INFORMATION SOCIETY
Technology, Knowledge, and Mobility

Mark I. Wilson, Aharon Kellerman,
and Kenneth E. Corey

ROWMAN & LITTLEFIELD PUBLISHERS, INC.
Lanham • Boulder • New York • Toronto • Plymouth, UK

Published by Rowman & Littlefield Publishers, Inc.
A wholly owned subsidiary of The Rowman & Littlefield Publishing Group, Inc.
4501 Forbes Boulevard, Suite 200, Lanham, Maryland 20706
www.rowman.com

10 Thornbury Road, Plymouth PL6 7PP, United Kingdom

British Library Cataloguing in Publication Information Available

Library of Congress Cataloging-in-Publication Data

Wilson, Mark I.
  Global information society : technology, knowledge, and mobility / Mark I. Wilson, Aharon Kellerman, and Kenneth E. Corey.
    pages cm. — (Human geography in the twenty-first century. Issues and applications)
  Includes bibliographical references and index.
  ISBN 978-0-7425-5693-5 (cloth : alk. paper) — ISBN 978-0-7425-5694-2 (pbk. : alk. paper) — ISBN 978-1-4422-2148-2 (electronic) 1. Information technology—Economic aspects. 2. Information technology—Social aspects. 3. Information society. 4. Knowledge management I. Kellerman, Aharon. II. Corey, Kenneth E. III. Title.
  HC79.I55W566 2013
  303.48'33—dc23

                                                              2013000540

♾™ The paper used in this publication meets the minimum requirements of American National Standard for Information Sciences—Permanence of Paper for Printed Library Materials, ANSI/NISO Z39.48-1992.

Printed in the United States of America

Contents

Part IV: Support Section

Preface

THE WORLD HAS UNDERGONE a major transition in becoming a global information society. This process has been complex and multifaceted, with special geographical dimensions not yet treated systematically. Furthermore, the topic is being taught under various disciplines without a proper text that students can consult.

As a result, we are pleased to have this opportunity to share with readers our collective lifetimes of research, travel, and observation about the global information society and knowledge economy. The three of us have been fortunate to have had these experiences. Further, we have been fortunate to have had these opportunities and experiences early in the evolution of information technology–based development around the global economy. Many of these early and longer-term reflections and researches have been captured and documented in our previous books.[1]

This book on the global information society represents our current perceptions and thinking about some of the issues that have been spawned by information and communications technologies and the concomitant deluge of information that has inundated the globalized society. The diverse multimedia flood of information that has resulted has in turn compelled us to reflect on some of these recent forces and dynamics that have captured our attention and concerns.

In many places around the world over the last several generations, civil society seems to have become less active. In an era of more information that is widely available and facilitated by increasingly pervasive information and communications technologies, it would seem that the current generation has a great deal of opportunity to reactivate civil society. For those who subscribe to or are inclined to be supportive of societal engagement using information to contribute to the public good and the diverse interests of the commons, the potential is there for such people to strengthen civil society. This book was prepared with such persons in mind, with the intention that information might be harnessed routinely to inform policy making and other societal decision making.

The knowledge shared here is intended both to improve *understanding* of the global information society and also to empower individuals to use this knowledge to *create* new and better futures for regions and localities world-wide. In particular, the current generation of younger citizens, businesspersons, and those in public service are encouraged to engage information and practice intelligent development. This is the generation that has grown up in an information-rich environment. This is also the cohort of the world's population that is comfortable with using and experimenting with diverse and ever-changing digital technologies. This is the first generation that was born and prepared to sort through and be positioned to selectively use this global-ized information and to mobilize it by means of near-ubiquitous information and communications technologies.

This approach has been formulated through our empirical work and inter-action around the global society with citizen volunteers, professional prac-titioners, and students at all levels. This is the rich body of diverse learners from which we have derived our approach to intelligent development—and it is also the diverse range of audience and readership for which this book has been prepared. We have learned that lower-division undergraduate students, especially in small-group settings, can master this hands-on learning-by-doing approach; the learner need not necessarily be a graduate student or otherwise highly educated. To illustrate, bright, committed, and disciplined adults who are competent to vote in a national election or to serve in a na-tion's military have demonstrated that they can use intelligent development frameworks to strategize better development futures for city-regions and other subnational regions. Simply put, the content and processes that are explicated in the book are for those who seek to function effectively in, and contribute to, the betterment of their parts of the global information society.

Limited space here does not permit a glossary of terms. Even if we were able to provide such support, we would not. This is an era of easy electronic access to search engines and endless browsing. As readers come upon unfa-miliar words and phrases, they should dig in the nooks and corners of cyber-space and derive the information needed to form a working understanding of the issues under discussion. Many suggestions in this book assume motivation and curiosity sufficient to engage in self-driven learning and exploration. Active engagement is expected.

Development practice throughout much of the global information society is led by persons and institutions that predate the digital generation. In order to enrich the debate and hasten needed policy change, local and regional society needs the participation and creativity of more members of the digital generation. It is our hope that this book might contribute to the engagement of members of this and all other generations with interests and stakes in imaginative intelligent development. Toward this end, this book points the reader to the general direction of intelligent development; it is up to the reader to intersect these understandings with the current empirical realities of his or her region in order to contribute to the creation of specific pathways to the destination of better future realities for the region.

Aharon Kellerman
University of Haifa
Haifa, Israel

Mark I. Wilson and
Kenneth E. Corey
Michigan State University
East Lansing, Michigan, USA

Note

1. Kellerman (1993; 2002b; 2006b; 2012); Wilson and Corey (2000); Corey and Wilson (2006)

Acknowledgments

A S DIGITAL IMMIGRANTS TO the information society, we greatly enjoyed learning more about the technology and geography of our subject. In addition to our own research interests, we also learned from our colleagues in the International Geographical Union's Commission on the Geography of Global Information Society. The collegial meetings of the commission provided the perfect environment for the exchange of ideas and perspectives.

Much of the work that informed and inspired the policy analysis and the policy planning material must be attributed to the Center for Community and Economic Development (CCED), Michigan State University (MSU). Director Rex LaMore and the center's staff of faculty and students have contributed importantly to the translation of development research into intelligent development practice. We thank also CCED's rural regional practitioner partners for engaging us, thereby enabling us to actualize this translational research and practice, and for operationalizing the intelligent development concept. These practitioner partners included the staff and officials of Eastern Upper Peninsula Regional Planning & Development Commission, Northeast Michigan Council of Governments, East Michigan Council of Governments, and Northwest Michigan Council of Governments. Our appreciation extends further to the U.S. Economic Development Administration, especially the Chicago Regional Office, for the ongoing grant funding to CCED that assisted these development practice opportunities.

The book benefited immeasurably from the research and feedback contributions of our MSU undergraduate Asia-Pacific course students who were supported with grant funding from MSU's Provost's Undergraduate

Research Initiative (PURI) and from MSU Honors College's Honors Students Research Program. These students included Anesah Mohsin Elhaddi, Anastasia Danielle Eby, Timothy James Smalley, Marissa C. Wahl, and Sarah Elizabeth Aldrich.

Our MSU Department of Geography master's degree student and graduate, Josh Watkins, contributed valuable editorial and substantive improvements to early drafts of the book manuscript. We are grateful for his insightful and fresh perspectives. Also, our thanks to Urban Planning student Eric Phillips for preparing the maps for this book.

We thank MSU Emeritus Professor Jack Williams for his wise advice and counsel on potential publishers for a book concept focused on the global information society.

Our thanks to Rowman & Littlefield and senior acquisitions editor Susan McEachern, associate editor Carrie Broadwell-Tkach, and the production team of Jehanne Schweitzer, Matt Evans, Rhonda Baker, and Rae-Ann Goodwin.

Dedications

The three of us owe a debt that can never be repaid to our spouses and families for their support, both direct and indirect, that has permitted and encouraged us to conceive and to complete this book. Thank you.

From Kenneth E. Corey to Marie Corey, Kenneth Corey (Sr.), Jeff Corey, Jennifer Mann, Paul Mann, and granddaughter Maddie Mann.

From Aharon Kellerman to his grandchildren: Zohar-Ruth, Eitan-Avraham, Malachi-Menachem, and Tal-Zvi.

From Mark Wilson to his family: Lisa Robinson, Andrew Wilson, and Kate Wilson.

I

ORGANIZATION AND THEMES OF THE GLOBAL INFORMATION SOCIETY

1

Introduction

INFORMATION SOCIETY, and related terms such as the *knowledge economy* and *network society*, is a term frequently used to explain the current status of our lives. The use of such terms reflects a need to understand the circumstances and changes we witness daily in the way we live, work, socialize, and find context and meaning for our actions. On one hand, the information age is represented as the next new thing, as a way of capturing a significant shift in the way the world functions. On the other hand, it is the arrogance of the present to ignore the fact that through history information has been essential. Hunters and gatherers needed information about food supplies, weather, and threats to survival in order to live. Agriculture depended on information, as did manufacturing and, more recently, service industries. What is different today is the scale of information in which we find ourselves immersed. Information society is not new; what is new is the dominance of information in our lives. It is the purpose of this book to provide some order and context for the information age so that individuals can identify their place and understand the implications of information dominance.

The concept of information society is global, reflecting the nature of current economic and social organization. The term *information society* is most often searched in Google Trends in Korean, followed by Portuguese, Greek, and then English. The term appears often in Asia, Africa, Europe, and the Americas, and across a wide range of academic and popular literatures. The International Telecommunication Union has designated one day annually as World Telecommunication and Information Society Day to promote recognition of its significance.

A central element in information society is the technology that enables it. Commonly termed information and communication technologies (ICTs), these devices facilitate the collection, management, control, and distribution of information. ICTs include computers, telephones, the Internet, radio, television, and digital image and music technologies. On a planet with more than one billion personal computers and more than seven billion telephones, most people find themselves surrounded by information and communication technologies and likely think little of their existence, as they have become so pervasive. While surrounded by these devices and systems, it is easy to forget that many did not exist until the past two or three decades. The personal computer dates from the early 1980s, the commercialization of the Internet to the early 1990s, the MP3 player to the late 1990s, and the iPod to 2001. The speed of electronic innovation and the development of ICT devices makes it seem to many that these technologies have long histories, yet many are recent.

Accompanying the rapid rollout of ICTs is the mind-set that forms through their adoption. Marc Prensky[1] captures the significance of mind-set through his comparison of digital immigrants and digital natives. Digital natives are those who have grown up with ICTs and see them as the first or only source of information or action. Natives have always been surrounded by information and cannot remember life without computers, mobile phones, MP3 players, and the Internet. Prensky notes that "today's students *think and process information fundamentally differently* from their predecessors."[2] In contrast, digital immigrants come to ICTs later in life and can understand how the technology affected their behavior. Natives are fluent and comfortable in their ICT-enabled world, while immigrants may be less comfortable, or more efficient with alternate information sources, such as books and newspapers. Over time, digital natives will become the majority, and information society will be significantly changed.

The challenge we face is that, as authors of this text, we are all digital immigrants. We "speak an outdated language (that of the pre-digital age), [and] are struggling to teach a population that speaks an entirely new language."[3] Our immigrant status does, however, provide some advantages, in particular the ability to compare life before and after the rapid deployment of ICTs in the 1990s. As scholars of ICT development since the 1980s, each of us has a perspective of studying the impact of ICT while it was being implemented. As immigrants we can provide a different mind-set, and as long-term scholars of information society, we hope that our accents are not too strong.

Conceptual Framework

Global Information Society seeks to empower its readers to understand the complexities of the networked global information society and to use that understanding to promote awareness and to positively effect change. Why is this goal important? Policy development and practice today throughout much of global society is led by persons and institutions that predate the digital generation. In order to respond to the needs of our communities, local and regional society needs the participation and creativity of the digital generation and those who recognize the significance of electronic and networking information technologies. So our focus, in the end, is practical but informed by theory. At the interface of theory and practice are translational research and translational practice that we have framed as "intelligent development," which closes the gap between theory and practice in planning development strategies.[4]

Over the last generation, the overwhelming proportion of literature on development planning has been academic-centric. Judith Innes documented the early stages of a paradigm shift from the then-dominant positivist and scientifically verifiable approaches to development planning theory and planning practice to the emerging paradigm of communicative action and interactive practice. So much of this new planning work has been devoted "on the one hand, to document what planners do and, on the other, to reflect critically on that practice."[5] Our book is devoted to the extension of these learnings by framing practical and informed actions for stakeholders to influence the local development debate.

The intelligent development approach informing this book, and discussed in chapter 12, is based on a number of components including the ALERT model, developed by Kenneth Corey and Mark Wilson to guide practitioners and scholars through the ICT and planning process.[6] Also informing this text is the communicative action theory of contemporary German philosopher and sociologist Jürgen Habermas. One of his most widely known and discussed concepts is *communicative action theory*, "in which actors in society seek to reach common understanding and to coordinate actions by reasoned argument, consensus, and cooperation rather than strategic action strictly in pursuit of their own goals."[7]

The translated writings and explanations of Habermas' theory of communicative action are abstract, but Roger Bolton provides a valuable introduction to the theoretical backdrop of Habermas' thinking.[8] Bolton's paper also introduces the complementary Habermas concept of *lifeworld*. This notion includes "background conclusions" and "one's worldview that is taken for granted and so anchored that it is difficult to change. Habermas sees communicative action as crucial in the rationalization process of one's lifeworld. "Rationalization is a process in which claims of validity increasingly are exposed to criticism and discussion rather than accepted merely on faith."[9] These processes are essential in reducing path-dependent mind-sets, thereby opening minds for more transformative and responsive understanding and actions in the global knowledge economy.

The influence of Habermas on our construction of the intelligent development system and the ALERT model has been indirect. The primary inspiration for our theoretical constructions came directly from Stephen Graham and Patsy Healey's article "Relational Concepts of Space and Place: Issues for Planning Theory and Practice."[10] Through Graham and Healey and through their use of Habermas, our work has been informed both indirectly and directly from a wide range of social theorists.

Trends for Information Society

Our social, political, and economic futures will be heavily influenced by three major elements: the knowledge economy, globalization, and network society. These elements appear in many forms throughout this book and will be discussed in detail in later chapters. For the moment, it is important to recognize the foundational issues on which our analysis rests and the approaches adopted to present this information. In considering these trends and the topics in this book, it is valuable to adopt a relational approach, as it offers a thorough approach to complex phenomena.[11] A relational framework recognizes relations and processes among actors, the significance of space and time, multiple layers of power geometries by place, and the power of agency in negotiating between the layers of power geometries. The lesson from this approach is not to look at society and technology in isolation, but to follow through to see the people, places, and institutions affected, and influencing, information society.

The knowledge economy captures the significance of science and technology as a driver of growth, and the need for an educated workforce to facilitate economic development. As Joel Mokyr notes, the knowledge economy is not new, as knowledge has always been a powerful element in economic and social change.[12] Forty years ago, Alvin Toffler and Daniel Bell predicted the shift to services and the realignment of the economy around knowledge and the production of services rather than goods.[13] Their predictions were realized, as the nature of the economy and work has changed in the interim. As economies have evolved, what is new is the rapidly growing significance of knowledge, the routinization of its production, and the commodification of its final form.

As structural change progresses in terms of what is made and how products and services are delivered, there is also a geographical restructuring, with production systems fragmented to locate in the lowest-cost and most advantageous areas. This globalization of production affects people and places as they now compete across the world rather than locally. Frances Cairncross and Thomas Friedman, among many, have shown how ICT and globalization have produced supply chains that cross thousands of miles for goods, or almost instantly link service centers for trade in information.[14]

The third phenomenon, network society, reflects the impact of information and communication technologies on how people live, work, and interact. With more than two billion Internet users and more than six billion mobile phones in use, many in the world are extensively connected to each other and to information.[15] The potential for ubiquitous computing is approaching reality in some locations, especially cities, and for groups and classes of people eager to adopt new ICTs.[16] As the ubiquity of ICT grows, individuals and societies need to decide how much to interact and to weigh the costs and benefits of ubiquitous access in both financial as well as personal and privacy terms.

Outline of the Book

Global Information Society builds on the analytical research of its three authors: Aharon Kellerman, Kenneth Corey, and Mark Wilson.[17] The social and technological phenomena, policies, and strategic processes outlined here are based on the ALERT model, which frames complex activities in the context of the global economy and network society. The ALERT model asks analysts, scholars, and policy makers to raise their Awareness of changing geographic (Layers) and technological (E-Business, E-Government, and E-Society) forces and to positively and creatively react (Responsiveness) through information and collaboration (Talk). The ALERT model is one way to organize thinking and action about information and communication technologies.

The first element, awareness, is particularly relevant for analysis of ICT and information society due to the rate of change produced and experienced because of these forces. It is easy to rely upon past knowledge and to assume that the future will reflect the past, but changes in ICT are so rapid that society will advance well beyond our current knowledge, data collection, and understanding. The landscape of information society ten years ago was very different from today, with many elements not evident, such as the role of social networking or the shift of Internet access away from desktop computers to laptops and mobile phones. This introduces the importance of mind-set, that is, the worldview we each hold that has evolved through experience and education, and the attitudes it informs.

As we make decisions based on our mind-set, it is essential that the knowledge we use for decision making be current. In a rapidly changing environment, such as information and communication technologies, reliance on information even a few years old can produce incorrect results. This book takes great pains to provide current information, but readers are encouraged to refresh their data, and mind-set, regularly in order to gain a clearer understanding of information society. To assist in this process, online sources are noted in the book, and readers are encouraged to seek current information.

The aware scholar needs to be familiar with the spatial trends in information society, as well as with the technologies and their forms. Given technologies and geography, there will be different responses to change. Individuals, organizations, governments, and societies will respond differently to the same technological force, and this responsiveness needs to be understood and harnessed to benefit society. The importance of response to our analysis is shown in part II where the geographic variation in ICT use is illustrated. Finally, one of the best ways for scholars to understand information society is to talk, to communicate with each other, to survey populations about experience with ICTs, and to be vocal about views and concerns so that the information society that emerges is one that was intended and not accidental.

This book has multiple goals, attempting to present contemporary information society from several angles: a general conceptual focus on the information society and its global-geographical nature, a descriptive-empirical analysis presenting the various information societies globally, discussion of the role of policy, and a resource section. The book is divided into four parts: Part I focuses on the organization and themes of the global information society, so that chapters 2 through 5 present foundational material on information society (chapter 2) and discuss the three pillars of such a society: *technology*—on which it is based (chapter 3); *knowledge*—which it produces and fosters (chapter 5); and *mobility*—which it facilitates (chapter 4). Part II frames the global information society by spatial organization of world region and country (chapter 6), with analysis of the Americas (chapter 7), Europe (chapter 8), Asia-Pacific (chapter 9), and the Middle East and Africa (chapter 10). The theoretical and spatial analyses in the first two parts of the book pave the way for part III focusing on the policy (chapter 11) and action (chapter 12) dimensions of global information society. Lastly, the book ends with the support section of part IV, with chapter 13 offering a charrette exercise that builds on the knowledge contained in the book and instructs readers how to apply it to their home regions as a case study.

Notes

1. Prensky (2001)
2. Prensky (2001:1)
3. Prensky (2001:2)
4. Innes (1995a)

5. Innes (1995a: 183)
6. Corey and Wilson (2006)
7. Habermas (1984: 86)
8. Bolton (2005)
9. Bolton (2005: 15)
10. Graham and Healey (1999)
11. Graham and Healey (1999); Corey and Wilson (2006); Healey (2007)
12. Mokyr (2002)
13. Toffler (1970); Bell (1976)
14. Cairncross (1997); Friedman (2005)
15. ITU (2011)
16. Sakamura (2003); Yusuf and Nabeshima (2006)
17. Kellerman (1993; 2002b; 2006b); Wilson and Corey (2000; 2006)

2

Foundations of the Information Society

W<small>E START OUR INTELLECTUAL JOURNEY</small> through the still-unfolding global information society by recognizing that we are a part of that society. Most readers of this book probably make extensive use of the Internet and mobile phones and are open to the adoption of a growing variety of communications devices and media. As such, we are both analysts and participants in the global information society. Our position gives us personal insights, but care needs to be taken to remain objective when assessing information society, as experiences vary greatly across people and places. In this chapter we introduce the information society, and in later chapters we build on this foundation to explore additional elements, aspects, and dimensions of contemporary society. The chapter begins with a presentation of definitions and concepts for information and knowledge. Then we will examine definitions for the information society, followed by an elaboration on the development of the information society. These three initial discussions will pave the way for an examination of some basic terminology for the information society, followed by an exploration of major elements of the information economy.

Information

Information is a term used in ambiguous ways, notably since the introduction of information technology, which has permitted the storage, processing, and transmission of enormous quantities of information in electronic formats. On the one hand, information is a kind of "umbrella spectrum" that includes a wide family of communicative, mostly codified, materials: data, information as a specific class of communicative material, knowledge, and innovations. As Theodore Roszak notes, "In its new technical sense, *information* has come to denote whatever can be coded for transmission through a channel that connects a source with a receiver, regardless of semantic content."[1] On the other hand, the term *information* is also used in a more restricted sense referring to a specific class of communicative materials, which will be defined in the next subsection. Information at large is obviously something intangible, though its containers or media have traditionally been paper products: books, magazines, letters, documents, lists, and similar objects. The emergence of electronic transmission and storage media, such as radio, TV, cassettes, discs, and MP3s, coupled with computers and the Internet, have once again accentuated the intangible and abstract character of information.

The Information Sequence

The four classes of communicative materials, namely data, information, knowledge, and innovation, have each received numerous independent definitions. However, it is also possible to refer to all of them jointly as a sequence, in which data lead to the production of information, which, on its part, may lead to the development of knowledge, as well as the other way around. Knowledge, on its part, may bring about the development of innovations.[2] Let us review some definitions for each of these four communicative materials: data, information, knowledge, and innovation.

Data: "A series of observations, measurements, or facts in the form of numbers, words, sounds and/or images. Data have no meaning but provide the raw material from which information is produced."[3]

Information: Information per se has received numerous definitions, estimated at over one hundred, proposed in about forty disciplines.[4] It was claimed *to be* an activity, a life form, and a relationship[5] and is further seen *as* resource, commodity, perception of pattern, and a constitutive force in society.[6] From a sequential perspective, information is data organized to reveal patterns and placed in context.[7] Marc Porat similarly defined information as "data that have been organized and communicated."[8]

Knowledge: Definitions of knowledge refer to its relation to information. It has been defined as "the application and productive use of information. Knowledge is more than information, since it involves an awareness or understanding gained through experience, familiarity or learning."[9] To Theodore Roszak "*ideas create information*, not the other way around. Every fact grows from an idea."[10] Other commentators, however, such as Max Boisot, argue that "knowledge builds on information that is extracted from data."[11] A kind of two-way relationship between knowledge and information was illuminated by Neil Postman as follows:

> I define knowledge as organized information, information that has a purpose, that leads one to seek further information in order to understand something about the world. Without organized information, we may know something *of* the world, but very little *about* it. When one has knowledge, one knows how to make sense of information, knows how to relate information to one's life, and, especially knows when information is irrelevant.[12]

Sociologist Daniel Bell added the nature of communications to the concept of knowledge: "Knowledge is a set of organized statements of facts or ideas, presenting a reasoned judgement or an experimental result, which is transmitted to others through some communication medium in some systematic form."[13] On the other hand, Fritz Machlup concluded that knowledge may also be created without information and communications: "Information is acquired by being told, whereas knowledge can be acquired by thinking. . . . Thus, *new knowledge can be acquired without new information being received.*"[14] By the same token, Michael Storper noted that information flows varied by direction: "Information transfer is always necessary to knowledge exchange, the reverse is not always true."[15]

Innovation: Innovation may be defined as the creation of new knowledge, through an intrinsically uncertain problem-solving process based on existing knowledge and/or information. Innovative knowledge may lead to the introduction of innovative products or the application of novel production process, either through radical breakthroughs or through incremental improvements.[16] Knowledge may thus be viewed as an asset, serving as an input (competence) that may lead to the production of innovation or an output. The newly created innovation becomes a new piece of knowledge.[17]

We may recognize four basic sequential processes among the four communicative materials we just defined (see figure 2.1). In the first, data are turned into information when data receive meaningful patterns and context, such as in the classification or categorization of data. In the second, information yields information, such as in a spoken or written exchange between two or more people, when one's statements lead to a response by the partner of the exchange. In the third sequential process, information turns into knowledge through the application and use of information. Knowledge, for its part, may yield information, and it is further required for the additional development of information, such as in the use of a theory or model as a form of knowledge, yielding information when the theory or model is applied to a certain

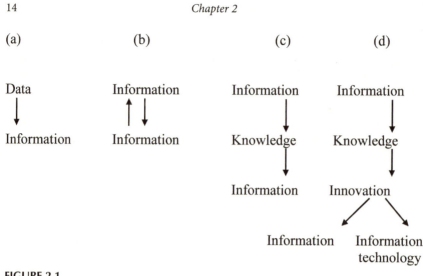

FIGURE 2.1
The Information Sequence (Kellerman 2002b).

case study.[18] Innovation, or the creation of new knowledge, is dependent on previously existing knowledge and information in order for it to emerge. On their part, innovations may yield new information technologies, among other possible innovations. Innovations may also produce new information when they are written down and obviously when they are applied.

Information Classification

There are various ways to classify information. One simple classification is by content: social, business, entertainment, news, or educational. Traditionally, there have evolved close ties among several of these information types through the technologies used for their production or transmission. Thus, books and articles share similar printing technologies, entertainment and news are transmitted through radio and television, movies also include voice and music, and the telephone is used for both business and social conversations. Computer-based multimedia technology was noted by Manuel Castells as enabling an "integration of all messages in a common cognitive pattern."[19] While the messages of an educational movie may differ from that of a news broadcast, their operational contexts may be similar, using icons, video games, audiovisual shows, and the like. Thus multimedia can be used to present a wide variety of cultural expressions. The most integrative information technology is the Internet, which functions as a comprehensive information storage system, containing all types of information, regardless of content or form.

Another most basic classification of information is by form: text, data, graphics, voice, and picture. From the perspective of information production and transmission, major developments in transistor and computer technologies as of the 1970s have turned all these information types into similar digital bit formats, differentiated mainly by the channel bandwidth required for their transmission. From the perspective of information users too, this classification has lost much of its significance through the introduction of the Internet in the 1990s, permitting integrative transmissions of information in every form through a single channel, transforming all information forms into electronic signals.[20]

A third simple classification of information has focused on information transmission, separating among information producers or senders, transmission media or telecommunications channels, and information receivers or users. However, as far as the Web system of the Internet is concerned, information may be produced and installed on websites, but these websites may not necessarily be accessed by anybody. In other words, if nobody calls for a certain site, it will neither be transmitted nor received or used. Thus, electronic information has to be classified into designated and undesignated information. Designated information is information which is transmitted to specific individual receivers (such as phone calls or fax transmissions) or to specific audiences (e.g., through cable television), whereas undesignated information is put on a transmission device (e.g., a website loaded on a hosting server) and potentially received by any number of users.

An alternative and fourth information classification, which would fit mostly electronically transmitted information, may look at information as something that does not stand for itself but is rather woven into wider contexts of social or economic processes. Information may thus be viewed as an economic process that can be either free of charge or involve a price for its use or purchase.[21]

Four types of information may be recognized by economic process according to Aharon Kellerman:[22]

1. *Pure information (type 1):* Personal, academic, and some business information, in the form of e-mails or website information, provided at no charge (other than for its transmission), and with no intention to create or promote purchases. Thus, some of this information is designated (e-mail) and some is not (websites).
2. *Information as part of sale processes (type 2):* Information transmission over the Internet has often become *part* of the sale process of both products (e.g., books) and services (e.g., airline tickets). This type of information is undesignated in most cases through commercial websites

offering products and services to the general public. However, such information may turn designated once purchase by a specific client is made (e.g., through order confirmation or progress reports). Such types of information are currently part of the marketing systems of almost all material products, as well as of many services.

3. *Information as product (type 3):* Information itself may be sold over the Internet (e.g., astrological forecasts) to any undesignated customers. Here, too, once a sale has been executed, the information transmission becomes designated.

4. *Products transformed into information (type 4):* Probably the only real product transformed into electronic information is also the most powerful one—money. Capital as a resource or as a product is currently transmitted almost exclusively over telecommunications channels, not necessarily over the Internet. The transmission of capital is obviously highly and most clearly designated.

The development of these four information types has been interwoven with the innovation and adoption of electronic transmission media. The transmission of pure information through voice telephony as of 1876, and later of text and graphical transmission through fax (information type 1), paved the way for the transmission of capital in the form of data as of the 1970s (information type 4). The construction of dense domestic and international telecommunications networks facilitated the evolution of the Internet as of the mid-1990s so that electronic information could be integrated into sale processes (information type 2) and information itself could be sold (information type 3). The emergence of the Internet has enhanced the transmission of pure information and capital, which can now be transmitted in more sophisticated ways.

Knowledge Classification

There are numerous classifications of knowledge,[23] tracing back to Aristotle, who distinguished among three types of knowledge: *èpistemé*, or theoretical and universal; *techné*, instrumental knowledge, practice related, and context specific; and *phronesis*, experience-based, normative, related to common sense, and context specific.[24] A recently proposed classification of knowledge into four types may be partially related to this ancient classification: know-what (facts); know-why (principles, similar to *èpistemé*); know-how (skills, similar to *techné*); and know-who (socialization).[25]

Another dominant classification of knowledge is into codified or explicit knowledge and tacit or implicit knowledge.[26] Codified knowledge is recorded or transmitted through symbols (letters and letters turned into words and sentences, digits, and drawings), whereas tacit knowledge develops through learning and is thus similar to know-how (skills). These two knowledge classes complement each other, and they are normally present in any specific "piece of knowledge." Codified knowledge can be converted into information and is mostly viewed as more easily transferable through information technology, whereas tacit knowledge is more readily transferred through the transfer of knowledge bearers, namely people.[27] It is arguable, though, whether tacit knowledge is becoming less important than codified knowledge, notably because "tacit knowledge remains a prerequisite in *all* knowledge activities."[28] Common professional education of students studying the same profession in different countries, thus "talking the same language,"[29] also assists in the transfer of tacit knowledge.

What Is the Information Society?

Following our exposure to the complexity of information and knowledge within a social context, we may turn our attention now to information society. The term *information society* has been increasingly in use as of the early 1980s, though earlier terms such as the *information age* date back to the early 1970s.[30] These and other terms have emerged within the wider context of attempts to coin societal transformations since the early 1950s. James Beniger counted seventy-five such terms proposed between 1950 and 1984, almost all of which have not been adopted for the naming of our current age.[31]

Manuel Castells noted that the information society "is based on the historical tension between the material power of abstract information processing and society's search for meaningful cultural identity."[32] Castells further differentiated between "information society" and "informational society."[33] Whereas the first relates to the role of information in society, which has always been of some importance, the second relates to "a specific form of social organization in which information generation, processing, and transmission become the fundamental sources of productivity and power because of new technological conditions." It so happened that what Castells termed *informational society* is what has come to be called *information society*.

The definition for *information society* favored by sociologist Frank Webster states that "*theoretical knowledge/information* is at the core of how we conduct ourselves these days."[34] Such a definition does not lend itself easily for comparative quantitative measurement, so that information society constitutes more of a process rather than a state of society. Webster was able to identify five definitions, or dimensions, for the information society:

technological, economic, occupational, spatial, and cultural. Jointly they seem to highlight the major facets of the information society. Let us take a short look at each of these five dimensions.

Technologically, and looked upon from a spatial perspective, the first phase in the emergence of the information society was the development and adoption of place-based connectivity beyond the telephone: the introduction of personal computers (PCs) in the 1970s and the generation of electronic computer communications, first via Telnet in the 1970s–1980s, followed by the Internet in the 1990s. This phase has been followed by a second one, namely placeless connectivity as of the 1990s, marked first by the widespread adoption of mobile telephony and laptop computers, and more recently typified by the fusion between mobile phones and laptops through the provision of Internet connectivity via smart phones and vice versa through tablets.[35]

At the economic end, it was claimed by the European Commission in the mid-1990s that "in an information society, information is the most important commodity."[36] Such economic conditions have not yet been reached, though one may argue that appliances using information and communications technologies, such as PCs and mobile phones, rather than information per se, have turned into most-important commodities. It still seems that it is more costly to purchase and maintain information machines, such as computers, printers, and mobile telephones, than to buy most of the information files which they transmit, process, and save.

Information society involves two major information processes: production and consumption. At the production end, several things may be produced. One major production process may be the innovation and wide-scale production of the hardware of information society, such as computers and telecommunications devices and equipment. Another major production process may be computer software, and a third may be information itself, notably electronic, such as Internet sites, television programs, and movies.

High levels of consumption of information may also be expressed in hardware, software, and information per se. The wide adoption of telecommunications and information devices such as PCs, telephones, and TVs is one indicator. Sale of software is another, as are the number and duration of domestic and international phone calls, or the proportion of homes connected to cable TV. A discussion of global variation in PC and television ownership is included in part II.

The occupational perspective of the information society was one of the first used in order to define and identify the information age. Jean Gottmann and Daniel Bell identified the quaternary sector as a new sector in the economy dealing with information.[37] The growth in information-related employment leads us to today: "We have achieved an information society when the preponderance of occupations is found in information work."[38] By the 1960s, a large proportion of U.S. workers were "information workers," employed in information-related occupations, or in the so-called "knowledge sector," followed later, in the 1970s and 1980s, by other leading economies.[39] The major problem with this approach and definition is the question of the exact nature of information workers. Can a worker in the printing industry, producing pamphlets, newspapers, or books while working with printing machines, be considered an information worker? It seems, therefore, more plausible to relate to the information society from an occupational perspective as a society led by people who are information rich, are information producing, and above all are engaged in the processing and manipulation of information.[40]

The information society also has a striking spatial dimension, although it is based on cyberspace, which is a virtual entity, to be discussed later on. One may define information society spatially as a society in which all information is available electronically anywhere, and interpersonal electronic communication is possible from anywhere to everywhere in all forms. As we will see throughout the chapters of this book, the world is rapidly moving toward becoming an information society from this spatial angle. The spatial organization of the global information society is complex behind the scenes in terms of the ICTs that make it work. However, from the users' perspectives, things become more and more simple. Each human being may be considered as a node in the global information/communications system when carrying a mobile phone, notably phones that permit access to the Internet (3G phones of various types). More complicated, from a human perspective, is the lack of time and space barriers for the receipt and transmission of information, thus fusing work and leisure activities.[41] By the same token, locationally fixed entities such as offices and classrooms become nodes in the global information/communications system once they are equipped with PCs and/or telephones.

The pipelines for the transmission of information are partially telephone and TV cables, but increasingly information is transmitted wirelessly, frequently aided by satellites. Thus the spatial system of nodes and pipelines is highly flexible and never fixed as the more traditional mobility systems of roads and fixed-line telephones are. As far as the types of information transmitted through this flexible system are concerned, the Internet constitutes a comprehensive information system, permitting the transmission of text, colorful still and streaming images, and voice. All of the information that has traditionally been printed or written on paper increasingly is available through the Internet. One of the attributes of the information society is growing mobilities, both corporeal and virtual, and these will be highlighted later on from various perspectives.

Culturally, the information society has been viewed by Yoneji Masuda as "a society that brings about a general flourishing state of human intellectual creativity, instead of affluent material consumption."[42] By this definition, information society may be viewed as a utopian vision that may never be fully achieved. Side by side with the enormous opportunities for intellectual growth that information technologies provide in many ways, such as through instant access to books and articles, e-learning, and the fast and intensive contacts among academics using e-mail, information technologies have also provided much opportunity for popular culture vis-à-vis, for example, MP3 and MP4 technologies, social networking via Facebook and Twitter, and movies transmitted over the Internet via YouTube, Netflix, and the like.

The Development of the Information Society

The rise of the information society during the last three decades has sometimes been viewed, explicitly or implicitly, as a single-phase process.[43] Some other commentators have argued for information as a major power continuously transforming American society since the very beginnings of European settlement in North America.[44] Just about fifteen years ago, some others still considered the term *information society* to be a concept rather than a mature phenomenon, claiming that Western society was still in a process of "informatization," thus lacking clear quantitative measures to demonstrate the existence of an information society.[45]

The following discussion outlines three phases in the development of the information society: information rich, information based, and information dominated (see figure 2.2). The incubation of the information society occurred first chiefly in the United States, and within four major societal elements: industrial society, capitalism, the Cold War, and culture as information. We will first examine these four elements and then explore the three phases for the emergence of the information society.

Whether industrial society has given way to information society by continuity or change, it has been extensively debated in the literature at the time.[46] On one hand, the development of information technology (IT) and the emerging need at the time for skilled workers who consume and produce more information were viewed as processes that nest within industrial society and the subsequent service economy. On the other hand, information technologies allow "a direct, online linkage between different types of activity in the same process of production, management, and distribution, establish[ing] a close, structural connection between spheres of work and employment artificially separated by obsolete statistical categories."[47] Thus, at a certain stage,

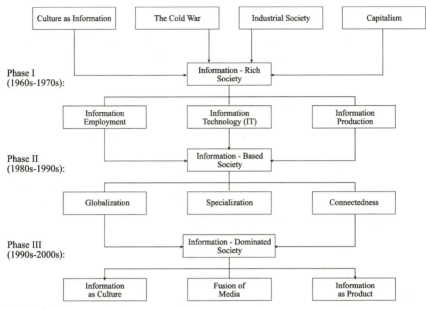

FIGURE 2.2
Phases in the Emergence of the Information Society (Kellerman 2002b).

information and knowledge may potentially replace labor and possibly also capital as leading production factors.

Capitalism has been recognized as a major force in the emergence of an information society by facilitating the transfer of information from the public to the private sector, or "the privatization of information."[48] This process involved the rise of a class of technocrats in the so-called "programmed society," in conflict with more disparate groups being governed or managed by them.[49]

A third major force in the rise of information technology and society in the United States was the Cold War.[50] Computers were widely required for missiles and defense from missiles, as well as for space exploration. Furthermore, the contemporary Internet network had its root in the Pentagon ARPANET alternative communications system for cases of telephone system collapse.

A fourth major dimension facilitating the emergence of the information society was the nature of cultural activity in developed societies, requiring a constant and rich transmission of written and oral information, such as literature and music, which used to be constrained by volume, form, time, and distance before the technological age. Thus, the very accent on information and information transmission in contemporary information society was not novel.

Information-Rich Society (1960s–1970s)

With these four elements for the development of the information society in action, the first phase in the evolution of the information society took place between the 1960s and 1970s, and it may be termed an *information-rich society*. The characteristics of this phase included growing societal emphases on information production and employment in information work, mainly vis-à-vis the introduction of information technologies.

Growing employment in information-related activities has been recognized as an early and central aspect of information societies: "The term 'information society' has been used to describe socioeconomic systems that exhibit high employment of information-related occupations and wide diffusion of information technologies."[51] Marc Porat and Fritz Machlup showed that a large proportion of U.S. workers were "information workers," employed in information-related occupations, or in the so-called "knowledge sector," as early as the 1960s,[52] followed in the 1970s and 1980s by other leading economies.[53] However, it was not until later phases in the emergence of the information society that information became a common thread in production as well as consumption, mainly through the introduction of PCs and a common channel of information flow, the Internet.

The introduction of information technology via computers and telecommunications and its rapid and wide diffusion and adoption have become the driving force of information society, interrelated with the growth of information employment. The impact of information technology over the years has been on two levels. On the one hand, it has constituted a major enabling force for society, allowing inexpensive recording and storage and fast processing and transmission of information.[54] But it has also become an extensive industry in itself, the high-tech industry, characterized by intensive research and development (R&D) coupled with entrepreneurship for the development and production of information technologies.

A third major aspect of the information-rich society of the 1960s and 1970s was the growth in information production. It seems obvious that the introduction of information technology and the growth of employment in information would lead to the production of larger volumes of information. However, this growth also had to do with the expansion of research and study in universities and research institutes during these decades, yielding ever-increasing numbers of books and journals.[55] Thus the number of books published in the United States increased between 1960 and 1970 from 15,012 to 36,071, or by some 140 percent.[56]

Information-Based Society (1980s–1990s)

The growth in the volume of information, technology, and employment in the 1960s and 1970s led to a second phase in the emergence of the information society: the *information-based society* of the 1980s–1990s. This phase was characterized by three trends, all based on developments in the first phase: globalization, specialization, and connectedness.

We will devote special attention to globalization later on, but it is important to note that the ability to move information instantaneously worldwide became possible with the rapid development of international telephony, the emergence of the Internet, and the introduction of cable/satellite television. These technological breakthroughs have reduced or completely removed international boundaries to the movement of information, thus weakening the role and control of national governments or statism in a wide sphere of human activities. This free international transfer of information has been evident in almost every economic, social, and cultural area, including news coverage, banking, commerce, and social contacts. The pace of information production and transmission has quickened with the shrinking of space in time.

The second phase in the rise of information society has also been typified by the rapid diffusion and adoption of "information devices," such as telephones, mobile phones, fax machines, PCs and laptops, television sets, and the like, a process that we will further highlight in the next chapter.[57] A third characteristic of information-based society has been increased connectivity. Internet technologies have permitted the recording and transmission of all forms of information, namely text, data, graphics, and voice in electronic digital format. Coupled with fast and low-priced telecommunications and PCs, they have allowed an increased connectedness of individual customers with service providers, as well as complex connections among goods producers and service providers among themselves. Furthermore, the interrelationship between electronic information and printed information has changed with the introduction of low-priced high-quality laser and jet printers and optic scanners, permitting nonprofessional users to produce high-quality printed information products. These developments have rendered society in developed countries increasingly information dependent.[58]

Information-Dominated Society (1990s–2000s)

Unfolding in the late 1990s toward the 2000s has been a third phase in the rise of information society which might be termed *information-dominated society.* Information production, transmission, and use have become lead-ing, if not *the* leading, economic and social activities in this phase, with information constituting both a product in itself and a service leading to the production or consumption of material products. As such, three additional characteristics have been added to the information society: information becoming a major product, information media beginning to fuse into each other, and information becoming a culture.

Information has increasingly become a commodity in its own right. By the late 1990s, revenues from the sale of information were matching those from the sale of material products and services. Major examples are the sale of data sets relating to Internet users and the tremendous growth in the sales of software and TV programs. A few years later in 2004, the worldwide sales of packaged software reached some $179 billion, representing growth of 5 percent over 2003.[59] The United States has become the world leader in the sale and distribution of electronic information at large, with one estimate that it held approximately 50 percent of the software production market.[60]

Liberalization trends in the provision of information services to house-holds, as well as technological advances, have brought about possible fu-sions among different forms of information, their transmission, and use. Thus it has become possible, for example, to use a computer also as a telephone, fax, and TV, and to receive these services from a single service provider. Even more striking, smart phones have emerged as multipurpose information communicators. Such fusions may lead to the adoption of single appliances for comprehensive information consumption and produc-tion, as well as so-called "public networks," providing fast and cheap access to data and software.[61]

The information society becomes at this third phase of its development a society with culture as information. Some commentators have seen this as "recognition of the cultural value of information through the promotion of information values in the interest of national and individual development."[62] Others believe that beyond promoting proper and aesthetic production, transmission, and consumption of information, the culture of information may turn into a culture of power:

> Cultural battles are the power battles of the Information Age. They are primarily fought in and by the media, but the media are not the power-holders. Power, as the capacity to impose behavior, lies in the networks of information exchange and symbol manipulation, which relate social actors, institutions, and cultural movements, through icons, spokespersons, and intellectual amplifiers. . . . Cul-ture as the source of power, and power as the source of capital, underlie the new social hierarchy of the Information Age.[63]

Another important cultural dimension of information is the changing significance of time and space. Instantaneous written and oral communications in global space intensify the pace of work and alter working times. In terms of cultural symbolism and reality, our source and anchor have changed from traditional national territory to a global virtual one. This brought Manuel Castells to declare that "the space of flows of the Information Age dominates the space of places of people's cultures,"[64] a statement we will examine further in the following subsection. Others, however, did not identify cultural imperialism in the blurring of national boundaries and saw no threat to domestic democratic institutions.[65]

The contemporary phase of the evolution of the information society has further marked an emergence of information societies in developing countries. The most striking element in this regard is the massive adoption and use of mobile phones, marking a leapfrogging effect, since in many regions there does not exist an extensive infrastructure for fixed telephones, and many of the mobile phone users have never seen or used a fixed telephone. About 70 percent of the population in developing countries already owned a mobile phone in 2011 (reaching over 40 percent in Africa). Attempts are further being made to introduce the Internet widely into developing countries, notably through school systems, coupled with the development of cheaply priced, solar or manually powered laptops (e.g., the Negroponte and Nokia projects). The possibility of interacting through communications technologies and the availability of information may aid development processes, but use of the Internet requires literacy. Too sweeping technology adoption may carry social risks though, as it may, for instance, threaten local social networks as well as existing social structures when people can suddenly reach out to global networks.

Basic Terminology for the Information Society

In this subsection we would like to introduce three basic terms for understanding the information society: *cyberspace*, *globalization*, and the *space of flows*.

Cyberspace

The introduction of the Internet in the mid-1990s has brought about a focus on cyberspace, originally proposed by William Gibson as a science-fiction notion and applied later to computer-mediated communications and to virtual-reality technologies.[66] *Cyberspace* was variously defined as (1) *artificial reality*: "Cyberspace is a globally networked, computer-sustained, computer-accessed, and computer-generated, multidimensional, artificial, or 'virtual,' reality";[67] (2) *interactivity space*: "Interactivity between remote computers defines cyberspace . . . cyberspace is not necessarily imagined space—it is real enough in that it is the space set up by those who use remote computers to communicate";[68] and (3) *conceptual space*: "the *conceptual space* within ICTs (information and communication technologies), rather than the technology itself."[69]

These three definitions, ranging from the early 1990s to the early 2000s, suggest that with the rapid development of information systems the definition of *cyberspace* has become wider, moving from a virtual, through an interactive, to a conceptual entity. The common thread among these three definitions of cyberspace is that the primitive notion of space has been used metaphorically for some new virtual entity stemming from the development of computers and information systems. Rob Shields referred, in this regard, to a contemporary "shifting relationship between the virtually real, and the material."[70] Moreover, Mike Crang and colleagues argued for "the virtual as spatial" and that "virtuality [then] is not just something which operates through and across space. It is at its heart a spatial phenomenon."[71]

Thus cyberspace was recognized to be "hardly immaterial in that it is very much an embodied space."[72] This "embodiment" is in a more metaphorical sense than embodiment in our physical daily life, since cyberspace cannot be turned into a physical entity. On the other hand, cyberspace may be viewed as embedded in physical space: "electronic space is embedded in, and often intertwines with, the physical space and place."[73] Furthermore, both spaces, the physical and the virtual, coevolve, in that they "stand in a state of *recursive interaction*, shaping *each other* in complex ways."[74] At yet another end, cyberspace was interpreted by Jay David Bolter and Richard Grusin as another form of Marc Augé's nonplaces,[75] which he originally proposed for real space, such as airports.

The Web may be viewed as a special form of social space. Like the more real social space, it constitutes a resource and a production force, for instance for the very existence and functioning of online shopping. Further like social space, cyberspace by its very nature may be looked upon as an invisible text and as a symbol for individuals and organizations, and it further serves as an organizational framework.[76] Several commentators claim it can also be interpreted as a landscape, a place, and even a social value.[77] In its Web form, cyberspace constitutes an imagined space of representation through its virtual imitation or virtual description of real spaces and places.

Real space and cyberspace may be viewed as overlapping: cyberspace is accessed from real space, and it contains data on material space, thus affecting it. Further, cyberspace keeps or imitates various features of physical space.

"Virtual environments contain much of the essential spatial information that is utilized by people in real environments."[78] Cyberspace has its own geography and is symbol sustained.[79] It further enables and constrains its users like real space.[80] However, cyberspace is distinguished from real space in many instances, as shown in table 2.1. These differentiations may be divided into three dimensions—organization, movement, and users—and these are discussed in detail elsewhere.[81] It would suffice here to notice that the physical space of virtual space, namely the hardware (e.g., PCs) for its operation, is auxiliary from a spatial perspective and seems to have no spatial significance of its own. Cyberspace permits simultaneous human co-presence in physical and virtual places, whereas a person can only be at one physical place at a given time.

From a cultural-geographic perspective, cyberspace has been argued to amount to a heavenly New Jerusalem.[82] As such, cyberspace was assumed to

TABLE 2.1
Real and Virtual Spaces

Dimension	Real Space	Virtual Space
Organization		
1. Content	Physical and informational	Informational
2. Places	Separated	Converge with local real ones
3. Form	Abstract or real	Relational
4. Size	Limited	Unlimited
5. Construction and maintenance	Expensive and heavily controlled	Reasonably priced and lightly controlled
6. Space	Territory/Euclidean	Network/logical
7. Matter	Material/tangible	Immaterial/intangible
Movement		
8. Medium	Transportation	Telecommunications
9. Speed	Depends on the mode of transport	Speed of light, constrained by infrastructure, costs, regulations, etc.
10. Distance	Major constraint	Does not matter mostly
11. Time	Matters	Matters, but events can suspend in time
12. Orientation	Matters	Does not matter
Users		
13. Identity	Defined	Independent of identity in real space
14. Experience	Bodily	Imaginative and metaphorical
15. Interaction	Embodied	Disembodied
16. Attitude	Long-term commitment	Uncommitted
17. Language	National-domestic	Mainly English-international

Sources: Table: Kellerman (2002b: 35); Kellerman (2007). Items 1–2, 8–12: Li et al. (2001); items 3, 14–15: Dodge and Kitchin (2001: 30, 53); items 6–7: Graham (1998).

move contemporary society from a mere conception of physical space to a more complex one involving an inner spiritual space, achieved through networks based on global information sharing.[83]

Cyberspace may be divided into two classes: information [cyber]space and communications [cyber]space.[84] Information cyberspace (IC) refers to digital information sets or systems consisting of information organized along spatial notions such as the Web, and therefore involving geographical metaphors such as sites, homes, and navigation/surfing. Information cyberspace further refers to digital information sets at large, such as data archives, library catalogs, and videos, such as YouTube.[85] All of these information sets are either textual and/or graphic and have some constancy in terms of their virtual availability to users so that they may be recalled. Most of these information files are meant to be shared by users: either the general public through the Internet, or segmented users through intranets. Contemporary search engines have permitted easy access to websites and files. Google has emerged as a leading company in this regard in addition to providing search into specialized information systems, such as satellite images, scientific articles, and books, turning into what Maria Paradiso termed a megaproject within a megaproject (the Internet).[86]

The second class of cyberspace is communications cyberspace (CC), referring to the cyberspace of persons who interact via various modes of communications: first and foremost through video communications, which include transmitted real space visible in the background of the communicating parties as well as callers' images, and second, through purely electronic and invisible spaces of interaction, using nonvideo communications media (mainly written e-mails, faxes, short message services [SMSs], and audio telephone calls).[87] Communications [cyber]space is mostly interpersonal or shared by a small group (though it may be more widely open to larger groups in social networking systems, such as blogs, Facebook, and Twitter). Much of the content of communications cyberspace is not recorded, and if recorded it is meant to be shared only by communicating parties.

The two digital/virtual spaces of information and communications are frequently interfolded, for example when e-mails are sent through an informative website rather than an e-mail interface, or in some of the messages transmitted through Twitter, blogs, Facebook, and MySpace, which may include pictures or data. Such interfolded and even fused information and communications [cyber]spaces attest to cyberspace oneness, beyond the shared communications infrastructure of the two spaces. However, each of the two cyberspace classes may frequently function independently of the other; for example, oral communications does not involve the transmission of textual data sets.

Globalization

The essence of globalization is transitions in the location and nature of production, distribution, and consumption of products, services, money, and information, from locally and domestically based systems to highly integrated global ones.[88] From a social perspective, "globalization involves the intensification of social exchanges of various sorts on a global scale."[89] This is not to say that cities, regions, and states have lost their locational significance. It means, rather, that more than one country is normally involved in the three major phases of the economic process (production, distribution, and consumption). Investors and owners of a firm might be globally distributed, and this may also be the case for the customers of products and services. A product may be assembled in one particular place whereas its components may be produced in various other countries. Thus, globalization implies "growing *interdependence* and *interpenetration* of human relations,"[90] as well as higher locational flexibility of financing, production, and consumption. It has further implied the emergence of transnational corporations (TNCs) or multinational corporations (MNCs), with multinational ownership, management, and operation.

To a large degree, the massive adoption of new communications technologies (notably the Internet and mobile devices), as well as the upgrading of older ones (notably through digital telephony and the provision of telephone and Internet services via cable TV), have implied direct globalization of virtual mobility and contacts. By "direct globalization," we refer to the very geographical expansion of destinations for frequent contacts with other countries. This applies to international telephone calls, the tariffs for which have been drastically reduced, even to the rates of local ones in many countries, and to Internet contacts, whether through e-mails or web searches, or online shopping communications sent to out-of-country electronic addresses. The Internet further permits free voice and video contacts from computer to computer via VoIP (voice over Internet protocol) services. "Indirect globalization" may refer to rather local and domestic out-of-town physical mobility, as well as to domestic telephone calls, all stemming from the globalization of activities, for example daily commuting to work for a multinational corporation or working for a globally exporting domestic company, or, on the consumption side, even having some food or enjoying entertainment in a facility owned or operated by a global chain.

The tremendous growth in personal mobilities has been extensively embedded within the wider scene of globalization. This embeddedness will be discussed in the following paragraphs and through figure 2.3, which presents mobilities within the framework of globalization. This framework applies to mobilities at large, referring to both personal mobilities and

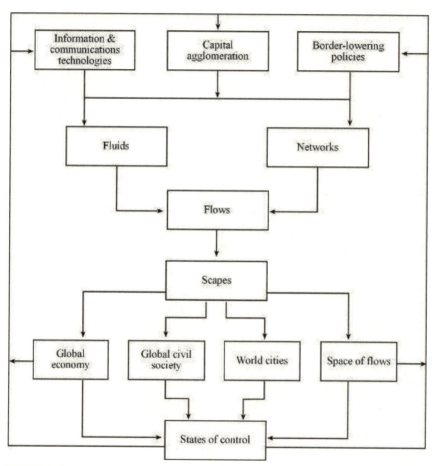

FIGURE 2.3
Globalization and Mobilities (Kellerman 2006b).

institutional ones using public transportation. The figure consists of three
parts: the first line includes three major facilitating processes for global or
globally related mobilities, namely information and communications technologies, capital agglomeration, and border-lowering policies; the boxes of
"fluids," networks, flows, and scapes, which refer to mobility components
per se; and the last two lines which refer to resulting entities in the economic, social, spatial, and political spheres. All of these elements will be
elaborated on in the following paragraphs.

Viewed from the perspective of political economy, Vincent Mosco considered the spatial agglomeration of capital as the source of globalization and as
having led to a changing geography of information and communications.[91]

Implicitly, then, it was the agglomeration of capital that provided a drive for continuous IT development and infrastructure construction. The changing geography of information and communications has meant that previously dominating major capital centers, such as New York and London, have enhanced their economic power through an expansion, or distanciation, of their area of influence on a global scale, facilitating almost limitless worldwide flows of information. This information revolution was coupled with the capital revolution, which permitted global flows of capital following the lowering of international barriers for capital flows due to the removal of state restrictions and the growth of multinational corporations. Thus capital turned into digital information: "Nowadays money is essentially information."[92]

These three facilitating processes and powers have involved virtual as well as corporeal mobilities at unprecedented scales. The various components of these mobilities have been presented by several writers, notably John Urry and Arjun Appadurai.[93] Urry used the metaphor of "fluids" as a general term for the things that are being moved globally, such as information, capital, risks, and the like: "Any such fluid can be distinguished in terms of the *rate* of flow, its *viscosity*, the *depth*, its *consistency*, and its degree of *confinement*."[94]

The transmission of these "fluids" or their flows is channeled through networks with varying degrees of flexibility. Social networks have emerged as the most flexible ones, with members or participants entering and leaving freely, and with the anonymity of members' identities preserved in many cases. Other forms of networking have been provided by commercial entities, with identities revealed and used by network management bodies. Some more rigid networks are intranet networks, usually open only to employees of specific companies. Even stricter in their access, and for obvious reasons, are banking or interbank networks, such as SWIFT.

The systems of networks and flows both constitute and aggregately create categorical scapes. Appadurai distinguished among five dimensions of global cultural flows, all of which he termed *scapes*, since, similarly to landscapes, they are looked upon differently by various actors, and since they are "fluid" and irregular. These five scapes are *ethnoscapes* (the migration of workers); *mediascapes* (television, movies, magazines, etc.); *technoscapes* (technology); *finanscapes* (finances); and *ideoscapes* (ideologies).[95] To this list one can add *commodiscapes*, for commodities that carry some cultural message on a global scale, such as pizza as an Italian food or Japanese cars,[96] and *infoscapes*, for information and knowledge globally transmitted mainly via the Internet and thus not included in mediascapes.[97]

Growing global mobilities simultaneously bring about and are enhanced by structural changes at the global scale. A leading development at the global scene has been the extensive emergence of the global economy, manifest in numerous ways. Such are complex business organizations, notably MNCs, and such are also globally anchored banks and capital funds, which survive on global mobilities of people, information, and capital, but simultaneously they call for more mobility for the continued flourishing of their firms. Side by side there emerged also globally transmitted public video information mainly through cable TV, as well as through the Internet (e.g., YouTube).

In the sphere of business management, Manuel Castells viewed the Internet as a medium that facilitates networks.[98] These networks, on their part, constitute flexible, adaptable, and coordinating organizational tools, which permit a *many-to-many* communications mode on a global scale. Castells further viewed Internet networking as reflecting globalization, freedom, and telecommunications technology. However, it does not seem real to assume that hierarchical business organization is about to disappear in the networking era. Though hierarchical business organization might have been weakened by Internet networking, the very integration of "old" hierarchical and "new" networked cultures and technologies of management has permitted the contemporary management of companies and transactions typified by their unprecedented scales of size and volume respectively.

At the social level, local and domestic societies cannot function independently of global ones. Sociologist Anthony Giddens defined globalization as "the intensification of worldwide social relations which link distant localities in such a way that local happenings are shaped by events occurring many miles away and *vice versa*."[99] As has been shown elsewhere, such global-local relationships may potentially evolve in three phases of global involvement with local processes. First is a disembedding of the local from the global so that global business activities in a city function side by side with local ones. This phase may be followed by a phase of phantasmagoria, in which global forces are concealed underneath seemingly local processes, so that local economic activity is powered by global demand for local products, or local economic entities are owned by global funds or companies. Finally, in a third phase, a fusion of the local and the global may develop, making it difficult to separate between local and global activities.[100]

Overall, Urry argued that "behaviour and motivation are less societally produced and reproduced but are the effect of a more globally organized culture that increasingly breaks free from each and every society."[101] Furthermore, a global civil society has emerged through new virtual communities, as well as through growing tourism and migrations. Castells pointed to the freedom of expression offered by the Internet in an era dominated by communications media.[102] However, the versatility of social networks does not permit an identification of a unified Internet communal culture. Rather, users are engaged in self-directed networking, looking for their own Internet destinations.

Geographically, global mobilities have been interrelated with two processes: the development of *world cities* and the possible emergence of the *space of flows*.[103] Globalization has been tied to the notion of world cities originally presented by John Friedmann and Goetz Wolff.[104] The system of world cities has been topped by three cities, New York, London, and Tokyo, and consisting of various lower levels of world cities. Global and world cities are typified by the concentration of globally spanning financial, management, and service activities in them, whether in the form of global bank headquarters, numerous foreign bank branches, global stock market activities, global business service activities, or global media concentrations. As mentioned already, all these activities have emerged through global mobilities of people, information, and capital.

The emergence of the global dimension in economic, social, and spatial spheres of society has involved some political change as well, which simultaneously nourished the previously mentioned changes. As Gilles Deleuze and Felix Guattari showed in 1986, later reinforced by John Urry, the traditional nation-state, based mainly upon territory and its symbolism, has taken the role of a controlling and regulating entity, focusing mainly on the management of mobilities.[105] This has been the case regarding domestic mobilities, whether in the form of car and drivers' licensing, or in the form of regulating the growing and privatizing communications services. This has further become the case for global mobilities, where the nation-state has become a rather sophisticated gatekeeper, licensing the activities of companies and people and thus maintaining an interest in economic and organizational goings-on beyond its territorial boundaries.

Space of Flows

Another perspective on global flows and location was put forward by Manuel Castells,[106] namely a dissolution in the significance of local place, coupled with the emergence of the global *space of flows*. The space of flows is defined as "the material organization of time-sharing social practices that work through flows,"[107] where "flows" include all possible ones, except for people: capital, information, technology, organizational interaction, images, sounds, and symbols. The space of flows, as developed by Castells, consists of three layers: the first one is technology, constituting a *circuit of electronic exchanges* embodied in networked cities; the second is a layer of places, *nodes and hubs*, hierarchically organized and topped by global cities, which serve as major loci of information production; and the third layer is people, the *managerial elites*, charged with the directional functions of the space of flows.[108] We noted already that one of the most significant aspects of the globalization of information flows is the active participation of laymen all over the world as both producers and consumers of information. This widely used access does not reduce the importance of the managerial elites: "elites are cosmopolitan, people are local."[109] These elites in flows creation have a more significant role in the very constitution of global flows as well as in the integration of such flows into their daily lives.

The exact relationships between the rather global space of flows and the domestic spaces of places have not been made clear in Castells' writings. In one place, Castells argued for "a space of flows substituting a space of places,"[110] and in another one he declared that "the space of flows of the Information Age dominates the space of places of people's cultures."[111] However, at yet another place he referred to "the historical emergence of the space of flows, superseding the meaning of the space of places."[112] Elsewhere, Castells attributed the supremacy of the space of flows more specifically to organizations in the informational economy.[113] The very idea of the superiority of the space of flows was criticized, with the observation that the locational anchoring of the space of flows is within the space of places and that the dialectic relationship between location and flows was ignored.[114] In any case, if the space of flows refers to mobility and the space of places to fixity, then still the latter, fixity, builds up mobility: "The impetus to motion and mobility, for a space of flows, can only be achieved through the construction of (temporary, provisional) stabilizations."[115] In other words, "the world is *both* a 'space of places' *and* a 'place of flows.'"[116]

Major Elements of the Information Economy

It was geographer Jean Gottmann who first identified the emergence of an urban information economy in the United States in his 1961 seminal *Megalopolis*, in which he defined the *quaternary occupations* as "those supplying services that require research, analysis, judgment, in brief brainwork and responsibility."[117] Abler, Adams, and Gould broadened the scope of the quaternary sector into *information activities*.[118] The quaternary sector was more widely defined by Daniel Bell to include trade, finance, insurance, and real estate.[119] The roots of the contemporary information economy lie, therefore, in the *postindustrial economy* and the *service economy* identified in the 1970s and 1980s. The concept of an *information economy* was first coined by Marc Porat, when he commented on the growing shares of information in the American GNP and labor force.[120]

Information may be considered as both product and resource or input for various uses by both individuals and businesses. It constitutes a product in the most simple way when it is sold, and it serves as a resource or input in many ways, such as information on market trends being used as an input for the production of material products. John Goddard was able to identify four characteristics of the evolving information economy: the increasing central-ity of information in the production of goods and services, the development of information technology, information becoming a commodity in itself, and economic globalization.[121] The very incorporation of information into the production of goods and services is not novel,[122] bringing some to comment that "every business is an information business . . . information is the glue that holds together the structure of all businesses."[123] The increasing centrality of information in the production of goods and services is thus related to the development of information technology. This technology, once wide-scale connectivity has been achieved, permitted the development of an information economy, dealing with information itself, notably as an electronically pack-aged and transmitted product. The four characteristics proposed by Goddard are thus interrelated.[124]

The information economy consists of five major elements, as shown in figure 2.4a:

- *Infrastructure:* made of information and communications technologies, including computers, communications appliances, and telecommunica-tions networks.
- *Information:* contents of all types, whether personal, business, educa-tional, or entertainment, to be delivered through the infrastructure to customers (users).
- *Media:* systems through which various types of information are con-sumed, basically the telephone, mobile phone, TV (and radio), and the Internet, devoted to different information types, at least from the user's perspective, and requiring different production, transmission, and re-ceiving systems and appliances.
- *Operators:* a very wide variety of companies that deal with the operation of businesses for production and servicing of the infrastructure (e.g., computer and telephone companies), information (such as news agen-cies and filmmaking companies), and the media (such as web design companies and TV stations).
- *Users:* all customers of the infrastructure, media, and information, whether households or businesses.

Traditionally these five major elements amount to three economic functions, namely supply (infrastructure and information), mediation (media and op-erators), and demand (businesses and households). The supply side of the

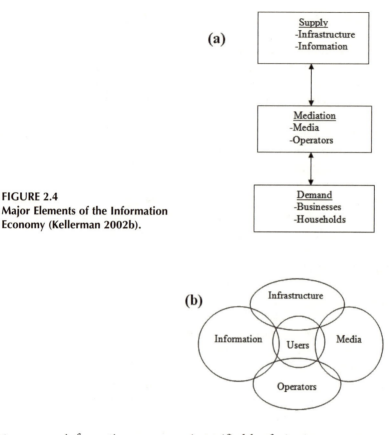

FIGURE 2.4
Major Elements of the Information Economy (Kellerman 2002b).

contemporary information economy is typified by fusion processes among these elements (see figure 2.4b), mainly because all information types have been turned into electronic bits, bringing about the development of a single channel for all information types: the Internet.

Notes

1. Roszak (1991: 13)
2. Malecki (2000: 104)
3. Roberts (2000)
4. See, e.g., Machlup (1983); Braman (1989).
5. Barlow (1994)
6. Braman (1989)
7. Roberts (2000); see also Borgmann (1999).
8. Porat (1977: 2)
9. Roberts (2000)

10. Roszak (1991: 105)
11. Boisot (1998: 12)
12. Postman (1999: 93)
13. Bell (1976: 175)
14. Machlup (1983: 644)
15. Storper (2000a: 56)
16. Feldman (1994: 2); Feldman (2000: 373–375)
17. OECD (2000: 13)
18. Roberts (2000)
19. Castells (1996: 371–372)
20. Kellerman (1997)
21. Zook (1998)
22. Kellerman (2002b)
23. Howells (2000)
24. Johnson and Lundvall (2001: n. 6)
25. Johnson and Lundvall (2001)
26. Cowan et al. (2000); Roberts (2000)
27. Cowan et al. (2000); Roberts (2000); Johnson and Lundvall (2001)
28. Howells (2000: 61)
29. Storper (2000b:157)
30. Kellerman (2000)
31. Beniger (1986:4–5)
32. Castells (1998: 67)
33. Castells (2000: 21, n. 31)
34. Webster (2006: 9)
35. Webster (2006:10)
36. European Commission (1996: 7)
37. Gottmann (1961); Bell (1976)
38. Webster (2006: 14)
39. Porat (1977); Machlup (1962); Hepworth (1990)
40. Castells (1996)
41. Grantham and Tsekouras (2004)
42. Masuda (1980: 3)
43. See, e.g., Schement (1989); Webster (1994).
44. Chandler and Cortada (2000)
45. Halal (1993); Martin (1995)
46. See, e.g., Gottmann (1961); Bell (1976); Kellerman (1985; 1993); Schement (1989); Masuda (1980); Lyon (1995); Castells (1996: 228).
47. Castells (1996: 228)
48. Schiller (1981); Schement (1989)
49. Touraine (1974); Lyon (1995)
50. Nye and Owens (1996); Lyon (1988); Masuda (1980)
51. Katz (1988: 1)
52. Porat (1977); Machlup (1962)
53. Hepworth (1990)

54. Martin (1988: 40); Steinfeld and Salvaggio (1989: 2–3); European Commission (1996)
55. Bell (1976); Steinfeld and Salvaggio (1989)
56. Swivel (2008)
57. Kellerman (1999)
58. Feather (1994: 2); Kitchin (1998: 131)
59. Software & Information Industry Association (2008)
60. Software & Information Industry Association (2008)
61. Halal (1993); Kellerman (1997)
62. Martin (1988: 40)
63. Castells (1998: 348)
64. Castells (1998: 349)
65. Kitchin (1998: 101–102)
66. Gibson (1984); Kitchin (1998: 2)
67. Benedikt (1991: 122); Kitchin (1998:2)
68. Batty (1997: 343–344)
69. Dodge and Kitchin (2001: 1)
70. Shields (2003: xv)
71. Crang et al. (1999:12–13)
72. Dodge (2001: 1)
73. Li et al. (2001: 701)
74. Graham (1998: 174)
75. Augé (2000); Bolter and Grusin (1999: 179)
76. Kellerman (2002b)
77. Dodge and Kitchin (2001)
78. Péruch et al. (2000: 115)
79. Benedikt (1991: 123, 191); Batty (1997)
80. Adams and Ghose (2003)
81. Kellerman (2002b: 33–38; 2010)
82. Benedikt (1991); Wertheim (1999)
83. Wertheim (1999)
84. Kellerman (2007)
85. Fabrikant and Buttenfield (2001); Couclelis (1998)
86. Paradiso (2009)
87. Kellerman (2007)
88. Dicken (2007: 8–9)
89. Drori (2007: 303)
90. Webster (2006: 69)
91. Mosco (1996: 205–206)
92. Thrift (1995: 27)
93. Urry (2000); Appadurai (1990)
94. Urry (2000: 32)
95. Appadurai (1990)
96. Knox (1995: 245)
97. Kellerman (2002b)

  98. Castells (2001)
  99. Giddens (1990: 64)
100. Kellerman 2002b: 43–49)
101. Urry (2000: 32)
102. Castells (2001: 54–55)
103. Castells (1989)
104. Friedmann and Wolff (1982)
105. Deleuze and Guattari (1986); Urry (2000)
106. Castells (1989)
107. Castells (2000: 442)
108. Castells (2000: 448)
109. Castells (2000: 446)
110. Castells (1985: 14)
111. Castells (1998: 349)
112. Castells (1989: 348)
113. Castells (1989: 169)
114. Merrifield (1993), Kellerman (1993)
115. Massey (2005: 95)
116. Dicken (2007: 18)
117. Gottmann (1961: 580)
118. Abler et al. (1977: 200)
119. Bell (1976)
120. Porat (1977), Hepworth (1990: 6)
121. Goddard (1990; 1992)
122. Miles and Robins (1992: 2)
123. Evans and Wurster (1997: 72)
124. Goddard (1990; 1992)

3

Technologies and Infrastructures

A<small>FTER BEING INTRODUCED TO</small> the information society in the previous chapter, you might realize that information and communication technologies constitute the basic vehicle for the evolution and operation of the information society. Thus, in this chapter, you will be introduced to ICTs per se, surveying the various technologies relevant to the emergence of the information society and its functioning, and considering the distribution of infrastructures needed for technological access to information. The major technologies that will be elaborated in the following sections are the telephone, the Internet, and mobile communications devices, notably the mobile (cellular) phone.

ICTs permit the virtual mobility of people, their thoughts and ideas, coupled with the transmission of information at large, whether it is entertainment related, such as TV broadcasts, films, or music, or whether it is institutional and commercial information of all types. The physical mobility of people at large was extended and enhanced primarily during the first part of the twentieth century through successive innovations involving various transportation technologies. These technologies have enabled a declining *friction of distance*,[1] or decreasing costs and efforts related to the overcoming of distance. They have further enabled three additional processes that we will discuss in the next chapter: an extended *distanciation*,[2] the *convergence of time-space*,[3] and *time-space compression*.[4]

By the same token, the telephone has permitted the virtual mobility of humans through interactive real-time voice communications. Innovations in telecommunications and information technologies, as of the second half of the twentieth century, have ultimately provided for almost instantaneous transmission of all types and forms of information, notably through the Internet, side by side with constant personal access to information and communications through the use of mobile phones and computers. A well-developed virtual mobility of people has thus emerged, becoming a dominant aspect of contemporary developed societies, and this virtual mobility of people has also diffused into developing societies, notably through the adoption of the mobile phone.

The emergence of contemporary virtual mobility as of the second half of the twentieth century has consisted of two major phases. In the first one, information technologies were developed, permitting the conversion of information of all types (text, voice, and still and streaming pictures) into electronic bits, stored and moved electronically. These developments were followed by the more recent introduction of sophisticated mobile information machines (laptops of various sizes and smart phones). The facilitation of information flows at the speed of light has brought some to assume the *death of distance*,[5] side by side with the emergence of *cyberspace*,[6] as well as that of the *space of flows*,[7] which we discussed in the previous chapter.

The vast development and enhancement of mobility technologies imply an intersection between enhanced physical mobility, or the growing ability of humans to move fast and efficiently across the globe, on the one hand, and their enhanced parallel virtual mobility via ICTs on the other. Passengers are able to carry with them their business and personal connections, as well as their personal "libraries," consisting of their electronic files, pictures, music, and favorite website addresses. Under well-developed telecommunications infrastructures, any performed physical spatial movement, or any journey from one place or country to another, does not change the spatial extent of the virtual mobility of the traveler: it remains global anywhere, assuming that travelers are equipped with the proper communications devices. Thus, whereas the physical spatial mobility of humans is still restrained by the time-bound friction of distance, the virtual spatial mobility of humans is not.

Communications media are normally divided into personal and public ones. The telephone, mobile phone, and e-mailing constitute *personal* communications means, extending the reach of the self through personal or personalized information, whereas radio and television are *public* media, extending the availability of given public information. The Web falls into both categories, as it permits public exposure of personal information through self-extending websites, blogs, and social communications, side by side with commercial and institutional public websites. The personal means of communication permit individual regulation of content as well as the geographical destinations/origins of information, whereas public media, varied as they may be in their content, are much more limited in this regard, providing almost always one-way communication from broadcasters to listeners/viewers. The tremendous speed and mobility of information, coupled with the wide availability of mobile information machines, are unparalleled with those offered by current corporeal transportation means, such as cars or airplanes.

The Telephone

We will highlight the telephone from various perspectives: first, we will briefly outline its development, followed by an elaboration of its social and spatial aspects, especially as compared to the automobile, and conclude with its use compared to physical personal mobility through automobiles.

The telephone was invented in the United States in 1876, nine years before the automobile, and was first conceived of as "a speaking telegraph."[8] It was turned into an independent commercial service much faster than the automobile, in 1878, just two years after its invention, following patenting by its inventor, Alexander Graham Bell. However, the first fifty years of telephone diffusion presented higher adoption rates by businesses than individuals.[9] Thus, it was only in 1946 that over 50 percent of American households were equipped with telephone communications. This benchmark was achieved some sixty-eight years after the commercial introduction of the telephone, compared to just nineteen years for the same phase in the adoption process of private automobiles. One of the reasons for this difference in the adoption rates of these two personal mobility media has to do with their transmission systems. The construction of telephone lines, owned by private companies, represented response to demand and did not spread sufficiently into U.S. rural areas until the 1930s, as compared to road systems which were constructed by governments and thus represented wider equality of access by privately owned cars as well as by public buses. Following the 1934 U.S. Telecommunications Act, which called for the provision of universal telephone service, the federal government had to assist private telephone companies in the development of proper telephone infrastructures, mainly in rural areas.[10]

The traditional fixed-line telephone, permitting audio and written (through fax) communications between two or more places, has been upgraded in recent decades through its digitalization, thus providing more diversified services, such as communications with computers, international direct phone calls, and its integration with Internet-based voice communications (VoIP). By the end of 2011 there were globally some 16.6 telephone lines per one hundred world inhabitants. In the developed world this percentage reached 39.8 in 2011, decreasing from a peak of 56.8 in 2000, whereas in the developing world this ratio reached 11.6, declining from a peak of 19.5 in 2005.[11] In both the developed and developing worlds, the penetration of fixed-line telephones has declined in recent years due to the growing penetration of mobile telephones.

Telephones constitute the most basic and oldest appliance and medium for personal virtual mobility. When weighed by electronic volume (bytes), Peter Lyman and Hal Varian[12] estimated for 2002 that 96.6 percent of electronic information flows worldwide were made over telephones (fixed and mobile), whereas just 3.0 percent were transmitted through the Internet. In addition, some 0.4 percent of electronic information flows constituted television broadcasts, and merely 0.04 percent of all electronic information bytes were transmitted over radio broadcasts. It might well be, though, that the share of the Internet would have been larger if the measurement were made by number of contacts. Telephone history has been documented elsewhere, as have its sociospatial aspects,[13] so our focus now will be on comparisons between telephones and automobiles.

Telephones and Automobiles: Comparative Features

Comparisons of telephones and automobiles are useful because each technology has the potential to change how and where we live and work. As we seek to understand the impact of information and communication technologies, it is instructive to understand how past technologies have shaped, and been shaped by, their adopting societies. While the initial mass production of automobiles was geared to the household market, the early commercial introduction of the telephone was meant for business use. Even after telephones started appearing in households in the United States in the early twentieth century, no significantly distinguished telephone models for home use were introduced. The telephone has always been a small appliance which normally has had to be attached to the body when used, rather than being a large-scale capsule enveloping the body as cars have been.

The telephone implies speed: it provides speedy and instant two-way communications, qualities which are unattainable for communications through postal services and the telegraph. The telephone is furthermore much speedier than the automobile, as it does not involve time and space frictions. These features of the telephone took several years of development at the time, since early telephone service required the time-consuming assistance of telephone exchange operators. Like automobiles, telephones provide flexibility in movement, when assuming that most households and businesses are connected to the system. Also like automobiles, telephones provide subscribers with personal autonomy and individualism,[14] at times most significantly for women and children who were partially deprived of these qualities. Telephones further involve the power of information sharing, as well as the pleasure associated with social contacts. Given the lack of time friction or traffic jams in its normal operation, the telephone may assist routine time organization, and it may involve a reorganization of daily lives when services can be obtained over the telephone.

The major differences for individuals between automobiles and telephones are the lack of laws and regulations for "driving" the telephone or "passing through" communication lines, and the lower dependence on maintenance and global supply industries in telephone usage, as compared to garages and gas supply for cars, respectively. Telephone use also involves several features that are irrelevant for physical mobility. Thus telephones provide for co-location in at least two places when a conversation is made, and telephone conversations amount to "disembodied sounds—of speech displaced in space and time from its origins."[15] The telephone is thus a time intruder when one is being called by another party.

From a social perspective the telephone and its use present various aspects and ramifications. Early or recent governmental attempts to assure universal availability of household connections to the telephone system assumed that personal virtual mobility constitutes a basic right, even if the provision of the service was not performed directly by government but was rather channeled through private companies. Sometimes such policies have been anchored in laws such as the 1934 American Telecommunications Act which we have mentioned already.

Informal social relations, as expressed through telephone conversations, may present some special nuances for audio interactions. Thus telephone contacts have created a telephone culture as to the way telephone conversations begin and end, their structuring, the time of calling, and so forth, and these nuances and cultures might differ among cultures and countries. Callers are expected to abide by such domestic "norms." Similarly to the driving of private cars, telephone use for social contacts may facilitate increased contacts with other places, and these contacts may bring about declining levels of localism. Such increased telephone contacts with other places may further contribute to a sense of placelessness or a feeling of similarity for all contacted places. The telephone may be considered a significant social device, but despite its social importance it has not become a status symbol like automobiles, because the fixed-line telephone constitutes a small appliance located inside the home.

From a spatial perspective, and contrary to automobiles, contemporary telephone infrastructures constitute a minor and declining land use, as most telephone cables are buried, and digital telephone exchanges are becoming smaller and smaller. Until the introduction of digital telephone services as of the 1960s, analog telephone exchanges required much space, so telephone buildings were present in urban landscapes. Also contrary to automobiles, telephones have not been considered an environmental pollutant. However, like automobiles, they have facilitated the suburbanization of populations, services, and production.[16] As such, telephones do not necessarily contribute to segregation, but they may facilitate personal physical isolation while still permitting the maintenance of virtual communications with and by solitary individuals.

Telephones and Automobiles: Use Comparison

Unfortunately, not much evidence exists on individuals' choices between telephone and car usage during the first century of telephone and automobile availability to households, though futuristic predictions in this regard were already being proposed as early as the introduction of the telephone.[17] However, the choice between the use of cars and telephones has been widely discussed and tested in the more recent transportation literature, evolving mainly as of the 1970s. At that time telephone systems gradually underwent digitization, thus permitting the networking first of computer terminals and later of PCs in both offices and homes. In addition, long-distance telephone services became cheaper and more direct, mainly in the 1980s.[18] Thus it is possible to divide the transportation-telecommunications relationship into three periods by prevailing communications technologies: first, telephone-based vocal virtual mobility until the 1970s; second, the period from the 1970s to the mid-1990s, which may be considered transitional, focusing on computer-supported telecommunications (notably the Telnet system, which permitted the introduction of remote desk terminals for larger computers); and third, the rather versatile, Internet-based era, emerging as of the mid-1990s.

Patricia Mokhtarian distinguished among four possible relationships between telecommunications and travel: "substitution (elimination, replacement), generation (stimulation, complementarity), modification, and neutrality."[19] Though these patterns may exist simultaneously, the accumulated evidence has pointed to complementarity and travel stimulation as the leading modes of relationship between physical mobility via automobiles and virtual mobility via telecommunications (telephones and computers).[20] This trend has been true for both the Telnet-based transitional period as well as for the more contemporary, Internet-based period. Of interest in this regard is the estimation that much of our physical travel is geared to the obtaining of information,[21] and as John Adams noted, "Those societies that make the greatest use of telephones and the Internet are also the most mobile physically."[22]

The two most frequent daily personal journeys are for shopping and commuting, estimated at 21 and 16 percent, respectively, of all trips in the UK from 1997 to 1999.[23] In the United States, commuting amounted to 30.4 percent of the total motor vehicle miles traveled already back in 1977.[24] Telecommuting has turned out to constitute a less-preferred alternative option to physical commuting. Just 3.9 percent of the American workforce worked at home in 2006,[25] merely 5 percent of the Swedish workforce worked from home in 1999, and some additional 6 percent were considered mobile workers.[26] Patricia Mokhtarian estimated that merely 16 percent of all U.S. workers could potentially telework or telecommute.[27] For various reasons, most of these potential teleworkers do not prefer to work from home, so that only 2 percent of the total U.S. workforce telecommuted on a given day, and since many of these teleworkers worked just part time and thus did not use carpools, the net potential decrease in physical travel by telecommuters amounted to just 1 to 2 percent! In addition, and even more importantly, teleworkers may be tempted to go on other new trips unrelated to commuting, so that the real aggregate decrease in travel brought about by teleworking is even lower.

In the United Kingdom, growth in teleworking due to the Internet was reported for occasional work only,[28] though the boundaries between work and home have been blurred.[29] These low estimates following the computerization of telephone services and the early use of the Internet may also shed some light on the first period of the transportation-telecommunications relationship, when telephone services constituted only vocal communications. We may thus assume that the more limited vocal communications provided by the telephone at those times could not generate significant substitution for physical travel to work. Hence, it seems that so far virtual mobility cannot be considered a significant replacement for physical mobility via automobiles for commuting.

As for shopping, the estimate for direct marketing in the United States for the late 1970s stood at around 10 percent of total retail sales.[30] This estimate included telephone sales, sales made through the postal service, and products and services that by their very nature could not be sold in retail stores. As Ilan Salomon has noted, the impact of the telephone and other forms of teleshopping on travel was not studied at the time.[31] However, the low percentage of total direct marketing using telephones and postal services hints to complementarity between physical and direct marketing rather than to massive substitution at the time. The more contemporary relationship between the Internet and physical travel for shopping purposes will be further highlighted in the following section focusing on the Internet.

The Internet

The Internet will be presented and discussed from various angles. We will begin by highlighting its very essence, followed by an elaboration of its evolution. We will then move to discussions of its structure, its social and spatial aspects, and finally its comparison to corporeal mobility through cars.

Essence

Basically, the Internet fulfills two major needs: It serves as the largest library on earth, available anywhere through wired or wireless communications of various kinds, and includes all forms of human-made information on all possible topics. As such, the Web part of the Internet constitutes *the most comprehensive information system*. The Web contains information in all possible forms: text, data, graphics, voice, and motion pictures. Unlike the telephone, it contains structured information, and unlike almost all of live radio and television programs, it is an on-demand system. The Internet fulfills another need in its being simultaneously a communications system through electronic mail (e-mail), which can connect two or more corresponding persons and which may transmit written, graphic, and audiovisual messages. Furthermore, the Internet at large, combining the Web and e-mail systems, is a comprehensive and interactive information system, permitting the performance of a variety of economic activities, such as shopping, work, financial transfers, and so forth. In fact, the Internet permits through the Web, as well as through e-mailing, the incorporation of all other electronic and printed forms of information (e.g., fax, voice telephony, radio, television, and newspapers). Through new generations of technology for mobile telephony, the Internet is turning into a wireless information system available through telephones rather than only through designated computers. As such, the Internet may be considered a *general purpose technology* (GPT), similar to electricity, railroads, and automobiles.[32]

By the end of 2011, there were some thirty-five Internet users per one hundred inhabitants worldwide. In the developed world this rate reached seventy-four by the end of 2011, whereas in the developing world this rate stood at the same time at twenty-six. A globally publicized initiative at the time by MIT professor Nicholas Negroponte is OLPC (One laptop per child), which called for the supply of specially designed laptops for schoolchildren in developing countries. These laptops were proposed to be cheap ($100–$200), without hard disks and manually powered, but making it possible for children worldwide to explore and express themselves within the global information system. This initiative was later partially materialized by Nokia and other computer and mobile companies.

The rapid adoption of the Internet, as well as that of mobile telephony, has been influenced by the prior existence of partial infrastructures through the telephone system, so that new connections to the system could be easily performed. Of no less importance, though, is the emergence of both the Internet and mobile telephony at a time when these innovations constituted technologies and means supporting and simultaneously being an integral part of the evolving information society, which puts a special emphasis on the production, processing, transmission, and consumption of information.

Another way of looking at the Internet is through the eyes of computer networks: "The Internet consists of a global network of computers that are linked together by 'wires'—telecommunications technologies (cables of copper, coaxial, glass, as well as radio and microwaves)."[33] An additional way of looking at the Internet is from the perspective of information technology, namely that it consists of computers interconnected by the protocol TCP/IP (Transmission Control Protocol/Internet Protocol). Yet another way of viewing both the Internet and intranets, which permit intraorganizational communications, is via the form of information exchanges, namely that they constitute networks that permit open and free information exchanges.[34]

Evolution

The Internet is currently an information and communications system available to the general public and geared to the needs of the widest possible customer sectors. It took a long period of twenty-five years of incubation and development of early security and academic electronic networks of communications and information until they eventually matured into a universal and commercial entity, the Internet, in 1994. However, it took much less time, just seven years, for the Internet to be adopted by one-half of Americans, either having access to it or being online at home. Its current universal availability has been considered the best example of the adoption of a technology for purposes completely different from those envisaged by its developers.[35]

Originally, the Internet was an outgrowth of the communications and information needs of two sectors, namely the U.S. military and academic communities. The U.S. Army was interested in the 1960s in a backup computer-based communications system in case the telephone system might be severely damaged by a nuclear attack. Early experiments with an intercomputer communications system were performed by the U.S. Army as of the early 1960s, and the experimental ARPANET (Advanced Research Projects Agency

Network) system was launched in 1969 connecting to a site at the University of California in Los Angeles.[36]

The early connections of the military system had been made to university research centers so that the new communications system, later known as e-mail, has brought about the development of academic networks, connecting universities and research centers. Side by side with the emergence of an electronic intercomputer communications system, there were developed information technologies needed for the establishment of an information system that later permitted the formation, storage, transmission, and retrieval of data, information, and knowledge bases, first known as Gopher and File Transfer Protocol (FTP), and later transformed into the World Wide Web (WWW). This system first served the specific needs of universities and research centers. The geographical diffusion and expansion of the system was aided by the development of the TCP/IP communications protocol in 1973, permitting the transfer of electronic information among computers with different hardware, operating systems, and applications software.

The 1980s witnessed three major developments spanning the United States and Europe: the maturing and diversification of computer communications networks, further developments of communications technologies, and the development of technologies for the establishment of the Web. Thus, in 1987, the originally military ARPANET was replaced by the civilian and educational NSFNET (National Science Foundation Network), based on a U.S. transcontinental backbone of communications lines and hubs. In 1981 Yale University and CUNY (City University of New York) were connected into what became another interuniversity system called BITNET (Because It's Time Network) in North America. As of 1984, BITNET was coupled with the IBM-sponsored EARN (European Academic and Research Network) network.[37] These two systems were based on the chain principle, so that each new linking university was connected to an already connected one, while permitting other joining institutions to connect through its computers. In 1995 the Clinton-Gore administration decommissioned and privatized NSFNET into what became the Internet, a unified nongovernmental, general-purpose, and global computer communications and information system, a *network of networks*.

In the 1980s through the early 1990s, the major European research center CERN, based in Switzerland, developed some crucial information identification and switching tools for the emergence of the Web: HTML, URL, and HTTP. At the same time, in 1986, the American Cisco company introduced the router, permitting route selection for the transmission of information between computers. Meanwhile, at the American academic R&D frontier, the server UNIX was developed at the University of California, Berkeley, and in 1993 the first browser, Mosaic, was developed and introduced at the University of Illinois,

Urbana-Champaign. This latter tool marked the beginnings of the Web as a collection of sites for downloading. The Mosaic browser served as the basis for the introduction of Netscape (1994) and Internet Explorer (1995). Thus, in 1994–1995, some twenty-six years after it was experimentally launched, the Internet had been established as an open, commercial communications system, as well as a rapidly developing comprehensive information system.

From a geographical perspective, it is interesting to compare the diffusion and expansion of the originally military ARPANET/NSFNET with the academic BITNET across the United States.[38] Being oriented to military centers and related research centers, ARPANET did not diffuse necessarily through the major population centers. Thus, in 1971, Los Angeles, San Francisco, and Boston were connected through several sites in each city, but New York hosted only one node at New York University. This trend continued when the backbone was established by NSFNET in the late 1980s, resulting in highly networked urban regions such as Seattle, Austin, and Boston. To the contrary, BITNET, as an academic network originating in New York, had the largest number of universities connected in New York, followed by California (Los Angeles, San Francisco) and later on by Massachusetts (Boston), Illinois (Chicago), and Texas (Austin). Given the chain structure of the network, the geographical diffusion of BITNET was contagious, connecting nearby universities, as well as hierarchical, connecting first the major institutions. Interestingly, the major nodes on both NSFNET and BITNET emerged in the 1980s as the major centers of information technology R&D and production.

Structure

The *domain name system* (DNS) is the system that identifies any hosting server by a numerical address, the *IP address*, and its equivalent alphanumerical address.[39] Responsibility for allocation and registration of IP addresses and domain names was first exclusively located in the United States, moving from government agencies through the NSF to a nonprofit organization, Network Solutions. As of the late 1990s, these activities have also been maintained by a European company, NetNames, and finally by a global agency, ICANN. In early 2008 the world total for domain name count was close to 58 million, headed by the United States and the United Kingdom.

Top-level domains (TLDs) are the suffix of any e-mail or Web address. Most, but not all, of the U.S. suffix codes constitute one of the following categories, the generic TLDs (gTLDs):

com: commercial company
org: nonprofit organization

net: network
edu: academic institute
int: international organization
gov: governmental department/agency
mil: U.S. military
info: information
biz: business
coop: cooperative
aero: air-transport industry
name: individuals
travel: travel
jobs: jobs
museum: museum
mobi: mobile

Outside the United States the TLDs consist of a two-letter code representing one of about 250 countries, the ccTLD, normally the common international country code, such as *uk* for the United Kingdom. This code is preceded by a two- or three-letter code representing gTLDs, such as *co* for commercial companies, *ac* for academic institutions, and *org* for organizations. Additional flexibility emerged in 2009, when TLDs could potentially be chosen by users, if they wished to do so, for a high registration fee.

The TLD is preceded in a domain name by the company/organization/individual full name or its abbreviation, or any other name that the registering company/organization/individual would like to carry for its identification on the Internet, if still available. This domain name may be preceded by a local host or server name or any subdomain. For example, the URL *exchange.haifa. ac.il* refers to the server exchange at the University of Haifa in Israel.

Domain names are traded, and registering entities may sometimes choose registration countries for various convenience factors.[40] Thus, there is no full symmetry between a company/organization's country of operation and country of Internet/host registration.[41] By the same token, within a given country the Internet registration address of an entity does not necessarily correspond to its street address or its major address of operation.

The Internet has been governed by an open code, which Lawrence Lessig considered the "heart of the Internet."[42] This open code permits unlicensed access for the production of Internet information, whether through the establishment of websites or through writing e-mail messages. It further permits open access to the consumption of Internet information, through the receipt of e-mails, as well as access to free-of-charge websites, thus providing for the uncontrolled flow of information from any origin to any destination. This open-code system also allows for innovations to be freely introduced and adopted, innovations that relate to both the production and consumption of Internet information. All of these activities are unrestricted by any minimum or maximum age of users, so that Internet use constitutes a completely informal activity as compared, for example, to the restricted and licensed driving of a car.

This nature of the Internet may be related to its origin in the United States and the accent of American society on free expression. The open-code nature of the Internet has been questioned by various forces of a regulatory nature, such as taxing authorities, copyright holders, and others. Lessig called for preserving the open-code status of the Internet.[43] The open-code of the Internet has had some additional expressions, for instance in the evolution of some informal communications codes, such as ways of approaching others in e-mail correspondence, which resemble face-to-face conversations. By the very nature of the Internet as a mainly verbal communications system, literacy requirements are much more needed for its use than they are for driving. Another informal requirement for Internet use is the knowledge of some basic computer operation. Knowledge of English is also almost imperative, as illiteracy of the English language implies no access to information contained in a large share of websites.[44] Culture and religion are some additional informal dimensions that may in some cases influence the extent of use of the Internet, for example when rather restricting codes or censorship are imposed on the use of the Web by various countries or religious groups.

The Internet and Telephones

The Internet has been considered to constitute "a metaphor for the social life as fluid."[45] The Internet is in many respects similar to its predecessor, the telephone, in virtual mobility facilitation. This stems from its very nature as a free and uncontrolled medium for personal mobility. Like telephones, there are no laws or regulations for "driving" the Internet or for "passing through" communications lines. Also like the telephone, the Internet provides for co-location in at least two places when a real-time interaction is made. On the other hand, one may also point to some differences between the Internet and the telephone. If not used for incoming telephone calls (VoIP: Voice over Internet Protocol), the Internet cannot be considered a time intruder. In other words, the Internet can be accessed and used at any time, but it does not force an interruption into the time of communicated partners as the telephone does through incoming calls. However, the Internet is similar to telephones, as far as spatial expansion is concerned, in that it permits long-distance and international messaging and calling. The Web further expands the lived spaces of its users beyond their real locations, since cyberspace represents additional real or imagined spaces.[46]

At the social level, the Internet has expanded the idea of personal virtual mobility as a democratic right by its very provision of instant written communications, as well as by its provision of access to information. It has practically extended personal virtual expression to unprecedented levels, through both the Web with its personal websites and interaction systems, and obviously through e-mailing. One basic dimension of this extended mobility and expression is the emergence of virtual communities and networks.

The Internet further permits co-presence in several places simultaneously.[47] Thus the Internet involves exposure of its users to virtual spaces as well as to geographically more dispersed social ties, and these may potentially be associated with increased placelessness.[48] As such, the Internet is closer to automobiles than to telephones, as it permits both an audio and a visual exposure to virtual spaces.

Virtual and real services provided through the Internet may potentially contribute to an increased and more extensive spatial dispersion of dwellings. Visions of future totally dispersed spaces of residence have accompanied earlier phases of telecommunications developments, but they have not materialized. So far, the first seventeen years of service provision through the Internet have not yet provided evidence for the emergence of community dissolution.

The Internet and Automobiles

The maintenance of the Internet and its spatial effects are completely different from those of automobiles. The use of the Internet involves some dependence on experts in telecommunications and computers, more than the use of telephones, but still at a much lower frequency than the periodic and unpredicted mechanical maintenance of automobiles. Contrary to automobile maintenance, computer problems can frequently be remotely fixed or taken care of by users themselves with expert guidance over the telephone. The Internet is transmitted through telephone lines so that it does not add any specific land uses other than computer stores, ISP offices and facilities, and the like. Like the telephone, and contrary to automobiles, the Internet per se does not add environmental pollutants, but its waste (such as hardware) may.

Back in 1982, Geurt Hupkes suggested "the law of constant travel time and trip-rates [which] stated that the average number of daily trips per person and the time budget allocated to transport show stability"[49] without regard to technological change. Patricia Mokhtarian and Cynthia Chen termed this notion *travel time budget* (TTB) and were able to date it back to the early 1960s.[50] They reviewed over a dozen empirical studies on the use of public and personal corporeal mobility media and concluded that a person devotes on the average some 1.1 to 1.3 hours a day for travel, and that the notion of TTB may possibly hold only at the most aggregate social level for reasons they claim not to be clearly understood. They concluded from their review that it is the principle of travel time as a disutility to be minimized that governs individual transportation behavior, so that individuals want to minimize travel time for their ability to perform a given set of activities rather than wanting to achieve the most attractive set of activities within a given TTB. The time devoted by individuals to travel depends on a variety of social variables, one of which is car ownership. However, this variable was shown in empirical studies to work in contradictory directions; sometimes it increased and at other times it decreased travel time expenditures, and in some additional cases it did not influence travel time expenditures at all.

The choice between using the Internet, on the one hand, and driving automobiles for household activities on the other is obviously a new one, but it too may yield one of the four potential options suggested by Mokhtarian: substitution (of travel by the Internet), generation (of new travel by the Internet), modification (of travel habits), and neutrality (no impact of the Internet on travel).[51] It is possible that the adoption of both cars and the Internet by households may bring about either more stationary or more mobile lifestyles.[52] Thus, if the law of constant travel holds, then the total time allocated to combined physical and virtual mobilities will not change compared to the pre-Internet era, at both the individual and aggregate levels. However, if the principle of travel time as a disutility to be minimized is valid for transportation-Internet relationships and it governs individual transportation behavior, then individuals will minimize travel time for a given set of activities, substituting travel by the Internet, but they will go on new corporeal trips. On the one hand, new communications technologies seem to call for substitution of travel, but social and other factors may inhibit a wide substitution of private physical mobility through automobiles by a virtual one via the Internet.

Findings for Sweden suggest that the Internet complements travel rather than leading to substitution.[53] It was further found in Germany that those who travel more also communicate more, and the other way around, which is a form of modification.[54] Similarly it was shown that those engaged in many activities outside their homes tend to use e-commerce.[55] Glenn Lyons compared the still-young Internet to Ford's Model T, claiming that major future modifications and improvements in the Internet should be expected, possibly bringing about travel substitution. He thus called for joint policy considerations of travel and the Internet.[56]

It recently turned out, however, that the introduction of video calls over smart phones has brought about combined physical travel with video personal communications. It was for William Leiss to comment back in 1976 that the geographical separation between the location of household dwellings and the location of people's spatial activities may increase more than the possible supply of means for personal mobility.[57] Thus the Internet could potentially assist in relieving urban traffic pressures. However, saving one trip through use of the Internet may generate another one.[58] The Internet could assist socially excluded populations, such as the handicapped, in the provision of substitutes for travel.[59]

The physical presence of employees at work seems to constitute a strong passion presented by both workers and managers, and it further seems that this has not changed with the wide adoption of the Internet.[60] The friction of time and distance involved in daily commuting has been frequently viewed negatively, but this seemingly "wasted" time also has a positive side in that it offers a buffer between home and work environments and responsibilities.[61]

The Internet, notably online exchanges and video conversations, might be complementary to, but not a substitute for, face-to-face social contacts. Though there are conflicting views on the social role of e-mail, its price is not distance sensitive as telephone contacts have been until recently.[62] The Internet permits us to keep social ties over long geographical distances, notably following a change of residence.[63] The Internet does not merely constitute a virtual personal communications system for households, but it is also an entertainment medium, possibly competing with or complementing other media such as television, notably with regard to time allocation for media usage.[64]

Mobile Communications

Two wireless communications technologies have been widely adopted in recent years: mobile, or cellular, telephones and computer wireless communications (Wi-Fi). These two technologies have been integrated in 3G (third-generation) smart phones. The mobile phone connects two or more people, rather than places, through voice, short text communications (SMS), and in 3G phones video communications. Mobile telephone technology was originally introduced back in 1906 by Lee de Forest who claimed then that "it will be possible for businessmen, even while automobiling, to be kept in constant touch."[65] The first limited mobile services were introduced in the United Kingdom in 1940 and in the United States in 1947, followed by commercial introduction in 1979.[66] Mobile telephony thus showed a rather slow evolution from the time of its original invention, early after the introduction of the telephone, to the 1980s–1990s. Mobile telephony had to await its final development until the release of the required wave spectrum in the late 1960s, when proper social and economic conditions emerged for such a long-awaited move by the American Federal Communications Commission (FCC).

Mobile phones have been rapidly adopted as of the 1990s.[67] In 2002, the number of mobile telephone lines worldwide for the first time exceeded the number of fixed telephone lines.[68] Mobile telephony has become the most widely and most rapidly adopted ICT device. By the end of 2011 its global penetration reached eighty-seven subscribers per one hundred inhabitants.[69] At that time, mobile phone penetration in developed countries reached 118 percent, as compared to 79 percent in developing countries. It was recently shown that penetration levels of mobile phones are related to personal income, notably in Oceania and Asia,[70] whereas the pace of penetration is higher in small and/or densely populated countries, permitting easier setup of wireless infrastructure.[71] Mobile telephony has a positive impact on economic growth, particularly in developing countries,[72] and it is generally of special significance in developing societies, notably in Africa, since this technology is frequently the only available mobility technology, representing a *leapfrogging process* in which a new technology is adopted while skipping the adoption of older ones, in this case namely the telegraph and fixed-line telephones.[73]

In more recent years, mobile phones have turned into diversified communication and organizational devices, including cameras, MP3/MP4 players, radios, calculators, and more, being further integrated with TV, the Internet, and GPS (Global Positioning System) through 3G technologies. SMS has recently transformed from an interpersonal medium, most popular among young people, into a business-to-clients medium as well. The British Kapow survey was able to rank the top-ten business types using SMS: recruitment agencies; entertainment information services; clubs and bars; Internet service providers and hosting companies; couriers; schools, colleges, and universities; hair salons, dentists, and surgeries; mechanics and body shops; charities; and insurance companies.[74] Of special importance for the urban scene are mobile LBS (location-based services) services, permitting users to receive information on specific functions and services in their immediate location.

The growing integration of mobile phones with Internet communications signals the completion of a major phase in mobile information society, permitting one to have immediate access to all personal and public information and permitting constant and universal communications in all possible forms. A contemporary urbanite, notably in developed countries, may already have access to all possible classes of information, whether she or he is sedentary at home or at work, or corporeally mobile, on the street or stopping somewhere, for instance in stores or in cafés. Some 46.3 percent of the population in Europe and some 25.9 percent in the Americas were connected to mobile broadband by the end of 2010.[75] Mobile telephone communications amounts not just to the addition of mobile communications to rather fixed communications, but it presents a new phase in the development and diffusion of virtual communications at large, including, in a more restricted sense, developing countries. Thus "mobility responds to communication and drives communication; communication responds to mobility and drives mobility."[76] Despite the location-free nature of mobile telephony, however, location telling is a common practice among users of mobile phones.[77]

Another unique aspect of contemporary mobile ICTs is that they do not require urban space for their adoption and usage, like roads and parking lots for cars and past spacious analog exchanges for telephones, nor do they facilitate new waves of urban spatial growth as automobiles and telephones did. They allow sophisticated uses of existing urban spaces, whether through navigation (via GPS) or through communications while on the road (via mobile phones), doing so without regard to the spatial organization of cities.[78]

A major feature of mobile phones is their small size and weight, despite their contemporary sophistication through the addition of functions such as cameras, radio, TV, GPS, and recording. Japan has led in the use of larger mobile phones than in other countries, permitting convenient SMS and e-mail typing so that phones are used more for written than for spoken communication. This has had to do with the small average size of Japanese homes, which limited the use of full-size computers at home.

Wireless laptop communications (Wi-Fi, standing for "wireless fidelity") was introduced in the late 1990s through the 802.11b communications protocol.[79] For general public use, it is still limited to areas where proper antennas are installed ("hot spots"), such as airports, cafés, and parks, though citywide installations of public antennas in urban areas are under way in many cities (e.g., San Francisco and Philadelphia). Studying what he called the "secret geography of Wi-Fi,"[80] Torrens was able to show for Salt Lake City an "adverse crowding of infrastructure in parts of the city and signs of saturation in the radio spectrum."[81]

The simultaneous introduction of SMS, Internet services over mobile telephones, and laptop Wi-Fi communications has implied the availability of two portable information machines, the laptop and the mobile phone, each potentially providing both Internet and telephone services. These technologies developed out of the previously developed telephone and Internet technologies, presenting a merger of mobility, computerized information, and communications. The ICT world is now in a process of merging the two information machines, the mobile phone and the laptop computer, and the recent introduction of tablets marks a new phase in this merging of mobile telephony and the Internet.

Wireless Communications and Other Mobility Media

The use of wireless communications in automobiles implies additivity between corporeal and virtual mobilities. It further implies a reconnection between the movements of people and information, following a long separation between the two, dating back to the introduction of the telegraph which enabled the transmission of messages without messengers.[82] From yet another angle, automobiles provide a special moving space of privacy for calls made over mobile phones.[83]

Wireless communications are in many respects similar to its predecessors in mobility facilitation. However, when compared to the telephone, it obviously facilitates flexibility in both physical and virtual movements, whereas the telephone permits only virtual flexibility. Wireless communications further simultaneously intrudes on users' time and place, as compared to a possible time intrusion by the telephone. The use of mobile phones thus nullifies possible isolation. The use of either mobile phones or wireless Internet connections implies a blurring between the private and the public, as well as between indoors and outdoors. Whereas telephones and computers were traditionally considered devices to be used indoors and involving some privacy of communications, the use of wireless communications media implies less privacy and a change of social boundaries regarding the acceptance of communications activity in the public sphere.

Barry Wellman viewed wireless communications as expressing a new phase in social communications and networking.[84] He termed nontechnological communications as *door-to-door* communications, typifying social relations within traditional, physical-place-bounded communities. The automobile and the telephone have permitted the development of a second phase of social relations and networking, *place-to-place* ones, replacing some of the local door-to-door relations. The Internet has enhanced place-to-place networks through its provision of continuous communications, whereas placeless wireless communications have implied the emergence of a third phase, *person-to-person* communications, detached from household location and its communications infrastructure.

Wireless communications devices may turn into status symbols as they present users' "emphasis on coping and continuous movement,"[85] and in this respect mobile telephones are different from fixed ones. Though smaller in size than fixed telephones, mobile phones are being carried and used in public, and the current variety of features for mobile telephones of various generations and makers may permit viewing some of them as status symbols.

Wireless communications constitute a minor land use, but the need for many antennas for its uninterrupted functioning is still considered a potentially hazardous radiation source and thus presents an environmental problem. Mobile telephones may permit the development of geographically more flexible clienteles for local services, given the ability to provide location-based services (LBS) to physically moving potential clients by identifying their exact location through GPS technologies. Wireless devices further encourage more travel, notably business travel, through the availability of virtual mobility while physically on the road.[86]

Anthony Townsend and Matthew Zook et al. noted that mobile phones may permit a faster, more efficient, and more flexible use of time and space by individuals, which may fit the more flexible social nature of contemporary cities.[87] They further noted the aggregately more efficient management of face-to-face contacts in central business districts, as well as a more efficient use of highways, when mobile phones are widely adopted, as this communication medium permits immediate contact when, for example, scheduling requires a change because of unforeseen traffic congestion. Leslie Haddon noted that mobile phones permit more spontaneity in time use.[88] For individuals, wherever located, mobile phones may further imply personal globalization, as overseas destinations may be reached instantaneously from any location, albeit frequently at high costs for vocal calls (and lower ones for SMS). Townsend commented that "accessibility became more important than mobility,"[89] but the two notions are strongly interwoven when automobiles and mobile communications are used simultaneously.

It is hard to assume any connection between household adoptions of automobiles and wireless communications, as the latter has been introduced when most households in developed countries already owned cars. Furthermore, given the mobile nature of wireless communications, it is, as we noted before, rather additive to automobiles, so that drivers and passengers can communicate while on the road. Another form of complementarity of wireless communications to physical mobility may be provided by technologies that permit more efficient driving and better way-finding. GPS are satellite communications devices providing vocal and visual navigation assistance, now frequently integrated into mobile phones. They permit easy, safe, and direct navigation, especially when driving through unknown urban environments. The penetration of GPS is still in its early phases as compared to mobile telephony. The United States is one of the three leading countries in GPS penetration (jointly with Japan and South Korea), with some 17 percent of its adult population using GPS devices in 2007, growing to 25.2 percent in 2010.[90]

Mobile telephones compete directly with fixed-line telephones, and as we noted already, some decline in household ownership of telephone lines has been registered already in response to the growth in household penetration rates of mobile phones. We have further noted already that the number of mobile phone lines worldwide exceeds the number of fixed lines. The intensive technological efforts to improve the operations of portable computers may potentially contribute to the replacement of PCs by laptops. These efforts include stronger electric power, lower weight, the growing extent of Wi-Fi coverage, declining prices, and the availability of modems connecting laptops to mobile phone systems.

Networking

At the core of contemporary electronic communications systems lies a process of standardization, referring to the transformation of different modes and types of information into standardized electronic bits. This is true even for the rather veteran analog telephone technology, which originally permitted only the transfer of human voices and instrumental sounds and music. The standardization process for information has reached its utmost in the Internet and its TCP/IP transmission protocol, through which all modes of information are transmitted or stored. The far-reaching standardization processes have permitted the emergence of networking.

In communications systems, there are two kinds of networks: commercial infrastructural networks of telephony, cable TV, and the like, and voluntary social networks typifying the Internet. Commercial communications networks are similar to the equivalent ones in transportation systems, albeit in communications systems the end users do not know of and are not interested in the channels of transmission and their geographies, as long as communications are achieved instantly and at fixed prices, regardless of the geographical routing of the transmitted information. Thus networking in terms of transmission channels is the responsibility and interest of the commercial service providers only. In cable TV systems, the end users do not even conceive of the system as a network if it is used for one-way TV broadcast reception only and not for telephone or Internet services.

Telephone networks have a kind of "passive" nature, consisting of subscribers identified by their phone numbers and communicating for a variety of reasons and purposes to frequently and infrequently called numbers. Compared to telephone networks, Internet networking has received a much more "active" connotation. Internet networks refer to communities defined around a specific area of interest, even if for chatting only. Members of such networks are not interested in the traffic arrangements and routes used, nor in the type of terminals (PCs, mobile phones, etc.) used by fellow members, nor in their geographical location. Their interest is concentrated on content or on the human social activity of members, per the network definition/purpose. These networks, therefore, are pure social ones, and they may reside on changing telecommunications network infrastructures. Normally, joining or leaving social networks is easy, and their geographical spread is potentially as wide as the globe. The networking dimension of the Internet was accentuated in the 2000s with the emergence of the social Web 2.0, in which users' blogs, Facebook, and Twitter have emerged, all facilitating and calling for social interaction. The penetration of Facebook has been extremely fast; by 2011 it was estimated that about one-third of global Internet users (650 million out of 2 billion) were Facebook subscribers.

Social networking has frequently led to significant changes at both the personal and societal levels. Personally, relating to personal relations, Aaron Ben-Ze'ev presented the evolution of romantic and sexual relations all the way from initial electronically written contacts through e-mail, real-time exchanges, blogs, and SMSs, followed by video conversations, to cybersex activities.[91] At the societal level, the social networking systems served as major tools for provoking and sustaining political unrest and revolution in 2011 in Middle Eastern and North African countries.

A darker side of networking is surveillance. Despite the seeming autonomous nature of personal virtual mobilities, communications may undergo surveillance and be turned into recorded mobility. Internet use by surfers may be recorded by commercial companies in order to channel proper advertisements, mobile telephone users may be located through GPS and other technologies, and telephone calls may be illegally recorded as well. Though these surveillance activities present diversified motivations, they imply an almost total potential and/or actual surveillance of personal mobilities. Paradoxically, people using personal mobilities of any type and thus expressing their autonomy of operations and contacts are much more vulnerable to surveillance than people who use public mobility services, at least corporeal ones, such as buses.

Transmission Systems

The entire spectrum of telecommunications is dependent on two major transmission technologies: satellites and fiber optics. Satellites were first introduced in the 1960s, and they are mainly used for TV and telephone contacts, whereas fiber optic cables were first introduced in the 1970s and are mainly used for telephone and Internet communications. Communications satellites are geostationary, meaning that they revolve around the globe at a similar speed to the globe's rotation. Thus they occupy a specific slot in space and cover a certain chunk of the globe's surface. Dozens of commercial satellites cover the whole surface of the globe, permitting, for example, the global use of satellite phones even in areas without any grounded antenna infrastructure for normal use of mobile phones. Fiber optic cables provide dense communications lines transmitted through thin optic cables at a very high speed and quality.

A major and more recent transmission development is broadband transmission of the Internet. Broadband transmissions of information from ISPs (Internet service providers) to end users (downstream) and back (upstream) have become norms for advanced connection and use of the Internet. Such transmissions imply faster Internet sessions, as well as quality transmissions of video information, which have turned into a normative application of the system, mainly for video clips (e.g., YouTube). Broadband access through smart phones and laptops further permits the performance of location-free e-commerce (online shopping), e-government (online governmental services), and e-learning (online degree studies).

Broadband transmission of information, though, is a relative term, referring to faster speeds than those provided by dial-up modems (normally at speeds of up to 56 kbps). By the FCC definition, broadband applies to speeds of over 200 kbps, so that ISDN (Integrated Services Digital Network) of 128 kbps is not considered broadband. However, broadband services become faster and faster, with 100Mb being a normative service and 200 Mb services currently widely available, mainly in the Pacific. Broadband transmissions are usually available to home subscribers through wired xDSL and/or through cable TV systems, as well as through the more recent last-mile fiber-optic wires and the wireless UMTS (Universal Mobile Telecommunications System) service provided by mobile telephone companies.[92]

Global leadership in percentage of the population using the Internet at large, and of broadband in particular, as with many previously adopted telecommunications media, has been by small European countries, notably the Nordic ones.[93] Thus for the Internet in March 2011, Iceland led (97.0 percent), followed by Norway (94.4 percent), Sweden (92.4 percent), Denmark (85.9 percent), and Finland (85.2 percent). For broadband (fixed and wireless), the ranking was a bit different: Netherlands and Switzerland (38.1 percent), Denmark (37.7 percent), and Norway (34.6 percent), followed by South Korea (34.0 percent), France and Iceland (33.7 percent), and Luxembourg (33.5 percent). South Korea was globally the leading country in broadband penetration in the early 2000s as far as the percentage of Internet users who enjoyed broadband service, followed at the time by Japan and France.

Conclusion

This chapter has briefly reviewed and discussed technological change. From a societal perspective, technological change was assessed to be a *"socially and institutionally embedded process*," reflecting capitalist values and facilitating "new organizational and geographical arrangements of economic activities," notably globalization.[94] However, the facilitation of globalization by ICTs may be viewed as just one side of the coin, and the technology–globalization relationship as a two-way process, since growing globalization processes call for additional developments of ICTs in order to manage growing global contacts.

From the perspective of individuals, space and distance were argued time and again to constitute a "tyranny" for people and societies who functioned under past technologies.[95] However, for the contemporary information age, Vincent Kauffmann stated that "space is [thus] undefined and open. It is a set of opportunities in perpetual reorganization."[96] Currently, ICTs have only begun to provide flexible locational opportunities for individuals in the form of online shopping, exposure to other cultures, and social interaction.[97]

The first three chapters have introduced two basic dimensions for our exploration of global information society, namely the information society itself and information and communications technologies that make it possible. The next two chapters will attempt to explore the significance of these two dimensions for society at large (chapter 4) and for individuals (chapter 5).

Notes

1. Falk and Abler (1980)
2. Giddens (1990)
3. Janelle (1968)
4. Harvey (1989)
5. Cairncross (1997)
6. Dodge and Kitchin (2001)
7. Castells (1989)
8. Standage (1998:197)
9. Carey and Moss (1985)
10. Brooker-Gross (1980)
11. ITU (2012)
12. Lyman and Varian (2003)
13. See Fischer (1992); Sheller and Urry (2000); Freund and Martin (1993); Kern (1983); Kellerman (1993).
14. Fischer (1992)
15. Mitchell (1995: 36)
16. Kellerman (1984)
17. Mokhtarian (1997)
18. For reviews, see, e.g., Salomon (1986); Golob and Regan (2001).
19. Mokhtarian (2000: 1)

20. Mokhtarian (1997; 2000); Salomon (1986); Lyons (2002)
21. Salomon (1986); Lyons (2002)
22. Adams (1999)
23. Lyons (2002)
24. Salomon (1986)
25. U.S. Bureau of the Census (2009)
26. Vilhelmson and Thulin (2001)
27. Mokhtarian (1997)
28. Lyons (2002)
29. Howard et al. (2002)
30. Kellerman (1984)
31. Salomon (1986)
32. Harris (1998); Malecki and Gorman (2001)
33. Dodge and Kitchin (2001: 2)
34. Nolan (2000)
35. Urry (2003: 63)
36. See Townsend (2001); Nolan (2000); Warf (2001); Dodge and Kitchin (2001).
37. Kellerman (1986)
38. Kellerman (1986); Townsend (2001)
39. Wilson (2001)
40. Wilson (2001)
41. Zook (2001)
42. Lessig (2001: 246)
43. Lessig (2001: 247)
44. Hargittai (1999)
45. Urry (2000: 40)
46. Kellerman (2002b: 35)
47. Urry (2000: 71)
48. Dodge and Kitchin (2001); Wellman (2001a)
49. Hupkes (1982: 38)
50. Mokhtarian and Chen (2004)
51. Mokhtarian (2000)
52. Vilhelmson and Thulin (2001)
53. Vilhelmson and Thulin (2001)
54. Nobis and Lenz (2004)
55. Visser and Lanzendorf (2004)
56. Lyons (2002)
57. Leiss (1976)
58. Lyons (2002)
59. Kenyon et al. (2002)
60. See, e.g., Salaff (2002).
61. Kellerman (1994)
62. Hampton and Wellman (2002)
63. Boneva and Kraut (2002)
64. Dupagne (1997); Haddon (2004)

65. Agar (2003: 167)
66. Comer and Wikle (2008)
67. Lacohée et al. (2003); Rogers (1995: 244–246)
68. ITU (2004); Castells et al. (2007)
69. ITU (2012)
70. Comer and Wikle (2008)
71. Castells et al. (2007)
72. Kauffman and Techatassanasoontorn (2009)
73. Comer and Wikle (2008)
74. Kapow Survey (2005)
75. ITU (2011)
76. Adams (2009: 186)
77. Arminen (2006)
78. Kellerman (2009)
79. Torrens (2008)
80. Torrens (2008: 72)
81. Torrens (2008: 81)
82. Sheller and Urry (2000: 752); Cooper (2001)
83. Kopomaa (2000: 15)
84. Wellman (2001b)
85. Kopomaa (2000: 14)
86. Castells (2001); Kopomaa (2000); Laurier (2001)
87. Townsend (2001); Zook et al. (2004)
88. Haddon (2004: 96)
89. Townsend (2001: 71)
90. *GPS World* (2007); *GPS Magazine* (2011)
91. Ben-Ze'ev (2004)
92. Kellerman (2006a)
93. OECD (2011b); *Internet World Stats* (2011); Kellerman (1999)
94. Dicken (2007: 73–74)
95. Toffler (1981); Duranton (1999); Blainey (1966); Mitchell (1995)
96. Kauffmann (2002: 8)
97. Kellerman and Paradiso (2007)

4

Societal Dimensions of Mobility, Information, and Knowledge Production

GLOBAL INFORMATION SOCIETY, as the title of this volume declares, consists of three major elements: technology, knowledge, and mobility. It is tempting to assume that information technology is the major "cause" for the emergence of global information society and that the development and wide adoption of this technology have brought about increased production of knowledge and wider mobility, jointly yielding a global information society. However, such a view is overly simplistic for various reasons. Contemporary society constitutes more than just an information society, and the relationships among its various characteristics and its emergence as an information society have to be explored. For example, technology-based personal mobilities may be considered as either stemming from some wider societal processes, as being facilitated by them, or as constituting an integral part of such macro processes: "We assume that mobility is a basic principle of modernity besides others like individuality, rationality, equality, and globality."[1]

Simultaneously, however, enhanced personal mobilities may be considered as major societal processes by themselves, leading to or bringing about some social change. This may be the case whether one views mobility as movement in space only or if one prefers to view mobility within a wider concept of social mobility. Thus, "spatial mobility is not an interstice, or a neutral liaison time between a point of origin and a destination. It is a structuring dimension of social life and of social integration."[2] In such a structure,

> incorporating the mundane practices of personal mobility (albeit often technologically assisted) transforms appropriate metaphors and sociological concepts.

Social processes have to be rethought as involving multiple mobilities with novel spaces and temporalities. Second, notions of such mobile persons can be transferred, metaphorically and literally, to the mobility of other entities, of ideas, images, technologies, monies, wastes and so on. In each case it is hybrids that are mobile, flowing along various scapes. Such networks comprise "physical" and "human" entities whose power derives from their complex mobile combination.[3]

These interrelationships, which will be outlined in the following sections, may thus be regarded as a societal structuration process, in which mobilities are structured, facilitated, and embedded within a wider societal unfolding of a new modernity, while at the same time, aggregate personal mobilities themselves may facilitate and bring about social change (aggregate in both the variety of mobility technologies and in the movements of numerous social agents).[4]

The focus of this chapter will be on society and societal processes. We will begin with an introduction to early thinkers on information society and the concepts developed by them, followed by coverage of contemporary thinking on the information society, focusing on the new modernity and attempting to stress differing approaches to the information society. These discussions will highlight the more flexible social, economic, and political structures emerging through the increased availability and exposure to information at a global scale. Following these rather general sections of the chapter, we will focus on some more particular dimensions from the perspective of the global information society: the network society, knowledge production, and the use of language.

Early Thinking on the Information Society

The identification of information and knowledge as major economic and social forces may be traced back to the early 1960s and stretching into the 1970s, focusing to a large degree on information/knowledge as a separate and quaternary economic sector, joining the three traditional ones: primary (agriculture and extraction); secondary (manufacturing or transformation); and tertiary (services personal, social, and supportive of production and distribution). Whereas the three veteran sectors have been based on modes of manipulation of materials and operations as criteria, information/knowledge is an object, and the information sector consists of its production, transaction, and consumption, including goods (e.g., books, computers); transmission systems (e.g., the Internet, telephone systems); and information per se (financial, for example).

The growing role of informational economic activities in expanding cities has brought, first, the recognition of information and knowledge as a separate leading economic sector. As we mentioned already, it was for geographer Jean

Gottmann to propose in 1961 "the quaternary occupations, those supplying services that require research, analysis, judgment, in brief, brainwork and responsibility,"[5] and "what might be called the quaternary forms of economic activity; the managerial and artistic functions, government, education, research, and the brokerage of all kinds of goods, services and securities."[6] Later, as the information society advanced, Abler, Adams, and Gould broadened the scope of the quaternary sector into "information activities."[7]

Daniel Bell defined two new sectors within what he defined as the postindustrial society, in addition to the veteran tertiary service sector (which includes transport and recreation): the quaternary sector (trade, finance, insurance, and real estate) and the quinary sector (health, education, research, and government).[8] No explanation was given at the time for this differentiation, which does not seem to explicitly recognize information and knowledge as a separate sector. However, Bell further proposed five elements for the postindustrial society, all of which are heavily dependent on information: the economic sector (changing from production to services), occupational distribution (the preeminence of the professional class), the axial principle (the centrality of theoretical knowledge), a future orientation (control of technology), and decision making (the new "intellectual technology"). Frank Webster criticized Bell's identification of a new postindustrial, or even information, society evolving because of these transitions.[9] As we will see later, the information society should be assessed as part of the emergence of the new modernity.

Whereas Gottmann and Bell focused on employment and economic activities as pointing to new economic sectors, it was for a third major early-bird thinker on information society, Marshall McLuhan, to focus on the media and to envisage the development of a global information society from the perspective of geographically expanding public media coverage and availability, notably through radio and TV.[10] The notion that McLuhan proposed for such a global information society, the *global village* (originally coined by Wyndham Lewis), has turned into a cornerstone for information society thought.[11] In this latter regard, the emergence of the Internet, as of the mid-1990s, has added another, and even more striking, global medium, this time for both public and personal communications.

The New Modernity and Mobilities

The development of social thought and conceptualization for the emerging information society, following its early identifiers and thinkers, has been rooted within the wider societal emergence of what has been variously called the *new modernity*, the *second modernity*, the *super modernity*, and the *reflexive modernity*. All of these titles seemingly constitute synonymous terms for describing Western societies in the late twentieth and early twenty-first centuries. The somehow related term, *postmodern society*, has referred to contemporary society as a rather "new" one, replacing the supposedly previous modern society, whereas the new modernity has been rather assumed to continue the first modernity.[12] Others have viewed *postmodernism* as a term for the description of an interim period stretching between the first modernity, simply called the *modern society*, and the second, current one, so that postmodernism may refer roughly to the 1960s to the 1980s/1990s.[13]

Modern society had its roots in the eighteenth century, at the beginning of the industrial society, and it reflected, at that time, transitions brought about by the industrial revolution in a wide spectrum of dimensions, stretching from social structures and values, through economic and political powers, to urbanization and mobilities. The reflexive/second/new/super modernity "is conceived as a process of unexpected, unseen and unwanted transformations of the general conditions of modern societies."[14] As such, the new modernity implies change within modernity, rather than a revolutionary transition imposed by some major, seemingly "external" force, such as the industrial revolution which brought about the emergence of the modern society.[15]

Generally, the new modernity may be viewed as less rigid and more complex than modern society, and its theorization focusing "on process, connectivity, and at the expense of an alleged former focus on boundedness, hierarchy, and form."[16] As such, metaphors for the description of the new modernity at large have been taken from the general sphere of mobility.[17] For modernity at large it was argued that "modern societies cannot be described without recognizing them as having a fibrous, thread-like, wiry, stringy, ropy, capillary character that is never captured by the notions of levels, layers, territories, spheres, categories, structures, systems."[18]

The flexibility of the new/second modernity is expressed, for example, in the nondirectionality of spatial mobilities. The directionality of spatial mobility in the first modernity meant clear origins and destinations for movements, as well as direct-line routing between these origins and destinations, thus expressing social values of certainty, planning, and predictability. The nondirectionality of spatial mobilities in the new modernity may be exemplified by the use of road numbers rather than their origins and destinations in conversations or in traffic reports. By the same token, metropolitan areas frequently include metropolitan ring roads without any distinct beginning or end. In virtual mobilities, nondirectionality is manifest in the geographical routing of information which is completely flexible and usually does not use the shortest route between origins and destinations, so that compressed time and distance might be of less importance when speeds of light are used for the transmission of information.[19]

As far as Web searching is concerned, one could even point to a double nondirectionality: first, the geographical sources or addresses of the searched websites might be highly flexible in terms of changing locations of the servers from which the information was imported to the Web searcher/surfer, and second, the geographical routing of the information from the hosting server of the desired websites to the information seeker might be highly flexible as well. Nondirectionality in a slightly different sense also typifies the production side of websites, as sites which are placed on the system may be reached from all over the world, or may never be reached by any surfer. It seems next to impossible for the producers of unsecured websites, or the supply side of Web information, to limit or focus potential site users by geographical location of the users, given that the system is completely open for searches. On the demand side, censorship may block access to specific sites.

Bonss and Kesselring differentiated among four historical mobility periods.[20] The first, *traditional mobility*, was the pretechnological one, lasting until the end of the eighteenth century, and was typified by either forced or privileged movements, without mobility as a societal value or goal. The second period of mobility, *territorial mobility*, corresponds to the emergence of nation-states in the first half of the nineteenth century, which permitted the social use of the adjectives *domestic* and *foreign*, *near* and *far*. The third period was termed as *globalized mobility*, relating to the late nineteenth and the twentieth centuries, when movements beyond national boundaries evolved side by side with domestic ones, attesting to extensive distanciation. Finally, the fourth, and contemporary, period, was termed *virtualized mobility*, characterized by mobility beyond space and time through time-space compression that typifies the use of telecommunications. Thus, in the first modernity, the emphasis was on movements of the masses, which was carried into the first modernity from traditional societies characterized by collective movements of families and tribes. In the first modernity, the movement of the masses was embodied by trains that permitted a modern continuation of old mobilities but that simultaneously provided for a new and more individualistic mobility using public modes of mobility.

In the transitional period between the two modernities, the accent in mobility studies moved to individuals, the mobile subjects: their motives, reasons, and perceptions of travel, as well as their decision-making processes. This change of accent has been embodied in the *Leitbild* of the automobile and its interpretation. Mobility in the second modernity was embodied in the Internet (or virtual mobility at large) and has been interpreted by Bonss and Kesselring as representing a societal structuration process. Individuals and collective actors constitute nodes in material and social global networks producing flows and scapes. On the one hand, they are equipped with a growing ability to act individually, but on the other hand, they are "forced to decide and structured by powerful social as well as material network configurations."[21] One may add to this view the potential for the cumulative behavior of mobile individuals to change material and social forces or norms. Examples of such changes in social habits are an emerging norm to report immediately on possible delays in meetings, deliveries, and the like through e-mail and mobile phones, as well as the emergence of new boundaries as to what can be exchanged between people virtually and what needs corporeal proximity.

Mobility during the second modernity is assumed to be of a potentially individualistic nature, given the increased sense of freedom and the availability of varied and sophisticated mobility technologies. However, technological developments of mobility media constitute continuous processes, and the sense of freedom is still restricted by social, economic, and cultural boundaries. The second modernity is thus typified by increased diversification among people, as well as by an atmosphere of continuous technological and related sociospatial change.

At a more practical level, the second modernity implies not just hybrids between drivers and cars, as separate from hybrids between communications devices and users, since hybrids emerge simultaneously among humans and both corporeal and virtual mobility technologies. This is evidenced in what has become obvious: using mobile phones and laptops while physically on the road. The hybrid, then, is between three entities: a driver, a car moving from one point to another, and a mobile phone moving voice or data to various points on the globe through phone calls made or received by the driver while on the road. As speedy as cars, trains, or even planes can be, the speed of virtual mobility is always higher, thus creating a discrepancy between simultaneous physical and virtual movements. Under certain circumstances the virtual movement may dictate the physical one; for instance, some virtual message may change the destination of the physical movement while on the road to an originally different destination. Virtual mobilities between a person on the road and called/calling parties may also bring about some change in the agenda of the traveling person.

An important societal and individual change concerning mobilities in the second modernity relates to identities. Vincent Kaufmann suggested a two-way relationship between mobilities and identities when he asserted that "all mobility has repercussions on identity and, inversely, that an identity is built on mobilities."[22] This is noticeable in repetitive/reversible movements such as commuting, the repetitiveness of which may bring about identity construction by both the moving persons and others. Such identities may disappear, though, once the repetitive movements cease to exist. Mimi Sheller termed such changing identities "identities-on-the-move."[23]

The use of technologies for personal mobility involves changes in the modes of usage of time and space, both as two separate dimensions and resources, and in their being a joint time-space dimension. Such changes develop because of the very nature of mobility technologies, permitting the overcoming of space through time at growing speeds. "New technologies appear to be generating new kinds of time which dramatically transform the opportunities for, and constraints upon, the mobilities of peoples, information and images. Mobilities are all about temporality."[24] Thus it has become impossible to trace the time-space of people's activities through the specific times of the day and the specific places in which they were traditionally performed, and on which Torsten Hägerstrand's time geography was based.[25]

Increased mobilities via transportation, and even more so through communications and information technologies, have brought *distanciation*, or the "stretching" of social systems in time and space, almost to their utmost.[26] Though the telegraph already permitted global information transmissions in some way similarly to the Internet,[27] the personal nature of telephone and Internet transmissions compared to the mediated one of the telegraph, as well as the speed and endless variety in terms of Internet content, has brought global virtual distanciation to maturity at this age. The Internet may permit an *extensibility* of human beings, in that it relaxes time-space constraints concerning mobility and activity space, as well as in its provision for more flexible temporal scheduling.[28] However these high levels of global distanciation and reach do not necessarily imply the disappearance of geographical differences between places.[29] Moreover, this increased distanciation may bring about increased consciousness by Internet users about remote people and places as part of the *global village*.

The introduction of information technologies and particularly the facilitation of imaginative virtual spaces have led to the perception of spatial barriers as collapsing, notably at the global and national levels. Nineteenth-century transportation technologies were perceived as annihilating space *and* time,[30] whereas late twentieth-century telecommunications technologies led to the metaphor of the annihilation of space *through* time.[31] The very notion of time-space compression, coupled with globalization and the evolution of spaces of flows, are not completely new trends. Improved intranational and international transportation and telecommunications networks have facilitated more flows, especially instantaneous flows of capital and information, so that old spatial barriers consisting of international and interregional borders, as well as the constraints of distance and time, have collapsed.

Time-space compression refers to the contemporary "*compression* of our spatial and temporal worlds," or a "pull" mechanism, induced by contemporary telecommunications.[32] For example, a telephone call taking place between Australia and the United Kingdom implies that one of the parties may be awake late at night or working at that time, so that both time and space distances between the two parties have been compressed. Time-space compression is thus both an outcome and a cause for distanciation. By the same token, time-space compression provides for both a separation and a combination between the local and the global, and hence the emergence of local–global dialectics. We mentioned in chapter 2 such global–local dialectics as involving three potential phases of disembeddedment, phantasmagoria, and fusion, reflecting varying degrees of the involvement of the global with the local.[33]

Time-space compression is not synonymous with Donald Janelle's *time-space convergence*, since compression relates to conditions of social space, whereas convergence is a measured index, defined as "the rate at which places move closer together or further away in travel or communication time."[34] Time-space compression reflects power relations: there are those who may sense this compression only passively or indirectly, if they are forced to move or if they are immobile (e.g., traffic control workers) in order to serve mobile people, whereas other persons are in charge of this compression through their handling of the local/global transfers, notably those of capital and information.[35]

The Network Society

Manuel Castells developed the notion of *network society*, arguing that "in all sectors of society we are witnessing a transformation in how their constitutive processes are organized, a shift from hierarchies to networks. This transformation is as much an organizational as a cultural question."[36] The new network society refers to a global entity within which he proposed the "space of flows," a concept we discussed in chapter 2, and which consists of well-connected global city systems and well-connected elites residing and working in them. The emergence of global network societies implies a lower significance for national borders but not necessarily the death of nation-states.[37] In the previous chapter, we noticed how network society accentuated person-to-person communications, as compared to previous accents on door-to-door and place-to-place communications.

"The contradictory experience of being somewhere and nowhere at the same time is perhaps the most obvious cognitive dissonance resulting from the use of the WWW."[38] The emergence of global social networks and the growing interaction with global information networks bears upon the sense of place of users and on processes of place production. Maurice Halbwachs proposed the terms *implacement* and *displacement* for social reactions to urban changes.[39] By the same token, the simultaneous sensing of local-physical and global-virtual places when involved in some form of long-distance communications may be termed *co-placement,* or *co-presence.*[40] The development of a sense of place around real places may sometimes be a fast process, and at other times a rather long-term process, but in both cases it constitutes a continuous process, which is not the case for instantly replaceable virtual places.

These *spaceless places* do not permit the physical sensing of places, nor do they provide for a third dimension of depth, natural movements, air breezes and winds, or smells and sunshine.[41] Virtual places also lack a cultural depth, since they have no history and may not have an impact on a collective memory. These differences between the real and the virtual do not necessarily contradict viewing the virtual as reinforcing the real.[42] Cyberspace and network society may further be interpreted in light of Henri Lefebvre's thesis on *The Production of Space.*[43] Lefebvre insisted that space is not a thing but rather a social process unfolding in everyday life, and thus one may ask, "Are we engaged in the production of new spaces and new social relations, or merely simulating social structures in a hyperreal form? How does our experience of the global and the local, the public and the private, alter in a network society?"[44]

Production of Information and Knowledge

Following our earlier discussions of information, knowledge, and the information society (chapter 2), technology (chapter 3), and the societal context of the emergence of information society (in this chapter), we can now examine the societal dimensions of knowledge production and innovation, with a special accent on their spatial context.

From a spatial perspective, information might be viewed as an "active" action that occupies time but does not occupy space at all,[45] or it may be defined as something that is only "passively" contained within one's mind when viewed as "anything that is known by somebody."[46] On the other hand, information might be seen as something that is constantly moving over space: "Information that isn't moving ceases to exist as anything but potential."[47] The spread or movement of information differs from the movement of material objects in that "it leaves a trail everywhere it's been . . . information can be transferred without leaving the possession of the original owner."[48] Thus its impact on places may potentially be much more significant when compared to those of other entities moving or being fully moved from one place to another.

In terms of location, information has been defined as a "compromise between presence and absence" since it represents a "form of something without the thing itself."[49] Communicating information is thus "being; persons literally occupy the media they use; their existence cannot be separated from these symbolic systems."[50] Information, though abstract and highly flexible for electronic processing and transmission, has a simultaneous presence in places of origin and destination. Toward its transmission over space, it may be packaged and transformed. Furthermore, its interpretation and uses may change from one receiver to another, and it may embed differently in various places, thus bringing about different aggregate geographical patterns.

These various definitions and features of information point to three major geographical dimensions that information at large possesses, similar to other human products: it can be produced, transmitted, and consumed or disseminated. None of these aspects is new or related in principle solely to the contemporary introduction of information technology. This technology has rather changed the scale and form of information production and consumption, as well as the speed of its transmission or flow. If the major traditional container of information was paper, joined later on by film and electromechanical signals (telephone transmissions), information technology has made it possible to transform all information forms and containers into standard electronic bits and has offered a singular channel for its transmission, the Internet. In principle, these innovations should have made the production, transmission, and consumption of information at large ubiquitous.

However, the production of information, in the narrower sense of the term, differs from place to place. It is not only dependent on the size of a place but also on the types of economic activities taking place and concentrated in it. Thus the finances industry is a major producer of information, so that cities which specialize in finances (such as New York and London) tend to produce more information than others. Since the development of this industry had its roots long before the introduction of information technology, the initial and cumulative advantages for this industry have created an early differentiation among cities in information production. As far as knowledge production is concerned, notably technological knowledge, the differentiation may be even more significant, with fewer places dominating the map of production, and with an initial and cumulative advantage obtained by cities with universities specializing in technological studies and research (such as Boston and Silicon Valley).

The transmission of information is dependent foremost on the availability of a transmission system. The more bandwidth a transmission system provides, the more information it may carry and the faster the transmission. Transmission systems thus refer to information by its size rather than to its content. On the other hand, however, the price of information may differ sharply by content, dividing mainly between information and knowledge. The transmission of information is considered a global phenomenon, normally no longer constrained by political boundaries. However, legal procedures, notably those relating to copyrights, may regulate the flows of various types of information, such as movies, and much of the flows of knowledge. It is also easier to move codified knowledge rather than tacit knowledge, though conferences and e-mail permit an accelerated transmission of this form of knowledge as well.[51]

The consumption and dissemination of information and knowledge may differ from one place to another, and again not necessarily because of differences in population size. There is a need for some sociocultural similarity or "contextuality" between the sender and the receiver of information in order for a significant dissemination of information to take place.[52] This relates to major aspects such as shared language, education, and economic development; these aspects are notable in the transmission of knowledge, with the transmission of codified knowledge depending on the level of tacit knowledge at the receiving station.

The spatial dimension of knowledge, mostly as an economic resource for the recently evolving knowledge-based economy, has been highlighted by numerous authors in both economics and geography.[53] Economic knowledge has gained a general importance, not just for high-tech industries. Information and knowledge are neither concentrated in one place nor universally distributed. They present complex geographies of production, flows, and consumption, dependent and regulated by numerous factors, notably technology, social and cultural aspects, economic development, and legal procedures. Let us first take a look at knowledge and innovation, or the production of new knowledge, and then explore regions of knowledge.

Knowledge ⇒ Innovation ⇒ Technology

The development and production of information technology is most heavily dependent on knowledge and innovation. As mentioned earlier in this chapter, the roles of knowledge and innovation, which are striking as far as information technology is concerned, extend much further than information technology, and technology in general.[54] "Knowledge and its applications for market success has become the primary source of competitiveness in the developed economies of the world."[55] Therefore, "in the competence perspective, the firm is essentially a repository of skill, experience and knowledge, rather than merely a set of responses to information or transaction costs."[56] Hence, the so-called *new economy* has been defined as "a global knowledge and idea-based economy where the keys to wealth and job creation are the extent to which ideas, innovations, and technology are embedded in all sectors of the economy—services, manufacturing, and agriculture."[57]

It was estimated for the United States that 80 percent of the value added in its manufacturing in the 1950s could be attributed to material products of all kinds and only 20 percent to knowledge, whereas by 1995 these proportions had changed to 30 and 70 percent, respectively.[58] It is, however, misleading to assume that the role of capital has declined. As we will see later, R&D activities are heavily capital dependent, whether in the form of public research monies, commercial in-company capital, or mobilized venture capital. Capital is further required for the education and continuous training of workers. Capital spending in the United States on information technology constituted one-third of capital spending on product technology in 1965, but exceeded it in 2000.[59]

Knowledge for Innovation

Knowledge is produced almost anywhere, and typical centers for the production of knowledge are universities. However, not every place of knowledge production constitutes by definition a place or center of innovation, especially technological innovation. Various conditions regarding knowledge, capital, and entrepreneurship are required for a place or firm to become innovative. Hence, in this section we shall focus on knowledge for innovation. The knowledge types and knowledge sources that serve as the basis on which technological innovation may emerge and flourish are varied. "Not only is knowledge a heterogeneous commodity and can be put to multiple uses; often, one kind of knowledge needs to be combined with several other kinds to produce a particular good or service."[60] The various types of knowledge required for innovation processes are complementary and indispensable.[61] Seven types of knowledge are outlined below:

1. *In-house tacit knowledge:* Tacit knowledge is by far the most important type of knowledge required for innovation to take place, with high importance attached to it all the way through, from basic R&D to early production stages.[62] Tacit knowledge becomes available through well-educated and well-trained human resources within an innovating firm,

or within a university or research organization. It is therefore firmly embedded within organizations.

2. *In-house "innovation star(s)"*: In her discussion of the biotech industry, Maryann Feldman defined a "star scientist" as "a highly productive individual who discovered a major breakthrough."[63] Innovation leaders are actually required within almost any R&D team or within an innovative company, even if many of these leaders are at a more modest scale of "starring." These stars not only embody knowledge and ideas, but they lead others in innovative thinking and scientific-technological vision and daring.

3. *Codified knowledge*: Knowledge available in texts of whatever form, whether freely available or for a price, is an important knowledge resource for innovation, even if those involved in the innovation process have already completed their formal studies. Major university libraries or research institutions are of high significance in this regard.

4. *In-region knowledge spillover*: This spillover consists of formal and mostly informal transmission of knowledge, notably tacit knowledge, among people engaged in innovation processes, as well as similar transmissions among firms. Knowledge spillover may be considered second to in-house tacit knowledge in its importance for the innovation process, serving as "knowledge externalities."[64] Ongoing, daily transmission of knowledge takes place within regions, and the special significance of regions in this regard will be dealt with in the next section.

   Like information, the transmission of knowledge from one person to another does not eliminate the transmitted knowledge from the transmitter.[65] Innovative firms are in a conflict of interest in this regard. On the one hand, they do not like to have knowledge gained within their companies spilled over to other companies. On the other hand, they appreciate the tremendous value of knowledge transmitted into their firms, as well as brainstorming through knowledge exchange. The codification of knowledge cannot substitute for face-to-face exchange of tacit knowledge. Even institutional attempts to do so, such as the MIT project to post on a freely accessible website all the course materials of their degree programs, only emphasize the extreme importance of class and lab experiences for degree certification.

5. *Extraregional knowledge spillover*: Knowledge spillover beyond the geographical limits of a given region, whether metropolitan or otherwise, is of a different and more limited nature, but it may carry benefits and significance even beyond the innovation process per se. Extraregional spillover processes may take several forms. First are *connections* with colleagues in other areas, or the emergence of *innovation networks*,[66]

which may be maintained through professional meetings or through the Internet.[67] Second is *trade*, notably international trade, which may bring with it knowledge spillover, coupled with enhanced competitiveness and outputs.[68] Third is *globalization* of innovation activities, in the form of either globally spread R&D activities of multinational corporations (MNCs) or through knowledge export. Beat Hotz-Hart counted among the advantages of global R&D the access to globally spread but locally pooled knowledge, but this involves high coordination costs.[69]

6. *Continuous learning:* An innovative firm or organization must have its employees involved in continuous learning and adjustment processes in order to thrive through the creation of new ideas, as well as improvement of existing ideas and products. In addition, such companies continuously hire recent university graduates in relevant fields. It further implies a firm policy of openness to required organizational changes. In all of these aspects of continuous learning, the regional setting is important, as we will see in the next section.

7. *Business knowledge:* This type of knowledge includes producer services that innovative firms can purchase through outsourcing, or they may be located, partially at least, in house. Among the most important services, beyond capital mobilization, are marketing, testing, patenting, and other legal services related to innovation and R&D activities.[70] Though lying outside the arena of knowledge/innovation formation, accumulation, and exchange, access to tacit knowledge in these fields is of critical importance for an innovation to mature into a marketable product.

   Business knowledge implies not just the way a business should be conducted and marketed. It also implies entrepreneurship, which is most vital for innovativeness at large and for technological innovation in particular. Entrepreneurship may be acquired through learning, but it also requires a drive for risky innovation, as well as a general entrepreneurial atmosphere. The role of government is crucial in this regard through the creation and encouragement of proper taxing systems, financial tools such as venture capital funds, the creation of R&D funds, and the promotion of a social appreciation of risk-taking entrepreneurs.

Regions of Knowledge and Innovation

The seven types of knowledge pertinent for innovation have to be localized within a geographical setting in order to yield innovativeness. This setting is the region, normally a metropolitan area, or an extended metropolitan region. For some commentators, the region, or geography at large, constitutes a mere *vessel* for the innovation process,[71] whereas others see it more actively:

"The *territory* itself plays a role, as a place of co-ordination and learning."[72] The region ties the required types of knowledge together and facilitates in-region spillover among actors within a localized embeddedness or culture of interaction of a specific local or idiographic nature. This is achieved through two major elements: social capital and industrial organization.

"Social capital refers to the values and beliefs that citizens share in their everyday dealings and which give meaning and provide design for all sorts of rules."[73] These rules include specific norms, codes, trust, and solidarity, among other things. The untradeable asset of social capital serves as a basis for companies sharing the same region when it comes to exchanges of tacit knowledge. Social capital may obviously develop and exist in regions that are not necessarily specialized in IT R&D and production. However, social capital, or region-specific trust and codes, are crucial for knowledge exchange and sharing.

A favored regional industrial organization for the development of knowledge spillover is one of the three types of the so-called *sticky places*, or attractive regions, namely the *Marshallian industrial districts*.[74] This type of industrial district consists mainly of locally owned small firms. In such a region, workers feel more committed to the region than to their firm, and thus they lean more toward tacit knowledge exchange.

Sustaining the advantages of knowledge spillover is a continuous regional task carried out through the continuous accumulation of knowledge; hence the term *learning region*.[75] However, if the level of innovation is measured through the number of patents achieved per city, then it has been shown for the United States that city size and historical industrialization may determine the number of patents.[76]

Knowledge exchange may be achieved in a number of ways. First, and most important, are repeated face-to-face meetings in order for knowledge to be disseminated.[77] Firms may engage in various forms of exchange, beginning with simple *barter*, and moving through *dyadic*, semistable exchange, to *network-relations*.[78] The latter form of exchange may be enhanced via electronic communications as well as through strong contacts with local universities.[79] Another mechanism for knowledge spillover is patent citations, which tend to be more extensive between firms and universities sharing a location within the same region.[80]

These mechanisms of tacit knowledge spillover bring about the clustering of high-tech innovative firms, so that the more innovation oriented a firm is, the more it tends to locate in the proximity of similar firms, as the spillover effect is restricted by distance.[81] Knowledge transfer may become stronger when firms of various specialties, based on similar scientific knowledge, cluster in the same region.[82] By the same token, small firms may enjoy knowledge spillover from nearby large firms.[83] It is questionable whether globalization increases regional clustering and regional concentration or just the opposite.[84]

The Innovation Process

The innovation process is depicted in figure 4.1, and though it may apply to innovation at large, it is of special relevance and significance for information technology. Edwin Mansfield estimated that the time lag between an academic research finding and production based on it was seven years, so that the innovation process described in figure 4.2 would represent a ten- to

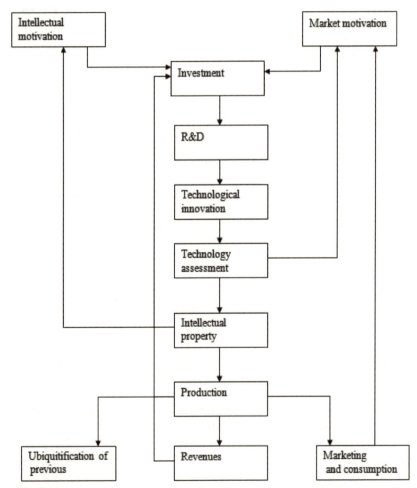

FIGURE 4.1
The Innovation Process: The Technology Perspective (Kellerman 2002b).

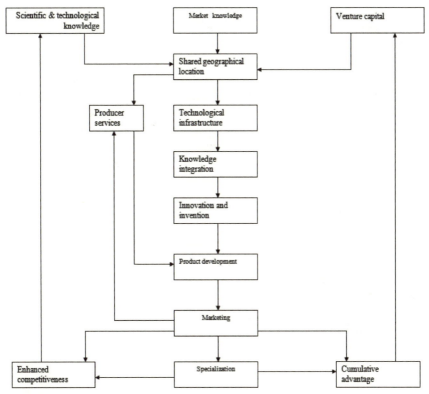

FIGURE 4.2
The Innovation Process: The Regional Perspective (Kellerman 2002b).

twelve-year span.[85] It is reasonable, however, to assume that the intensified R&D processes in the 1990s have shortened these time spans.

Innovation may be driven by two different motives leading to R&D, and these are normally located within two separate types of organizations. Market motivation typifies commercial companies, small or large, whereas an intellectual motivation may compel universities and research centers. As noted already, the geographical proximity of companies and universities within a regional setting may benefit both. The innovation process involves several investments and costs, but the initial one, the financing of R&D, usually constitutes the heaviest one. Sources for financing depend on the organization leading the innovation process. Universities may receive most of their research funds from public foundations, but they may receive research funds from industry as well. Private industry may finance R&D from corporate funds or through venture capital, mobilized directly or through dedicated funds. In some countries, government may assist innovative industrial R&D directly, on the assumption that successful production will pay back royalties.

Successful R&D, as part of an innovation process, implies producing a technological innovation. Such an innovation, whether achieved through academic or commercial research, requires an assessment of its development into a product vis-à-vis the market in order to reach a production decision. Such an assessment of an innovation may lead to further development of the innovation in order for it to fit market needs, or it may be suspended. Once finalized, the innovation has to be protected, either through patenting or through licensing in the case of software, which is not patented. Patenting may serve as a starting point for additional innovative research, mostly within universities. Universities may sell patents developed by their faculty following a technology assessment by potential buyers.

The phases described so far normally take place within one organization, whether academic or commercial, located in a single region. Production, though, may potentially take place elsewhere. However, since technological products involve complex processes before they become standardized, production at early stages may take place within the R&D region or close by, thus enhancing the development of these regions and further permitting knowledge spillovers from the production process as well.[86] Once standardized, production may move to other areas, either fully or partially, notably to regions specializing in mass production by large companies.[87]

Production may yield three results as far as innovation is concerned. First, marketing and consumption of a product may bring about a new round of market motivation for innovation, since the use of a new technology may bring about demand or potential demand for new products. Second, revenues from the successful marketing of a new product may finance new rounds of R&D; and finally, new technologies may bring about a *ubiquitification* of older knowledge, technologies and products.[88] For a company to keep its competitiveness, it has to be continuously involved in innovation processes.[89]

The Innovation Process and the Regional Economy

Information technologies were defined by Manuel Castells as "a specific form of productive organization, deriving their specificity from the distinctiveness of their raw material (information), and from the singularity of their product (process oriented devices with applications across the entire spectrum of human activity)."[90] Local concentrations of high-tech industries, in the form of planned industrial parks, were termed *technopoles*,[91] while a regional concentration of such industries was called a *technopolis*.[92] As of the late 1990s, the national scale has become increasingly significant for the development of high-tech industry, as numerous nations, notably small ones, have developed national policies toward high-tech R&D and/or production.[93]

Sweden and Finland are more veteran nations in this regard, whereas Ireland, Singapore, and Israel constitute more recent examples.

The emergence of technopoles (and of technopoli at a later stage) is based on three macroprocesses: the rapid developments in information technology, the emergence of a global economy, and the evolution of the informational economy, based on the generation of new knowledge. These three processes are interconnected.[94] The sweeping growth of the Internet has brought about new rising industries as of the 1990s, notably in the form of start-up enterprises, coupled with changes in the production scheme of existing industries, such as the telecommunications industry. The early to mid-2000s signified a similar process regarding mobile telephony, despite stock market and economic crises, serving as a major vehicle for venture capital mobilization for the industry.

From the regional/industry perspective, it is possible to trace the following process chain for the high-tech industry, leading from knowledge and capital formation, through innovation and invention, to production (see figure 4.2).[95] The industry is based on three major production factors: scientific and technological knowledge, market knowledge, and venture capital. As shown in previous sections, abundant scientific and technological knowledge, in the form of well-trained human resources, coupled with the proximity of major university and research institutions, is the most important locational factor, at both the local, regional, and national levels. Scientific technological human resources are still the relatively least flexible production factor from the locational perspective, notably at the international level, despite the globalization of professional human resources.[96] Cultural-national attachment of trained workers still plays an important role in this regard, slowing down international migrations of technologically trained professionals.

As we have seen already, market knowledge refers both to the understanding and assessment of demand for new ideas and products as well as to the entrepreneurship required for the development of new products and their marketing. This knowledge does not necessarily have to be locally or domestically based for each enterprise, though profound levels of market knowledge serve as prerequisites for the emergence of national or regional loci of innovation.

Venture capital has been assumed by various writers as a locationally inflexible factor, so that it has to be regionally embedded and mobilized.[97] The increased globalization of capital flows has permitted investments of venture capital at a global scale, so that, of the three major production factors, this has become the geographically most flexible one.

For a technopole or technopolis to take off, local availability of producer services of all kinds, notably telecommunications and finances, is crucial. Producer services play a major role for both the domestic and global activity of the industry, notably at the market development phase. This is also the sector that may benefit most from the innovation-production process chain, as it serves both innovation and production.[98]

Knowledge integration, becoming possible through the availability of capital and services, may finally bring about innovations and inventions. This integration was termed by Manuel Castells as the *milieu*, namely "a specific set of social relationships of production and management, based upon some common instrumental goals, generally sharing a work culture, and generating a high level of organizational synergy."[99] Further, he says, "an industrial complex becomes a *milieu* of innovation when it is able to generate within itself a continuous flow of the key elements that constitute the basis for innovative production of information technologies, namely new scientific and technological information, high-risk capital, and innovative technical labor."[100]

As we have noted already, industrial production based on new innovations does not necessarily have to take place in the location or country of innovation, though the location of initial experimental production is normally adjacent to the R&D location. From a regional perspective, if innovation, production, and marketing all share the same location, they may bring about enhanced competitiveness, specialization, and cumulative advantage, which on their part may enhance the conditions for new rounds of innovation.[101] Moreover, this specialization may attract additional innovative firms.[102] There is only partial evidence on possible geographical decentralization of production, even within metropolitan areas.[103]

Through continuous learning and resulting innovation rounds, high-tech regions constantly engage in the enhancement of their *sustainable advantage* through continuous improvements of technology and human resources.[104] The discussion of the innovation processes and landscapes described so far in this and previous sections may be concluded by Feldman and Florida's assessment that they constitute "agglomerated and synergistic social and economic institutions welded into a technological infrastructure for innovation."[105]

Language and Virtual Mobility

Language constitutes the major communications vehicle for the moved object in virtual mobility, namely information, and as we will note below, it further serves as a major means for the handling of corporeal mobility. The growing importance of language is noticeable in virtual mobilities because of its expansion from vocal electronic communications (through the telephone) into written electronic ones (through the Internet and SMS). However, even in corporeal mobility, the expanding use of automobiles and the growth in flights implies an expanded use of language, since new places and services have been created, requiring lingual expressions. The emergence of "mobility languages" for driving, surfing, or SMS sending emphasizes the growing centrality of mobilities in the second modernity.

It is possible to identify three trends, as far as the relationships between mobility and language are concerned: transubstantiation, individualization, and spatialization. By *transubstantiation* we refer to two-way exchanges between expressions referring to computerized communications and those typifying human relations. As Richard Stivers and Nigel Thrift have each noted, computers are referred to as "humans," since they are said to have "memories," "languages," and "intelligence," whereas human relations are viewed as possessing computer-like qualities, such as "networks" and "interfaces."[106]

By *individualization* we refer to what Marc Augé described as personal interpretations of information, as part of the growing individualism in the second modernity. "In Western societies, at least, the individual wants to be a world in himself; he intends to interpret the information delivered to him by himself and for himself."[107] Such an individualization, therefore, refers neither to the transmission of terms from one context to another, nor to the innovation of new terms, but rather to the personal use of conventional language in one's mind and speech for the interpretation of information. Though by their very nature such individualized interpretations have always existed, such processes have become significant with the flourishing of virtual mobilities, bringing about individualized interpretations of large volumes of public information available on websites, as well as the more obvious case of individualized interpretations of growing personal communications.

Spatialization is probably the most extensive of the three linguistic aspects of mobilities, relating to uses of spatial expressions for various aspects of virtual and physical mobilities. Stephen Levinson noted that "spatial cognition is at the heart of our thinking. It has long been noted that spatial thinking provides us with analogies and tools for understanding other domains."[108] He further noted that spatial thinking is always relative in nature, rather than absolute, telling, for example, about "far" and "close," and it is further egocentric and anthropomorphic in nature, focusing on individuals and on human beings at large. Augé noted the central role of vocabulary vis-à-vis space, in that it "weaves the tissue of habits, educates the gaze, informs the landscape."[109] Rebecca Solnit noted specifically on travel and thought,

> So stories are travels and travels are stories. It is because we imagine life itself as a journey that these symbolic walks and indeed all walks have resonance. The workings of the mind and the spirit are hard to imagine, as is the nature of time—so we tend to metaphorize all these intangibles as physical objects located in space. Thus our relationship to them becomes physical and spatial.[110]

Thus, the spatialization of language is a deeply embedded process, exemplified by numerous expressions, such as "steering straight, moving toward the goal, going for the distance, getting ahead. Things get in our way, set us back, help us find our way, give us a head start or the go-ahead."[111]

Space serves as a metaphor in the rather novel language of the Internet through terms such as *traveling, navigating, cruising,* or *surfing* the Internet system.[112] Geographical notions are also used to describe one's position on a network, or relative fixity, through phrases such as "See you online!" "Let's meet online," or just "I'm here."[113] Metaphors make it easier to learn and grasp. Spatial metaphors are attractive since they are well known to computer users from their daily lives, they are simple to use, and they make things tangible, though it may turn out to be difficult to separate metaphors from social realities.[114]

One could have expected the development of sophisticated linguistic expressions for mobilities, notably for virtual ones, for several reasons. First, the second modernity is typified by an "overabundance of events, spatial overabundance, the individualization of references."[115] Second, the very ability to surf visually through the Internet is novel; and third, there is the co-presence of individuals permitted in electronic exchanges with partners and in using websites describing visually remote places. More complex co-presences may involve, for instance, surfing the Internet globally during a discussion with others who are located physically next to the surfer, or talking over a mobile phone to any location while traveling from different origins to different destinations than the location being called. However, despite the variety of potential reasons for a growing development and use of spatial language for the Internet, it must be kept extremely homogenized and simplified in order for it to be understood by people of different cultures and languages who make use of the Internet. This may explain the rather shallow and simple global spatial language applied for the use of the Internet. This rather simple language may be in conflict with much richer domestic spatial languages.

Computerized networks may partially replace real space as a mediator and context for the emergence and maintenance of human relations, yet space and spatial language may play an important role in the functioning of computer-based social networks. Some global networks actually developed around an initial physical location (e.g., the San Francisco–based WELL network); others, such as MOOs, were organized around a symbolic city, implying centrality and agglomeration in the volume and intensity of communications to specific "rooms," "buildings," or "neighborhoods."[116] The spatial structuring of virtual communities constitutes a fusion of local and global spaces, in that concepts and ways of behaving that were originally shaped and originated locally, such as manners of approaching fellow network members, are fused into global social networks, which may set their norms of behavior accordingly.

The dominance of the English language in the world of mobilities is interpreted by Marc Augé as the use of a rather basic generalized vocabulary.[117] The English language has constituted the most dominant language on the Web. In 2000, some 78 percent of all websites were in English, whereas only 50 percent of all Internet users were native English speakers.[118] In 2004, the percentage of English-speaking users declined to some 35 percent, and in 2010 it went further down to 27.3 percent, but it was still the most frequently used language on the Net. This decline was probably coupled with a decrease in the percentage of English websites, but they would still amount to over one-half of the total websites.[119] The Web has reinforced the status of English as the most international language in a globalizing world, but the Internet also allows many linguistic and cultural forms to find new audiences, as we address in part II.

Contemporary corporeal mobility is characterized by some new terms. Augé referred to new transportation hubs, such as airports, as *nonplaces*. He noted that the formation of these hubs implied the coining of new words. Thus, the mobile *transit*, as compared to the veteran fixed *residence*, the *interchange* where no meetings take place, compared to *crossroads* which permit and even encourage human interaction, and *passengers*, defined by their destinations, rather than *travelers* defined by their routes.[120]

Conclusion

This chapter, devoted to the societal dimensions of the information society, attempted to address two major dimensions: first, highlighting the development of thought on information society with a special accent on mobility, and second, elaborating on the role and significance of information and knowledge production in society. The first part of the chapter may be summarized through table 4.1. It may be seen that the dimensions of the study of information society have become more complex as the information society has unfolded, starting with a focus on information and society and reaching the contemporary joint accent on information, space, society, and individuals. This growing complexity of study has been the outgrowth of the introduction and adoption of new communications technologies and notable spatial and social changes. Information economies emerged as being typified by growing temporal intensities of production, which have become spread globally and thus characterized by flows. Socially, widespread and even global networks have become a central element in social life, involving nondirectional personal mobilities.

TABLE 4.1
Phases in the Sociospatial Study of Information Society

Years	Dimensions	Concepts	Leading Scholars	Technological Context	Socioeconomic Context
1960s	Information + society	Quaternary sector Postindustrial society	Gottmann Bell	Telephone; early computing	Service economy
1970s–1980s	Space + society	Distanciation Compression Production	Giddens Harvey Lefebvre	Automobile; plane	Metropolitanization
1980s	Information + space + society	Space of flows	Castells	Telnet; Satellite communications	Globalization
1990s–2000s	Information + space + society + individuals	Network society Mobilities Nondirectionality	Castells Wellman Urry	Personal communications (Internet and mobile phone)	Individualism

The second part of the chapter has shown that information technology is not only critically important for contemporary information production, transmission, and consumption, but that its own development and production are based on various types of knowledge leading to innovation. The most important source of knowledge in this regard is the personally unique accumulation of knowledge, capabilities, and experience of those engaged in R&D, so-called tacit knowledge. For this type of knowledge to be productive and innovative, cross-fertilization is crucial, even beyond the boundaries of employing firms. Hence the importance of the geographical location of R&D within specific regions, permitting and fostering knowledge spillover.

The geography of innovation in information technology becomes more complex given the need for venture capital, as well as additional infrastructure requirements for the industry to emerge and flourish.[121] The increased globalization of capital flows, made possible by information technology, permits a wider global distribution of high-tech centers, though veteran industrial cores are still dominant. Information technology further permits the creation of global networks among these centers, something essential for centers that house plants owned by MNCs. It is, thus, up to constantly innovative information technologies to permit the growing use and handling of information, while existing information technologies, as well as information per se, facilitate the further development of such technologies.

Notes

1. Bonss (2004)
2. Kaufmann (2002: 103)
3. Urry (2000: 188)
4. Giddens (1990)
5. Gottmann (1961: 580)
6. Gottmann (1961: 774)
7. Abler et al. (1977)
8. Bell (1976)
9. Webster (2006)
10. McLuhan (1964)
11. Lewis (1948)
12. Bonss (2004)
13. Kaufmann (2002); Bonss and Kesselring (2004)
14. Kesselring and Vogl (2004)
15. Bonss (2004)
16. Simonsen (2004: 1333)
17. Shields (1997)
18. Latour (1997: 2)

19. Bonss and Kesselring (2004); Avidan and Kellerman (2004)
20. Bonss and Kesselring (2001)
21. Bonss and Kesselring (2004: 13)
22. Kaufmann (2002: 21)
23. Sheller (2004: 49)
24. Urry (2000: 105)
25. Hägerstrand (1970); Couclelis (2009)
26. Giddens (1990)
27. Standage (1998)
28. Adams (1995); Kwan (2001a; 2001b); Kellerman (1989; 2006b; 2012)
29. Harvey (1989); Hubbard et al. (2002)
30. Schivelbusch (1978); Marvin (1988)
31. Harvey (1989); Kirsch (1995)
32. Harvey (1989: 240)
33. Kellerman (2002b)
34. Janelle (1991: 49)
35. Massey (1994)
36. Stalder (2006)
37. Webster (2006)
38. Kwan (2001a: 26)
39. Halbwachs (1980: 134)
40. Shields (1996)
41. Ogden (1994:715)
42. Levy (1998)
43. Lefebvre (1991)
44. Nunes (2006: xxiii)
45. Barlow (1994)
46. Machlup (1980: 7)
47. Barlow (1994: 7)
48. Barlow (1994: 7)
49. Latour (1987: 243)
50. Adams (1995)
51. Roberts (2000)
52. Johnson and Lundvall (2001)
53. Dunning (2000a); Bryson et al. (2000); Clark et al. (2000)
54. Bryson et al. (2000); Malecki (2000)
55. Hotz-Hart (2000: 432)
56. Malecki (2000: 107)
57. Atkinson and Gottlieb (2001: 3)
58. Stewart (1997)
59. Dunning (2000b)
60. Dunning (2000b: 9)
61. Antonelli (2000a; 2000b)
62. Audretsch (2000: 72)
63. Feldman (2000: 381)

64. Audretsch and Feldman (1996)
65. Malecki (2000)
66. Camagni (1991)
67. Malecki (2000)
68. Storper (2000a); Ben-David and Loewy (1998)
69. Hotz-Hart (2000)
70. Feldman and Florida (1994)
71. Feldman and Florida (1994: 210)
72. Malecki (2000: 113)
73. Maskell (2000)
74. Markusen (1996)
75. Florida (1995); Jin and Stough (1998); Maskell and Malmberg (1999b)
76. Ó hUalacháin (1999)
77. Audretsch (2000)
78. Maskell (2000)
79. Antonelli (2000b)
80. Jaffe et al. (1993)
81. Dunning (2000b); Audretsch and Feldman (1996)
82. Feldman and Audretsch (1999)
83. Feldman (2000)
84. Sölvell and Birkinshaw (2000); Dunning (2000b)
85. Mansfield (1991)
86. Audretsch and Feldman (1996)
87. Felsenstein (1993); Markusen (1996)
88. Maskell and Malmberg (1999a)
89. Maskell and Malmberg (1999a)
90. Castells (1989: 71)
91. Castells and Hall (1994)
92. Scott (1993)
93. See, e.g., Lundvall and Maskell (2000).
94. Castells and Hall (1994)
95. Feldman (1994)
96. Castells (2000)
97. DeVol (1999); Cooke et al. (1998); Zook (2005)
98. DeVol (1999)
99. Castells (1989: 72)
100. Castells (1989: 88)
101. See Pred (1977: 90); DeVol (1999); Shefer and Frenkel (1998).
102. Malecki (2000)
103. Malecki (2000); Hackler (2000)
104. Florida (1995)
105. Feldman and Florida (1994: 226)
106. Stivers (1999); Thrift (2004)
107. Augé (2000: 37)
108. Levinson (2003: xvii)

109. Augé (2000: 108)
110. Solnit (2000: 72)
111. Solnit (2000: 73)
112. Schrag (1994)
113. Harasim (1993)
114. Schrag (1994); Graham (1998)
115. Augé (2000: 40)
116. See Rheingold (1993); Schrag (1994).
117. Augé (2000)
118. Lyman and Varian (2000)
119. *Global Reach* (2004); *Internet World Stats* (2011)
120. Augé (2000: 107)
121. Zook (2005)

5

Individuals in the Information Society

S O FAR WE HAVE BEEN exposed to several basic elements and processes of the information society: we have focused on the information society as a concept, moving to elaborations of information technologies, as well as to discussions of societal dimensions of the information society, with a special accent on knowledge production. This final chapter of the first part of the book will complement these discussions by shedding some light on us as individuals living and operating within the information society. We will begin the treatment of this dimension of the information society through explorations of two "internal" processes within our minds—curiosity and cognition—both of which have attained some special significance in the information society. We will then move to elaborations on differences and gaps among people in their exposure to the information society and then continue with discussions of several novel activities that individuals perform within the information society. We will conclude our survey of individuals in the information society with a short presentation of potential consequences of the growing daily global activities of individuals, namely the possible emergence of a global civil society.

Curiosity: The Human Urge for Information

Geographer Torsten Hägerstrand noted that "humans seem to have an in-born tendency to be explorers."[1] The human urge for information expresses highly varied motivations, much beyond the search for professional tacit and codified information, or our urge to meet people, to visit places, and to attend events. Basic daily routines involve, for example, a desire to become updated on close family members, resulting in telephone calls, or they may involve needs for some specific pieces of information at a given time, such as an updated landing time of a flight, leading to a web search over the Internet or to a telephone call.[2]

Of special importance for understanding the human urge to search for information is curiosity, defined as "the desire for information in the absence of any expected extrinsic benefit,"[3] and leading to exploratory behavior in order to satisfy needs for information.[4] In daily life the term *curiosity* is used in a wider and more permissive sense than benefit-free searches, relating to urges for information tied to some potential benefit derived from obtaining it. Curiosity has gained special importance in contemporary life, as the Internet-based World Wide Web has accentuated untargeted curiosities for information through browsing and for social outreach through networking. Traditional libraries in principle may bring about and satisfy curiosities for information, but the Web provides unprecedented satiating satisfaction to curiosity with its provision of instant, in situ, and extremely varied and multisensory pieces, chunks, or packages of information. To paraphrase Marshall McLuhan's famous phrase that the medium is the message, the Internet is not just the medium and the message, but it constitutes simultaneously a motive for curiosity as well as a channel for exploratory behavior.[5]

Numerous origins for human curiosity have been proposed by a number of scholars. Biologically, the brain's natural tendency to perform normally as a cognizing organism constitutes a primary source for curiosity, whereas physiologically and psychologically, curiosity may constitute a secondary drive stemming from more basic ones such as hunger for food. Curiosity may further be considered a primary drive for resolving specific uncertainties, in ways different from the mind's resolution of other simultaneous or previous uncertainties. For example, in the case of hunger, satisfying it by one food makes all foods unappealing following satiation, but satiating curiosity regarding one specific issue does not reduce curiosity for information on other issues. A fourth explanation for the origins of curiosity sees curiosity as rising from a gap between existing and desired knowledge.[6] In any case, one cannot normally reach a full rest from curiosity but merely experience times of relative or partial rest, whether one is awake or sleeping. Such relative rest from curiosity may amount to a form of *apathy* in the sense of incuriosity rather than as a personal characteristic.[7]

The urge for reception of information is manifest in both virtual and physical mobilities. This statement seems almost obvious as far as virtual mobilities are concerned, as they are all about information transmission and reception.

However, physical mobility provides a wealth of information too, regardless of whether the travel objectives are people, places, or events, because of the rich spatial contextuality that corporeal mobility involves by moving to a new destination through a road and the landscapes it involves. Tacit information exchanges always involve some enveloped contextuality, even if performed through e-mail messages, because of their informal nature and the spatial setting of the parties who are involved in the information exchange. Such spatial contextuality is normally not the case for codified information reception.

Information enjoys an enormously wide connotation, since information covers human life in all of its aspects, and hence also the extensive meanings of satiating curiosity for information that we have just discussed. Therefore, for certain types of information, one might achieve full satisfaction only once physical face-to-face contact is established, even if the travel effort involved in reaching such satisfaction is immense. People tend to invest such efforts when close social relationships are involved, or when major business affairs are dealt with. On the other hand, getting information on routine issues, such as the balance of a bank account, is the same whether it is received through the Internet or through walking into a bank branch. By the same token, apathy, in the sense of incuriosity as a required human condition for rest from curiosity (rather than as a personal characteristic), is a relative condition. The deepest condition of rest/apathy is achieved during sleep, but sleep may produce unconscious dreams as a form of information that reflects curiosity. Also, one may rest from one type of curiosity (e.g., resting at home from work-related curiosity), but curiosity may then rise from some personal or other topic that is not work related.

Exposure to Information through Virtual Cyberspace

Curiosity may lead to experiences of exposure to information, which by their very nature are multifold, and our attention here will be devoted to the rather special, novel, and contemporary cognition of virtual cyberspace as information. When assessed from the perspective of personal experiencing, cyberspace constitutes a "different human experience of dwelling in the world; new articulations of near and far, present and absent, body and technology, self and environment."[8] Thus, cognitive cyberspace, as a personally cognized cyberspace, may differ from the personal cognition of real space even if the cognition processes of the two space classes, real space and cyberspace, may seem similar. As we saw already (table 2.1), virtual and real spaces differ from each other in a variety of ways, but they are also interrelated, even if only in indirect ways. For instance, it was shown that persons who navigated successfully through a virtual maze were also more successful at finding their way in real space.[9]

Generally speaking, information, knowledge, and experience constitute mediating forces between the construction and reshaping of both real and virtual spaces. Thus, for example, navigation and manipulation of cyberspace through the Internet involve a metaphorical spatial experience through the extensive use made of geographical language, symbols, and tools, such as *homepage, surfing, navigating, site, cursor,* and so forth. The constant discourse between real (material) and virtual (imagined) spaces through knowledge and information (vis-à-vis perception and cognition), as well as through spatial experience (real and imagined ones), accentuate the oneness of the material, the perceived and the imagined modes of social space. Prior to the introduction of the Internet, David Harvey noted regarding the interrelationships between imagined spaces and real ones, "The spaces of representation, [therefore,] have the potential not only to affect representation of space but also to act as a material productive force with respect to spatial practices."[10]

In chapter 2, we presented a classification of cyberspace into information and communications cyberspaces at large, and we will turn our attention now to the cognitive spaces of these two classes of cyberspace. We believe that similarly to individuals' cognition of real space, people recognize the two classes of cyberspace in special ways. Hartwig Hochmair and Andrew Frank proposed a metaphorical cognitive mapping for semantic information space consisting of four fields: action affordances for events, physical object hierarchies for substances, attributes for qualities, and user intended actions for activities.[11] Studies focusing on way finding in virtual reality and studies of web navigation have both shown some similarity between the Web and virtual reality, on the one hand, and real space, on the other, as far as way finding and navigation are concerned.[12] Still, though, it turned out to be more difficult for individuals to navigate in cyberspace than in real space when using virtual navigation technologies available in the mid- to late 1990s. As far as the cognition of virtual landscapes is concerned, Internet surfers see only one visually restricted web page at a time, which makes it difficult to fully cognize a virtual landscape.[13] This limitation, though, may change in the future if further technological developments, such as 3-D, which has recently been introduced, permit different page/screen visualization possibilities.

Technologies of web search have developed immensely during the 2000s, for both textual and visual/spatial searches and navigations. Textual search is now mostly based on vertical-hierarchical structures, permitting search from general to more specific terms, rather than the simple, and horizontal, spacelike searches of specific terms only in the 1990s. Spatial search and navigation through virtual environments now permit the use of directions and angles, as well as looking at virtual landscapes from the perspective of walking persons. Locating addresses on virtual maps and navigating to these addresses have become standard procedures on the Web, as well as in car driving. Also, one may download a satellite image of a certain location and add information to it or manipulate it. In general, then, textual search and spatial manipulations in information cyberspace have been made widely possible and have gotten more sophisticated.

Cognitive maps for cyberspatial elements such as virtual landscapes, virtual maps, and navigational entities differ from cognitive maps for real space, which persons may have stored in their minds and which they may at times draw on paper. The basic source of difference between these two types of cognitive maps lies in the basic difference between real space and cyberspace. Real space is experienced bodily and mentally through all the senses. By the same token, cartographic maps of real space are concrete documents and stable entities of information. Cyberspace, on the other hand, is a more flexible and changing mode of information, sensed in restricted ways, normally through visual or audiovisual modes only. Based on the work of Reginald Golledge, Mei-Po Kwan claimed that "without the sense of location, distance, and direction necessary for the formation of configurational spatial knowledge, and without a habitual movement pattern essential for developing route-based spatial knowledge, an articulated cognitive map of cyberspace cannot be established."[14]

Internet users may over time get used to, and thus cognize, surfing procedures for reaching selected websites or software and then navigate through them, but they may have difficulties cognizing and eventually drawing cognitive maps of virtual landscapes or of virtual cartographic maps that they may have been exposed to in restricted sensory ways over the Internet. Furthermore, virtual landscapes or maps can be manipulated in varied ways, such as changing their scale, size, directions, colors, and richness of information, and virtual texts too can be manipulated by changing their formats, fonts, and color. Such manipulations may add to the difficulty of cognizing cyberspace presentations in memorable ways. As Kwan noted for real space, space and its maps are two completely separate entities, whereas in cyberspace these two entities may converge.[15]

Exclusion and Inclusion: Gender and Age in the Information Society

Following the discussion of the two "internal" individual processes of curiosity and cognition, we turn now to a more "external" dimension of individuals, namely their status in the information society, notably as it relates to their personal mobility. Enhanced personal mobility in the contemporary era, through the use of mobility technologies, cannot be viewed as a universally patterned social behavior. This reflects those who have to stay immobile in order to permit others' growing mobility (such as traffic controllers), as well as those who are forced to be mobile (e.g., commuters across long distances), both reflecting the *politics of mobility*.[16] Improved personal physical mobility via the acquisition of private cars may weaken public transportation systems and may reduce the physical mobility of those who continue to depend on them. Thus the contemporary *digital divide*, relating to access to virtual mobility media, is coupled with similar patterns concerning corporeal mobility in the public sphere. By the same token, the introduction of new media for virtual personal mobility may weaken existing public ones. Thus, higher levels of adoption of mobile phones may reduce the number and hence the availability of public fixed phones, and by the same token, growing levels of Internet household penetration may reduce the number of Internet cafés.

Mobility may be socially differentiated by other dimensions as well, notably by gender, race, and bodily abilities to move.[17] Mobility at large, and personal mobility in particular, may also be differentiated by cultural tendencies and codes for the permitted and the forbidden in the creation and maintenance of social relations, and in the exposure of individuals to the public sphere, especially of women. Recent surveys reveal digital divides and gaps along age, income, and social indicators other than race.[18] Vincent Kaufmann noted that access to the contemporary wider variety of mobility media and their use "now become potentially important factors of differentiation and social distinction."[19] Thus "there are those with access and those without access. It is no longer geographical space that differentiates but virtual space."[20]

Enhanced personal mobilities may bring about more complex patterns of social segregation. Social spatial segregation among various social groups and sectors emerges in its simple spatial form through continuous territorial enclaves that share similar social attributes.[21] However, enhanced personal mobilities may call for rather complex patterns of segregation comprising spatially dispersed but socially similar households reaching each other instantly through telecommunications and speedily through automobiles driven over expressways. Mimi Sheller and John Urry noted the combination of flexibility and coercion of the automobile as a means to overcome distance within the framework of urban sociality.[22] Contemporary telecommunications, though, present more flexibility than coercion, as they permit either immediate and synchronous interactions through voice communications, or lagged and asynchronous ones through a variety of media (e.g., SMS, e-mail, fax, voice messages).[23] Space-transcending technologies further permit a reorganization of economic space, as production may be dispersed in order to maximize location-based profits.[24]

Virtual mobility, notably the Internet, may potentially serve as an alternative and substitution for physical mobility, including for social networking. This option may materialize primarily for groups that suffer social exclusion, or "relative deprivation," when automobiles cannot be freely used as means for personal mobility, such as for the handicapped.[25] A politics of mobility is still required for the handicapped so that differences in "the mobile body" will be socially recognized, notably the special needs of the handicapped.[26]

In her analysis of women's mobility, Robin Law referred to "transport-disadvantaged groups."[27] It has been shown in numerous national contexts that women travel shorter daily commuting distances than men, reflecting their home and family responsibilities.[28] However, women's mobility at large also reflects "self-imposed precautionary measures [that] limit mobility significantly."[29] And even more generally, "gender shapes access to resources, notably time, money, skills and technology. Access to each of these resources will influence travel behavior (how often trips are made, where and when they are made, and the mode of transport used) as well as the experience and social meaning of mobility."[30] Manuel Castells and colleagues noted, in their international comparative study, that adolescents and young adults have led in the utilization of mobile phones for SMS communications, since it has been easier for them to adopt this technology and since its use is cheaper than voice calls. They further noted that with growing rates of adoption of mobile phones within given national populations, gender differences in adoption rates decline, though women tend to make more social uses of the technology than men do.[31]

Individual Uses of Information Technologies

Information technologies may be used by individuals for a variety of activities and services, presenting major personal information uses, which imply curiosity and cognition, on the one hand, and users' status within the information society on the other. Such activities and services include, for instance, surfing, searching, chatting, banking, and shopping. There are several activities that have changed their geographical extent for citizens of the information age. People may now use the Internet at home for remote social, cultural, entertainment, and economic activities, which were in the past either confined to or for practical reasons performed within the local physical reach of individuals, in a kind of "destiny" of geographical location.[32] We will focus our attention in the following two subsections on two major information activities of individuals performed through the Internet: online shopping and e-learning.

Online Shopping

Our discussion here will focus on what for merchants is called B2C (business-to-customers) e-commerce and for customers is termed online shopping. The electronic medium of the Internet permits us to perform virtually all the phases of physical shopping, except for touching and trying: searching for products, viewing products and information about them, price comparisons, and eventually even purchasing them. Shopping has thus become geographically extended into a potentially global sphere of "opportunity." One may still ask, though, do people actually make use of this opportunity, or do they prefer to stick to physically accessed stores? This question is even more interesting when online shopping is divided between domestic shopping websites ("closer" ones, geographically and culturally) and foreign ones (more "remote" ones, respectively).

For many contemporary customers, shopping may involve a mixture of online activities and physical ones. Thus, one may browse the Internet for products, makers, and prices and then eventually shop in a physical store, or vice versa. Evert-Jan Visser and Martin Lanzendorf estimated that e-commerce complements in-store shopping by stimulating further shopping or by modifying travel behavior.[33] Thomas Golob and Amilia Regan have claimed that each saved shopping trip is meaningful, but at the time they were writing it seemed that not too much travel could be saved.[34] This has possibly changed more recently with the sophistication of online shopping websites.

We will concentrate here on online purchasing, as this concluding phase implies domestic or international transfer of funds by customers, as well as remote domestic or international guarantees by sellers. Our focus will be neither on the aspects of financial volume of spending by individuals nor on the financial extent of B2C e-commerce. Rather, we will concentrate on the behavior of customers in order to see whether the opportunity to shop indifferently from a locational perspective is really materialized, or whether the physical location "destiny" for shopping in physical stores still governs shopping behavior.

As far as online shopping at large (domestically and in foreign countries) by percentage of the total population, it seems that the use of this medium has become quite popular in North America and less so in Europe. Thus, already in 2003 some 40 percent of Canadian households made online purchases. However, Ontario accounted for almost one-half of total online spending.[35] Data for the United States, the most veteran and most developed e-commerce economy, have presented rather modest Internet shopping in the previous decade.[36] Back in 2001, some 21 percent of the total population purchased online,[37] but in 2000, e-shopping and mail-order houses comprised only some 19.8 percent of total retail sales, or about double the percentage some twenty years earlier.[38] Nevertheless, most of the growth occurred in the more traditional mail-order houses, as e-shopping comprised in 2001 just 0.9 percent of total retail sales. Online shopping rose rather modestly to 2.4 percent of total retail sales in 2005,[39] and 3.6 percent in 2008.[40] For the first quarter of 2012, e-commerce accounted for almost 5 percent of retail sales, or more than $53 billion; e-commerce retail sales were expanding at a rate more than double that of traditional retail.[41]

Interestingly enough, in 2002 the leading material products, in percentage of online spending in the United States, were all information items: software (32.2 percent), PCs (32.1 percent), peripherals (22.4 percent), books (11.5 percent), and music (8.7 percent). All other material products ranked much lower. Hence it seems that the electronic information economy operates within a vicious cycle: computer equipment is required for Internet use, which in return is used for the purchase of computer equipment, and at lower percentages also for the purchase of more traditional information products (mainly books and music).

Based on OECD data for 2002, it was estimated that some 10 to 25 percent of households used e-commerce at least once.[42] Several years later, in 2005–2006, 27 percent of the population in the European Union shopped online, and this percentage was equal to the share of the population purchasing through the more traditional method of remote shopping via the postal service.[43] The European Union was highly diversified, including countries with high population percentages of domestic online shopping, led by Denmark and the Netherlands (46 percent), Sweden (45 percent), and the UK (41 percent), going all the way down to 0 percent in Cyprus and 1 percent in Greece (see table 5.1). The more recent growth trend for cross-border online shopping in the European Union is suggested to be generally high, with several countries doubling the percentage of their population involved in cross-border online shopping from 2002 to 2006. By 2010, the OECD reports an average of almost one-third of residents of member countries shopping online. Among the leaders were the UK (60 percent had shopped online) and over half in Norway, Denmark, South Korea, and the Netherlands. Data for online banking show even higher levels, with almost 40 percent using this service across the OECD and more than 75 percent in the Nordic countries.[44]

Purchasing abroad may be considered an advanced form of online shopping, as it may involve money exchange in some cases, trust in a foreign company, as well as overcoming an image of remoteness. Here, too, there

TABLE 5.1
Percentage Population Shopping Online in EU Countries and/or
Domestically, and Percentage Home Internet Connection, 2005–2006

Country	Shopping in EU Countries	Shopping Domestically	Home Internet
Luxembourg	28	7	65
Denmark	19	46	74
Austria	18	21	48
Netherlands	15	46	85
Sweden	14	45	79
Finland	13	34	66
Ireland	12	19	46
Belgium	12	17	56
Malta	11	4	51
UK	7	41	53
France	7	26	46
Germany	4	30	52
Estonia	4	17	48
Italy	4	11	31
Slovenia	4	10	52
Spain	4	9	38
Cyprus	4	0	34
Czech Rep.	3	21	38
Latvia	3	11	25
Poland	2	16	31
Portugal	2	3	23
Greece	1	2	17
Slovakia	1	5	19
Hungary	1	8	18
Lithuania	1	4	23
EU general	**6**	**23**	**44**

Sources: Kellerman and Paradiso (2007). Data source: European Commission (2006: illustrations D46 and QB1.1).

was found a major difference between North America and the European Union. Whereas in Canada in 2003, one-third of online purchases were made through foreign websites,[45] probably mainly American ones, in the European Union in 2005–2006, the percentage of purchases made in other EU countries stood at only 6 percent. This was so despite the convenience of possibly using the same currency, the euro, for most purchases.[46]

Contributing to the growth of international retail sales online is the ability of consumers to benefit from currency movements. The dramatic rise in the Australian dollar during the past five years, combined with a costly domestic retail sector, led to a surge in personal imports through online sales. Related to this is growing protest over the cost of information goods such as software and music, which often carry different prices depending on country of residence and yet are downloaded by consumers from the same server. In 2012 the Australian government is launching an inquiry into the online pricing policies of firms selling software, games, and music.[47]

The European Commission performed a survey in 2005–2006 of some 25,000 citizens in its then twenty-five member countries that referred to domestic and foreign (in other EU countries only) online shopping (see table 5.1). The country data for these two geographic extents of shopping do not lend themselves to formal statistical analysis because of the rather small samples in countries with low Internet penetration rates and low rates for online shopping. Still, however, when ordering the countries by decreasing magnitude of foreign purchases, two factors seemed to govern European online shopping behavior.

First, country size matters. Citizens of small countries tended to perform more foreign shopping then those of larger ones. Thus, Luxembourg led the list of foreign shopping with a percentage (28) that was four times larger than the percentage of domestic online shoppers (7), followed by various other small countries. This same factor applied also to small countries that presented much more modest values of online shopping at large. Thus Cyprus had no domestic online shopping at all, whereas the Maltese population tended to have almost three times as many purchases internationally as domestically (11 and 4 percent, respectively). The opposite trend was true for three of the larger European countries, namely showing more domestic than foreign online shopping: UK (41 percent for domestic shopping versus 7 percent abroad); France (26 and 7 percent, respectively); and Germany (30 and 4 percent, respectively). Online shopping opportunities were larger in bigger countries, so that the very availability of foreign online shopping provided an opportunity foremost for smaller countries. This trend is of interest since other factors have been proposed for magnitude differences in international B2C e-commerce: Internet infrastructure, economic development, and cultural factors.[48]

The second factor for international online shopping in the European Union was national Internet penetration rates. The Scandinavian countries have led the adoption of Internet and telecommunications media globally since the introduction of the telephone.[49] They also lead in foreign and domestic online shopping. The Internet has thus changed, to some degree, the shopping habits of Scandinavians as well as those of residents of other small and well-developed EU countries.

The overall picture of rather modest percentages of the population performing online shopping seems to suggest that geographical location "destiny" is still there as far as shopping is concerned. Habits, trust, and uncertainty are three primary obstacles to online commerce, but the desire to touch and to try merchandise, as well as shopping also constituting a kind of entertainment, are additional factors slowing down the wide adoption of online shopping.

On the supply side there are some additional constraints. Merchants have to invest more in foreign countries in order to attract customers, primarily over the Internet, targeting mainly the younger generations for whom cross-border activities at large might be more liberated. Needless to say, websites have to be multilingual in order to facilitate foreign shopping, notably if there evolves some competition between domestic and foreign websites.

E-Learning

Another opportunity becoming potentially available to individuals in the information age is e-learning through the Internet, both at domestic institutes and through cross-border education. One may study via the Internet at various levels. Tacit knowledge may be acquired through enrichment of the traditional frontal study by browsing the Web or via virtual consultations with remote colleagues. Codified knowledge, on the other hand, may be achieved through formal courses or full academic degree studies. Whereas the first two options are informal and may range in volume from time to time, formal degree studies are similar to e-commerce in that a product, knowledge, is bought online. There are, however, several differences between the sale of products and services (such as airline tickets), on the one hand, and the acquisition of formal codified knowledge on the other, which may bring about differing levels of their adoption.

From the supply side, language is a much more crucial element in e-learning than in e-commerce, by the very nature of learning. Standards are another and even more crucial dimension of formal degree study when compared to internationally recognized quality standards for products and services (e.g., ISO 9000), since a domestic or cross-border academic degree has to be recognized by national higher education councils as well as by potential employers. At the international level of higher-education standards for an opening and globalizing world, several efforts have been made to assure such standardization, for example, the EU Bolognia agreements, as well as global GATS (General Agreements on Trade in Services) agreements.[50]

From the demand side, the purchase of an online degree program implies a prolonged purchase process spanning several years, as compared to a few minutes when buying other products and services online. It further requires a much more extensive investment by the customer in terms of cost, time, and intellectual effort. This latter intellectual effort may make online studies inferior to face-to-face ones, from the perspectives of both students and universities and colleges. As far as product durability is concerned, an academic degree constitutes a lifelong product as compared to the disposability or limited lifespan of other products and services.

All of these reasons have turned online formal academic education into a widely debated issue, albeit still relatively modestly used by potential students, even compared to e-commerce.[51] The eUSER Population Survey 2005 performed by the European Union in ten member countries did not inquire about online full-degree studies.[52] It yielded low results for the more modest option of online studies of at least one course. In terms of percentage of adult learners (and not percentage of the total population), the results ranged from the rather low 3.3 percent in Germany, which ranked much higher in domestic e-commerce, to the leading UK (10.7 percent) and Ireland (10.0 percent). The relatively higher values for the UK and Ireland may be related to the wider availability of study opportunities in English, as well as to the impact of the British Open University. The need to overcome traditions, habits, and conventions by potential students and the hesitation of many universities and colleges to fully teach over the Internet require careful attention for the possible future development of study opportunities over the Internet.

In the United States, some 56 percent of degree-granting institutions offered distance courses in 2000–2001, but not necessarily full-degree studies. These offerings ranged from merely 16 percent of the private two-year colleges to 90 percent of the public two-year colleges, and from 40 percent of the private four-year institutions to 89 percent of the public four-year institutions.[53] The major differences between the two sectors of universities and colleges reflect academic differences regarding e-learning as well as possibly some wider responsibility toward potential clientele located in peripheral areas by public institutions. By 2007–2008, over 4 million students were taking online courses through U.S. universities, more than one-fifth of the total student population. While online courses are popular, less than 4 percent of students took all of their program courses online.[54]

Individuals as Global Citizens

Do the opportunities for global online activities and their wide or modest materializations create a potential for individuals to become citizens of a global information society, at the expense of or in addition to their national citizenships? "The idea of national citizenship loses some ground to more universal models of membership located within a de-territorialized notion of a person's universal rights."[55] This perspective may highlight growing global components in the identities of contemporary individuals in developed countries, replacing or joining their national cultural and political identities.

Mobility at large has been a major characteristic of modernity, as well as of the second/new modernity. "Modern society is a society on the move,"[56] with its individual citizen constituting *Homo viator*.[57] Contemporary humans are considered as constantly moving in both society and space. This wide availability and growing significance of mobilities may potentially bring about expanding locational flexibilities and opportunities for both individuals and geographical-societal entities (cities, regions, and countries).[58]

Space and distance have been argued time and again to constitute a "tyranny" for people and societies functioning under past technologies.[59] However, for the contemporary information age, Vincent Kauffmann states that "space is [thus] undefined and open. It is a set of opportunities in perpetual reorganization."[60] This change from tyranny or destiny provided individuals with the emergence of flexible locational opportunities—for example, in the form of online shopping—but these have been only partially, though increasingly, adopted. This tendency reflects long-established habits for local and domestic geographical anchoring of basic human activities. As Susan Hanson colorfully stated, "Life on the ground is surely more complex than life entirely off the road; but then life entirely off the road is an oxymoron."[61]

Citizens of the global information society are also typified by growing travel by air, or physical global mobility. The term *aeromobility* was originally proposed by Karl Høyer for air travel and tourism at large.[62] It may also refer to values, practices, norms, and patterns of individuals, society, and space associated with a growing use of flights by households, notably for international travel.[63] At the societal level, increasing frequencies of air travel by numerous and growing segments of society may be accompanied by an assessment of aeromobility as a democratic right, permitting free spatially expanded movement. Still, as of yet, one cannot identify a kind of civil society of aeromobility. However, more frequent flying, as well as the diffusion of flying along social strata, has brought about an emerging culture of aeromobility, suggesting norms and codes for flight behavior in terms of baggage styles, dress codes for vacation flights, on-flight social codes, and so forth.

Aeromobility has gained some status, despite its constituting public transportation, through the availability of several flight classes that differentiate among passengers not only during flight but also during check-in, as well as through the provision of separate and upgraded waiting lounges in airports. Airlines attempt to promote the turning of such services into a class symbol. For a still rather small segment of society, namely the "cosmopolitans," their high frequency of flying may involve a decline in localism. However, only in more rare cases, such cosmopolitans may live in one community and socialize in a remote one, mainly if during weekdays work is performed in one city/country while weekends are spent with family in yet another one.

Passports, which are the strongest individual expression of national citizenship in the global arena, play a special role for passenger identification, tracking, and regulation, notably throughout international airports,[64] and their presentation and checking may involve some tension by passengers.[65] So far no kind of international mobility identity document has been introduced, and passengers may receive preferred or discriminated treatment at points of departure and destination depending on their country of citizenship as expressed by their passport.

The global information society can be considered as one ingredient in the more general and still evolving "world society," which constitutes a global civil society, and in which individuals maintain and foster voluntary relations among themselves beyond the boundaries of nation-states, which are, therefore, changing but not necessarily dismantled and replaced by a world society.[66]

Conclusion

The variety of issues presented in this chapter regarding individuals in the information society accentuates the current status of this society as one that is still in the making. The growing role of virtual communications, notably through the Internet and its e-mail and Web components, side by side with mobile telephony, may bring about stronger and wider experiences of individual curiosity and cognition. It seems that curiosity receives a higher importance in the information society because it can be satiated easier and faster vis-à-vis the Internet. By the same token, spatial cognition receives a different and maybe novel significance through the emergence of cyberspace and its cognition, as compared to the cognition of real space.

The higher importance of curiosity in the second modernity might be related, first, to the very availability of new technologies, as well as to their affiliated organizational patterns (e.g., networks). It might further be attributed to the very nature of the second modernity, which implies, among other things, ambiguity, risk, uncertainty, "fluidity and liquidity," change, and unpredictability. Knowing more instantly, and without regard to the geographical distance of the information sources (or an intensified time-space compression), may assist people in coping with the nature and challenges of the second modernity.

The cognition of the rather novel virtual cyberspace may still undergo changes with continued technological developments, which may bring about wider uses of three-dimensional computerized interfaces coupled with different cognition experiences of cyberspace. This may also apply to widely available and more sophisticated mobile video technologies. Declining prices of information technologies for individual consumption at large may assist in wider and more egalitarian social participation in the information society. Furthermore, growing dependency on information devices may bring about wider varieties of uses for information technologies.

Adopting new ways of communicating and getting used to new experiences of curiosity and cognition may assist in the road-paving process for wider and more sophisticated uses of the Internet and mobile phones, whether for information searches or for more committed activities such as shopping and learning. By the same token, a wider and more egalitarian adoption of virtual communications technologies may bring about in the more remote future the emergence of a global civil society at the expense of traditional domestic ones based on sovereignty and national cultures.

Notes

1. Hägerstrand (1992: 35)
2. Kellerman (2006b)
3. Loewenstein (2002: 1)
4. Fowler (1965)
5. McLuhan (1964)
6. See Fowler (1965); Loewenstein (2002) for reviews.
7. Fowler (1965)
8. Crang et al. (1999: 1)
9. Péruch et al. (2000)
10. Harvey (1989: 219)
11. Hochmair and Frank (2001)
12. Dodge and Kitchin (2001)
13. Kwan (2001a)
14. Golledge (1995; 1999); Kwan (2001a: 26)
15. Kwan (2001a)
16. See, e.g., Massey (1993).
17. Massey (1994); Longan (2002); Sheller and Urry (2000); Wajcman (2000)
18. Rice and Katz (2003)
19. Kaufmann (2002: 19)
20. Kaufmann (2002: 29)
21. Freund and Martin (1993: 103–104)
22. Sheller and Urry (2000)
23. Raubal et al. (2004)
24. Freund and Martin (1993: 115)
25. Haddon (2000); Grantham and Tsekouras (2004); Kenyon et al. (2002)
26. Imrie (2000)
27. Law (1999)

28. Blumen and Kellerman (1990)
29. Law (1999: 570)
30. Law (1999: 578)
31. Castells et al. (2007)
32. Kellerman and Paradiso (2007)
33. Visser and Lanzendorf (2004)
34. Golob and Regan (2001)
35. Statistics Canada (2004)
36. U.S. Bureau of the Census (2003)
37. NTIA (2002)
38. Kellerman (1984)
39. Malecki and Moriset (2008)
40. U.S. Bureau of the Census (2011)
41. U.S. Department of Commerce (2012)
42. Visser and Lanzendorf (2004)
43. European Commission (2006)
44. OECD (2011a)
45. Statistics Canada (2004)
46. European Commission (2006)
47. Peatling and O'Rourke (2012)
48. Hwang et al. (2006); Kshetri (2001)
49. Kellerman (1999)
50. Knight (2006)
51. Breton and Lambert (2003)
52. European Union (2006)
53. U.S. Bureau of the Census (2006)
54. U.S. Department of Education (2011)
55. Urry (2007: 190); see also Keane (2003); Lechner (2009).
56. Lash and Urry (1994: 252)
57. Eyerman and Löfgren (1995)
58. Kellerman and Paradiso (2007)
59. Toffler (1981); Duranton (1999); Blainey (1966); Mitchell (1995)
60. Kauffman (2002:8)
61. Hanson (1998:248)
62. Høyer (2000: 155)
63. Kellerman (2006b)
64. Salter (2003, 2004, 2007), Kellerman (2008)
65. Iyer (2001), Salter (2003)
66. Lechner (2009)

II

MAPPING THE GLOBAL
INFORMATION SOCIETY

6

Spatial Organization of the Global Information Society

THE INFRASTRUCTURE AND context of global information society are varied and evolving in different ways. The first part of this book shows the many elements and theoretical foundations for understanding information society. In this section, emphasis shifts to analyzing information society in terms of its global organization and distribution.

What is apparent from the spatial patterns of global information society is the localization of information and communications technologies and their melding into different forms. Information and communications technologies reveal different experiences over time and in different places. The diversity of technology is somewhat recent; initially telephony had a similarity in technology and form globally, with telephones recognizable and used in similar ways across space, but over time, local innovations and preferences have changed the form and practice of making a telephone call.

With the proliferation of information technologies, from telephones to computers to cameras and the Internet, however, ICTs in any one location are now complex sets of different technologies and systems. One country may be mobile phone oriented, another dependent on personal computers, while yet another obtains information from more traditional sources, such as newspapers, radio, and television. The bundles of ICTs used in any one country or place are not random but the result of decisions made in the past and presently by consumers, regulators, and businesses.

One way to represent the nature and development of ICTs globally is through analogy to natural selection, where species evolve over time based on local territorial conditions. Conditions would include the state of economic development, consumer behavior, preexisting relationships with information technology, government policy, and investments by ICT businesses. Against this context of many stakeholders and interests, new technologies are introduced. Into this mix come new ICTs such as the Internet or mobile telephony. Technologically, they can be identical organisms, but when separated and placed in different contexts, they are likely to change over time as they adapt or perish.

ICTs represent a wide range of technologies that started identically, yet when used in different places—cities, regions, or countries—they take on different attributes related to place. In this case, place represents not only geographic coordinates on the planet but all that places capture in terms of environment, society, culture, government, and development. ICTs can therefore be represented as a set of identical technologies that, when introduced into different places, result in changes in form and function.

This chapter presents four realms of ICT characteristics. Each dimension is a classification employed across space to show the scale and scope of ICT use. Within each dimension there is a range of experiences evident across global information society so that it forms a spectrum. The four spectra that help define information society are devices, access, culture, and governance. Devices concern the technology, such as a computer or mobile phone, while access reflects the willingness and ability of residents in a place to use a new information technology. Culture captures the unique characteristics of a location into which the new ICTs find a role, and governance reflects the policy environment that shapes ICTs, their use, and the behavior of users and suppliers.

Each spectrum captures the variety across space of the technologies and contexts that shape, and are shaped by, information society. For each location, individuals, households, and the population in general owns or accesses a bundle of devices for which culture and governance play a role in where and how the devices are used, and in the form and content of information available. In the following chapters, these spectra will be used to show the richness and diversity of information society across world regions of the Americas, Europe, Asia, and the Middle East/Africa. In addition to the information society spectra, each chapter will also address population, income, and human development conditions.

Information Society Data

Before continuing, it is useful to discuss the data used in this section of the book. In addition to the summary data presented in this chapter, the following chapters devoted to world regions contain tables and statistics to illustrate patterns of information society. Given the rapid changes associated with information technology and society, it may be worthwhile to update the data you use on a regular basis. To date the data sources used have been consistent and should be easily accessible online.

The data sources used in part II include (1) population by country from the U.S. Census;[1] (2) gross national income in US$ adjusted for purchasing power from the World Bank;[2] (3) the Human Development Index (HDI) from the United Nations Development Programme;[3] (4) televisions per one hundred population from the U.S. Central Intelligence Agency;[4] (5) personal computers (PCs) per one hundred population from the United Nations;[5] (6) the Digital Opportunities Index (DOI) from the International Telecommunication Union;[6] (7) telecommunications data on landline and mobile phone subscribers, Internet users, and broadband access from the International Telecommunication Union database;[7] (8) Internet cost based on twenty hours' use per month in US$ from NationMaster;[8] and (9) freedom of the Internet and of the press from Freedom House.[9]

Devices

The technologies of global information society range from telephony to computing to the Internet. While initially distinct, there is also the growing merger of devices as mobile phones incorporate the Internet and computers serve as telephones, as television is adopted by phones and computers, or as telephones and cameras merge. The spectrum of devices employed by information society ranges from telephones (fixed line and mobile) to computers (desktop, laptop, and mobile phones), with functions such as e-books, television, and GPS navigation possible for each. Globally, and for each place, the spectrum of devices available and in use varies significantly, as do the trends of use for each.'

While storytelling and the book are certainly among the first forms of information technology and form, the first electronic device to shape society was the telephone. The International Telecommunication Union reports that there were 1.16 billion fixed telephone lines in 2011 and 5.8 billion mobile subscribers.[10] In 1997, mobile subscribers represented less than a third of the number of fixed lines globally, with 215 million mobile phones to 792 million landlines. By 2002 mobile subscribers exceeded landlines 1.2 billion to 1.1 billion, and in 2011 mobile phone subscriptions were five times the number of landlines. As a recent technology, mobile phones have been adopted widely in places that had limited landline access. In developing countries such as Tanzania and Rwanda, mobile phone subscriptions outnumber landlines by as much as one hundred to one.

The spatial patterns associated with an ICT device are evident in figures 6.1 and 6.2, which show the global distribution of landline and mobile phone subscriptions per one hundred residents. The patterns contrast landlines, which tend to be most extensive in the developed world, with mobile phone use, which is used extensively worldwide.

The extraordinary growth of mobile phone usage continues, while for the first time landline numbers have declined from 1.28 billion to 1.27 billion lines between 2007 and 2008. During that year, the slight loss of landlines was matched by an increase of more than 800 million mobile subscribers. The growth in mobile phones between 2007 and 2008 equals almost two-thirds of the global stock of landlines at the same time. In general, advanced economies show a drop in landlines and rapid growth in mobile telephony, while developing countries have very low bases of installed landlines with extensive mobile phone ownership.

With almost seven billion land and mobile lines globally in 2011, there would seem to be a lot of connectivity available, but the distribution is not equal. It is not uncommon for affluent households in the developed world to have one or two landlines and more than one mobile subscription per person, while the poorest locations and countries share very few lines or subscriptions. For example, in 2011, Macau had 206 mobile phone subscriptions per one hundred residents, while the global average was 86.7 subscriptions, and countries such as Somalia and Burma had fewer than 7 subscriptions. The 2011 global average for landlines was 16.6 per one hundred population, ranging from highs of 96 lines per one hundred in Monaco to a low of 0.06 lines per one hundred in Congo.[11]

Television is a major source of information in most societies, a technology that has rapidly developed over the past thirty years with the expansion of cable and satellite delivery systems. With the rise of the Internet, however, interest in television data collection has waned, and recent data are difficult to find. CIA estimates for 2003 show 1.4 billion televisions worldwide, with most in China (400 million) and the United States (219 million).[12] Most advanced economies have more than 90 percent of households with a television, although there are thirty-five countries with television penetration rates less than 20 percent and many African countries with less than 10 percent penetration.[13] It is not simply a matter of economic advancement, however, as the United Kingdom, Sweden, and Australia report approximately fifty televisions per one hundred population, while Georgia, Brunei, and Oman exceed fifty-three to fifty-five televisions per one hundred.[14]

The number of televisions is only part of the infrastructure needed for this ICT sector to function. Also essential is a broadcasting system comprising local, cable, and satellite delivery. Until the advent of satellite television,

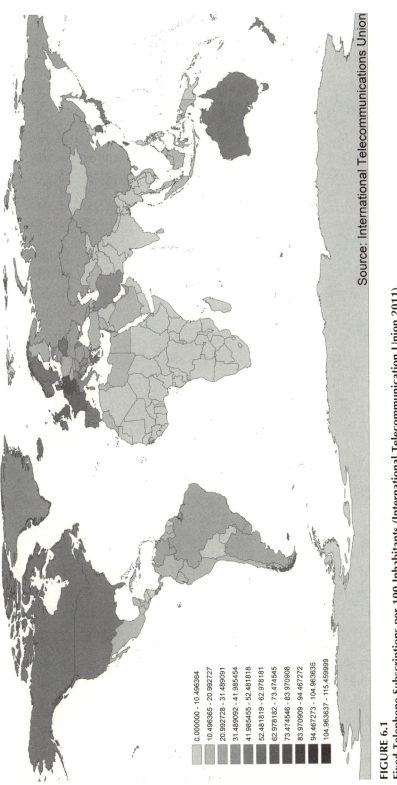

Source: International Telecommunications Union

	0.000000 - 10.496364
	10.496365 - 20.992727
	20.992728 - 31.489091
	31.489092 - 41.985454
	41.985455 - 52.481818
	52.481819 - 62.978181
	62.978182 - 73.474545
	73.474546 - 83.970908
	83.970909 - 94.467272
	94.467273 - 104.963636
	104.963637 - 115.459999

FIGURE 6.1
Fixed-Telephone Subscriptions per 100 Inhabitants (International Telecommunication Union 2011).

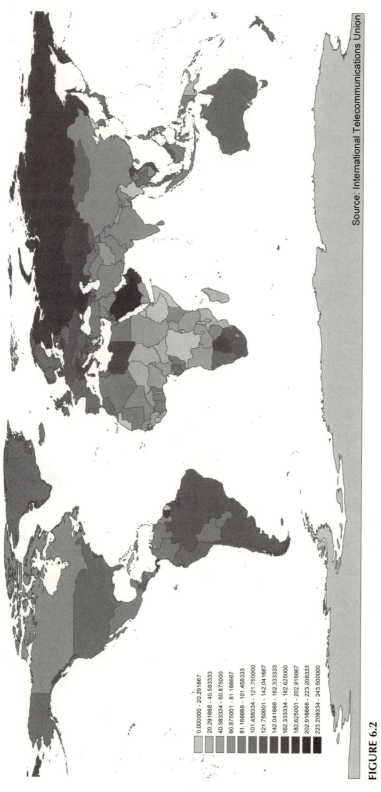

	0.000000 - 20.291667
	20.291668 - 40.583333
	40.583334 - 60.875000
	60.875001 - 81.166667
	81.166668 - 101.458333
	101.458334 - 121.750000
	121.750001 - 142.041667
	142.041668 - 162.333333
	162.333334 - 182.625000
	182.625001 - 202.916667
	202.916668 - 223.208333
	223.208334 - 243.500000

Source: International Telecommunications Union

FIGURE 6.2
Mobile-Cellular Subscriptions per 100 Inhabitants (ITU 2011).

residents of many locations were limited in their access to television-based information. Broadcast systems are important as an indicator of accessibility, and the number of broadcasters suggests availability of differing viewpoints. Concentrated media ownership, limited broadcasting sources, or government-controlled broadcasting all suggest a lack of diversity in viewpoint and ideology in media available to residents.

Computers represent the core technology of information society and have the potential to replace televisions for visual information and entertainment, while in many cases the merger of mobile phones and computers is a primary source of Internet access. The linking of computers and telecommunications made possible the Internet and the structure of information society experienced during the past two decades. The computer as envisaged by Charles Babbage as a universal machine is taking on increasing functions and living up to its heritage. The convergence of telephony and computing is providing a range of devices that form the foundation of information society. Computers can take many forms, from mainframes, to desktops, to laptops and notebook computers, to Internet-enabled mobile phones. The merging of technologies clouds data analysis as the mobile telephone today offers more computing power than early desktop computers.

Estimates of global computer numbers are of 787 million personal computers in 2004–2006,[15] while the International Telecommunication Union estimates 808 million PCs globally in 2005.[16] Forrester Research estimated that there were one billion PCs in use in 2008 and that two billion PCs would be in use by 2015.[17] It is important to note, however, that there is growing interchangeability of technologies. In one country, the popular choice for Internet access may be though a desktop, but in other places it could be a laptop, and elsewhere an Internet-enabled mobile phone.

In the chapters that follow, data will be presented for each world region and country showing the different devices used, such as televisions, computers, fixed landlines, and mobile phones.

Access

Access to information and communications technologies seems on the surface to be a simple case of the presence or absence of the technology itself. Access, however, is far more complex, with the use of ICT reflecting a series of decisions, abilities, and technologies. First is the cognitive ability or desire to access ICT, second is ownership or presence of ICT, and third, the cost of ICT use.

The first stage of access is the ability of an individual to use ICT and having the numeracy or literacy to use the technology. Telephones, especially landline systems, offer a simple device that only requires the use of ten digits to communicate. More advanced technologies, such as mobile phones or computers, require literacy for effective use. UNESCO estimates global literacy at 82 percent, although lower rates occur in sub-Saharan Africa (59 percent), South and West Asia (60 percent), and the Arab states (71 percent). UNESCO finds for 2005 that almost 700 million people are unable to read and write and therefore are effectively excluded from the ICTs of global information society.[18]

ICT is often presented as an end in itself, yet the reason we demand and use these technologies is for the communication or information that they provide. Desire for the technology is the desire for the services they can provide. Part of our understanding of access is the realization that use of ICTs is not mandatory, and that not everyone will find the same utility in ICTs. One parallel historically concerns Henry David Thoreau's observation about the telegraph in the mid-nineteenth century: "They tell us that Maine can now communicate with Texas. But does Maine have anything to say to Texas?"[19] Central to issues of access to ICT is the need for there to be something of value gained from the technology. Technologies are used to achieve something, yet often access alone is seen as an end in itself.

Given the presence of ability and desire, access then becomes an issue of physical possession of the technology, through ownership, position (student using school ICT, access at work), or temporary use (Internet café, purchased telephone call). ICTs are globally sourced technologies that are often made in the same factory for global use. Given international sourcing for components and a global market, the technology should cost the same worldwide. Even though often sold or rented in competitive markets, taxes, regulations, markets, and pricing conventions can lead to variations in price and cost across countries. For example, the OECD shows annual median mobile phone use costs ranging from US$131.44 in the Netherlands and Finland to US$635.85 in the United States.[20] Even with similarly priced technology, the social and economic context of ICT use has a significant impact on cost.

Internet service access usually comprises two costs, an Internet service provider (ISP) subscription and the cost of connecting to the ISP. ISP subscriptions are either an hourly rate or a set rate for unlimited access. With unlimited access, users have the freedom to consume bandwidth and time exploring and using the Web, while hourly users face an increasing cost as their time online increases. Countries with low-cost unlimited access will have a more sophisticated Internet user because the pricing structure allows greater familiarity with the Internet. Surveys across different countries show different Internet access rates for various reasons, but cost of access needs to be incorporated into comparative measurement.

Equally important in some countries or locations with dial-up Internet service is the cost of the telephone call to access an ISP. Countries with telecommunications services that allow an unlimited-length call for a local charge, such as Australia, Canada, or the United States, provide low-cost access to ISPs. Countries with metered local telephone charges, or people living in locations that require a long-distance call to reach an ISP, face far higher access costs.

While the cost of Internet access may show some variation, the income available from consumers to access ICTs varies far more; it is the ratio of Internet costs to income that is a major determinant of use. What is important is not the absolute cost of ICT use but the relative cost, taking into account the disposable income available to residents of a place or country. For example, Internet access costs US$147.80 per month in the Central African Republic, where the average income, adjusted for purchasing power, is only US$730 annually. In that case, Internet access costs double the annual average income. In contrast, in much of Western Europe, Internet costs approximate US$10–20 per month in countries where average incomes per capita exceed US$35,000 annually.

Culture

Culture is an important element of information society and ICT use as it shapes the forms of information available, ICT content, and where and how that information is used. Culture reflects beliefs, traditions, and languages and their role within a society, or the roles of multiple cultures within one country or location. Culture is important for understanding information society and ICT use, as it directly affects the relationship between technology and society. Culture and its relationship with ICT vary in many ways, such as how mobile telephones are answered and used; whether television is viewed by individuals, households, extended families, or entire villages; or the norms of Internet interaction through chat and messaging.[21] Culture also affects adoption rates and openness to new ideas and technologies, such as e-commerce.[22] As culture varies so much across space, so do the behaviors associated with the use of ICTs.

In almost all cases, ICT use requires language for telephony and television, and literacy for Internet use. Of concern is the ability to use ICT using native languages. In terms of the Internet, the current leading languages are English (478 million users and 28 percent of Internet users); Chinese (384 million, 22 percent of users); and Spanish (136 million and 8 percent of users), followed by Japanese, French, Portuguese, German, Arabic, Russian, and Korean.[23] In many cases, especially with the Internet, users must use a second language due to the limited range of content in local languages. David Crystal reflects on the many conventions associated with Internet communications and how the Web is affecting use of language, while Erin Jansen presents a dictionary of web terms and slang that often enter language as common foreign terms and cross linguistic borders.[24]

UNESCO recognized the importance of culture and social identification and recently included in its mission the use of ICT "to contribute to the promotion of freedom of expression, linguistic and cultural diversity, education, and access to information, particularly information in the public domain."[25] One of the central elements of culture is language and the way people communicate with each other. As important tools for communication, ICTs have the power to make interaction easier, or possibly more difficult. Marcel Diki-Kidiri shows concern over the ability of languages to be lost with the rise of dominant global online languages such as English, Chinese, and Spanish and expresses the need for space to be made for existing and threatened languages in cyberspace. He notes that of six thousand languages globally, twelve languages account for 98 percent of web content.[26]

One of the advances in terms of linguistic diversity and cultural identity is the implementation of global character sets that incorporate more than three hundred languages into the structure of URLs. In October 2009, the Internet Corporation for Assigned Names and Numbers (ICANN) announced internationalized domain names that could use over 100,000 characters. Until this step, domain names were available only in English and were a cause for concern about linguistic diversity and the spread of the Internet to non-English speakers. This decision should provide greater accessibility, as Internet users will be better able to navigate in a language, character set, and keyboard that they understand.

In addition to language, content is also part of culture, and the form of web and other ICT information will affect the popularity of content. Individuals use ICTs as a means to access information and to communicate; it is rarely an end in which the use of the technology alone provides satisfaction. Use of ICT will therefore depend on there being content available that interests users, which in turn anticipates content that will be of interest in terms of topic, language, and relevance. The early growth of the Internet required use of a narrow range of languages and information targeting an educated audience. With the growth of access, Internet users seek information that they can use; otherwise there is little to attract attention.

Governance

Governance concerns the ways that systems and societies are managed and organized. New technologies introduce new circumstances that require both informal and official protocols for behavior. Informal protocols include ways of answering phones, how mobile phones are used near others, and acceptable behavior on bulletin boards or for text and chat. Official protocols use the legal system and regulation to shape ICT infrastructure, content, and use. As ICT use grows, so does government regulation of the systems.

One set of regulations determines the provision of service for telephones, television, and the Internet. Laws often determine the number of service providers, with many countries having a state-run monopoly on telecommunications services. Access to spectra for broadcasting and mobile telephony is determined by regulation, as is licensing of Internet service providers. The infrastructure of ICT—landlines, radio and TV broadcasting, and mobile phone licenses—is determined by public policy that also controls ownership (local versus foreign), competition, rates and fees, and service areas. The regulatory environment allows the state to control most, if not all, aspects of ICT infrastructure and content.

Beyond the regulatory environment for infrastructure is the control of content, such as what is allowed or acceptable on television, cable TV systems, and the Internet. Part of the control desire is to minimize harmful content, especially to vulnerable populations such as children. This results in content limits, such as Nazi material on German websites or access to gambling and pornography by children in many countries. One motivation of policy, therefore, is the protection of society from what may be considered inappropriate content. The opposing view, however, is that content limits on radio, TV, and the Internet only serve as censorship or a way to protect state assets from competition (online gambling versus government lotteries). At the core of this debate is the question of who determines what adults in a society can freely choose to access, as one person's protection of society is another person's censorship and limits to freedom. The answer to this question lies in how states and countries govern themselves and in who determines the regulatory environment.

One example of the conflict associated with ICT regulation has been the 2011 and 2012 debates about access and control of content in the United States and Europe. In the United States, the Stop Online Piracy Act (SOPA) was a bill promoted by law enforcement to gain better control over intellectual property, although opponents said it would limit freedom of speech. The bill was defeated but remains an ongoing regulatory issue. A similar legal framework was established as an international treaty, the Anti-Counterfeiting Trade Agreement (ACTA). While a number of countries are signatories, attempts to include the European Union led to dissent and protest in 2012 that led to the EU rejecting the treaty.

Freedom House offers a typology of freedom issues associated with Internet use globally, which serves as a good example of many content and access issues for ICT. In the report, Karin Karlekar and Sarah Cook identify five negative trends in online freedom.[27] First, there is censorship through filtering, removal of content, intimidation, or legal challenges that force removal of online material. Second, there is the privatization of censorship, where monitoring and control of content is handled by private firms, often ISPs or telecommunications operators. Third, there is a lack of transparency or accountability that identifies the rationale for blocked content or that offers an explanation or guidelines for controlling content. Fourth, legal threats and action are used to silence content providers, bloggers, and writers to limit their influence and readership. Finally, there are technical attacks where denial of service and hacking are used to prevent content from being available. The report does note that due to decreasing costs, Internet access is growing and providing a platform for diverse views, while organizations are being established to monitor online freedoms.

The *Freedom on the Net* report ranked countries as free, partly free, or not free, with limited assessment of online content for only 15 countries, but analysis for press freedom is far broader and is a good proxy as data are available for 195 countries. In the following chapters, press freedom is used as a surrogate for Internet freedom due to the wider scope of that analysis, although Internet freedom will be referenced when data are available. The ratings of press freedom were based upon three measures: obstacles to access, limits on content, and violations of user rights. Using this rubric, seventy countries (36 percent) were identified as free, sixty-one countries (31 percent) as partly free, and sixty-four countries (33 percent) as not free.

Spatial Data and Analysis

In the following chapters, different social and spatial dimensions of global information society are presented. These chapters are not meant to be exhaustive surveys of each world region but examples of ways the four spectra of ICT characteristics discussed in this chapter can be applied. For each region and subregion, current issues associated with ICT are analyzed. This same approach can be applied to any scale or region you choose, from neighborhood to city, state/province, or country. ICT analysis in general, and its spatial dimensions in particular, are rich subjects for study due to their rapid change and variety of forms.

In undertaking spatial analysis, perhaps the greatest challenge is data collection, as information on recent trends in ICT tends to lag, and even recent data can be outdated. This is exemplified by the annual addition of one billion mobile phones, so data even a few years old are unrepresentative. As with any newly arrived social or economic phenomenon, the apparatus of statistical analysis is often poorly developed and applied. At a time when agricultural and manufacturing data are available across countries and industries, the information on services and ICT lags greatly. Tasks that might seem simple, such as finding the number of televisions in use, produces very little data, especially at the subnational level.

Information society is not yet well defined or documented, and as an evolving statistical arena, definitions and standards differ across the world. The analysis in this book tends to focus on national data because often that is the only information available and the only consistent information across countries. Our attempts to find data across cities and regions found few, if any, reliable sources.

The data presented in the following chapters have been chosen as they are freely available and can be updated easily by the reader. Sources such as the International Telecommunication Union, the United Nations, and the World Bank offer data online, while proxies for information society, such as web freedom, are available from nonprofit organizations such as Freedom House. National and state/province data through the census and statutory bodies can provide local information, although this is not always comparable with other areas. As always, searching online for data can provide rich sources of information, but users need to verify the source and intent of the contents.

Conclusion

After more than a century of telephony and twenty years of the Internet, the world presents a mosaic of the application and use of information and communications technologies. The mix evident in any location reflects the four spectra of ICT use presented in this chapter: devices, access, culture, and governance. For any location, analysts can explore the reasons for the preferences expressed for an ICT device, understand the economic and social factors shaping access, consider the role of culture in ICT use, and note the role of governance and policy in managing ICTs.

In the following chapters, major world regions are examined in terms of a set of common ICT measures associated with the four spectra, with additional information about how each region has adapted and shaped ICT. The results show a great deal of variation across space as represented by countries, but it is important to remember that similar, if not greater, scales of difference occur within countries and across cities and metropolitan areas. At the core of our geographic study is understanding how information society is evolving and recognizing that there are many paths associated with ICT use.

Notes

1. U.S. Bureau of the Census (2012)
2. World Bank (2011)
3. United Nations Development Programme (2008)
4. CIA (2003)
5. United Nations (2012)
6. ITU (2008)
7. ITU (2011)
8. NationMaster (2009)
9. Freedom House (2011a; 2011b)
10. ITU (2012)
11. ITU (2012)
12. CIA (2003)
13. NationMaster (2009)
14. CIA (2003)
15. NationMaster (2009)
16. ITU (2008)
17. Forrester Research (2008)
18. UNESCO (2008)
19. Arrow (1985: 320)
20. OECD (2009)
21. Chan, Vogel, and Ma (2008)
22. Gong (2009)
23. *Internet World Stats* (2009)
24. Crystal (2006); Jansen (2006)
25. UNESCO (2003)
26. Diki-Kidiri (2008)
27. Freedom House (2011a)

7

The Americas

INFORMATION SOCIETY VARIES across space, and in this and the following chapters we illustrate access and use of information technology by world region and country. For each region, a set of common statistics is presented along with examples of the cultural and governance elements of information society. These illustrations are not meant to be exhaustive but to show different dimensions of life as they are influenced by information and communications technologies. This chapter will analyze the scale and scope of information society in the Americas, divided into Canada/USA, the Caribbean, and Latin America. The region contrasts the largest single information generator, the United States, with populous and rapidly growing information societies such as Brazil, Mexico, Chile, and Argentina. The Western Hemisphere has over 900 million residents speaking English, Spanish, Portuguese, and French and contains a range of information societies.

Canada/USA

The United States and Canada, with almost 350 million people, are leading centers in the global information society, with data summarized in table 7.1. The countries are affluent and highly developed. Media penetration and use is high, shown by data such as high rates of television ownership (Canada 65.5/100, United States 74.1/100), and PC ownership (Canada 65.5/100, United States 78.7/100). Both countries have the same Digital Opportunity Index of 0.66, which would rank the countries seventeenth

TABLE 7.1
Information Society in Canada and the United States

		Canada	USA
Population millions	2009	33.5	307.2
Income per capita US$PPP	US$ 2008	36,220	46,970
Human Development Index	2005	0.961	0.951
TVs per 100	2003	65.5	74.1
PCs per 100	2005–2008	65.5	78.7
Digital Opportunity Index	2005–2006	0.66	0.66
Telephone lines per 100	2008	54.87	49.62
Mobile lines per 100	2008	66.42	86.79
Internet subscriptions per 100	2008	32.21	23.56
Internet users per 100	2008	75.43	74
Broadband subscriptions per 100	2008	29.59	23.46
Internet cost US$ per month	2005	8.9	14.95
Press Freedom Index	2009	19	18

Sources: See information society data discussion in chapter 6.

globally. There are similar levels of landline use (Canada 54.87/100, United States 49.62/100), but mobile phones are more common in the United States (86.79/100) than Canada (66.42/100). There are more Internet subscribers in Canada (32.21/100) than the United States (23.56/100), but the use rate is similar, around three-quarters of the population. Broadband access is higher in Canada (29.59/100) than the United States (23.46/100), and Internet access costs are lower in Canada (US$8.90) than in the United States (US$14.95). Both countries have a free press with the expectation of free access to post and use information electronically.

North American Information Society: Digital Divides and Net Neutrality

It seems ironic to start this discussion of North American information society by recognizing that not everyone participates. Approximately one-fifth of Americans in 2011 were not online, which can be accounted for by personal preference or by economic constraints.[1] During the 1990s there was a lot of interest in the United States in making access possible for as many people as were interested. The gap in access was termed the digital divide, which was the subject of a series of reports starting with *Falling through the Net* in 1999.[2] For several years access to information technology drove policy and discourse; but several years into the millennium, such concerns were lost from American political debate, and equity of access is no longer a driving policy issue. Although less evident, access remains an important social and economic issue given the personal and business benefits of a connected society.

In its May 2011 survey, the Pew Internet Project found men and women in the United States equally likely to be online (78 percent), but only 42 percent of Americans aged sixty-five years or older were online compared to 95 percent of those aged eighteen to twenty-nine years. Gaps also existed by education, with 42 percent online with less than high school, rising to 94 percent for those with a college education. Income was also a factor, with 63 percent online for those earning less than US$30,000 annually, but 96 percent for those earning more than US$75,000. Finally, approximately 80 percent of urban and suburban residents were online compared to 72 percent of rural residents.[3] So, twenty years into the Internet era, there remain one-fifth of Americans who are not online.

Access to information technology remains important because of its centrality to daily life for many people. Internet and mobile phones have moved from being desirable technologies to being essential. Owning or using these technologies is important for many functions, making them necessities rather than optional. For example, many high schools offer access to textbooks and assignments online, and while these can be accessed from schools, those with home access to the Internet have far greater educational resources available. In many jobs, use of technology is expected or required, as is home use of the Internet. Another factor is the cost savings possible through use of the Internet. Initially e-commerce did not penalize those who used telephones to make airline reservations or who shopped in brick-and-mortar stores, but today the cost of not being online can be significant. Banking and travel are two examples where online access offers lower-cost options than using a bank branch or travel agent. The growing ubiquity of access is often presented as a benefit and desirable social outcome, which it is. What is often forgotten is that as ICT access approaches ubiquity, it is assumed that all have access, and systems are designed accordingly. This means that only costlier options remain for those unable or unwilling to be online.

One segment of American population that tends to be ignored in terms of access is rural residents, who face higher costs and lower levels of service than urban and suburban residents. The lower numbers and higher costs of service provision mean that rural residents have less access. In some ways, the potential benefits are greater for rural residents through access to educational and health services not usually available outside metropolitan areas. Also, limited rural retailing can be overcome through online e-commerce. Rural populations in both Canada and the United States suffer lower access rates, although Canadian government initiatives have extended the reach of Internet in that country.[4] Canada's policy was driven by the need to link First Nation populations in rural areas, as well as serving rural schools and libraries. The United States also provided federal support to improve rural access, while at the state level there were a range of actions. Both Canada and the United States have focused on improving access through public policy, although Canada places greater emphasis on digital literacy and cultural content.

Canada and the United States share a number of issues relating to information society. One is net neutrality, which is the way that Internet service providers (ISP) manage the flow and access to information. Net neutrality argues that there should be no controls by government of ISPs on access to information. The term signifies that the technology should be neutral and that there should be no controls on content, platforms, or flow. With the growth of Internet use and the rapid popularity and use of online games and media, users may find that ISPs become slow or limit access by heavy users. Users are also concerned that websites may be able to pay for priority access or to block competitors so that choices are made by the provider and not the user. Net neutrality pits users against service providers, who wish to use the Internet for commercial purposes. Another element is government's desire to occasionally shape information use policies. The debate is seen by Christine Quail and Christine Larabie as the clash of market-based versus public-interest perspectives.[5]

In some ways, the net neutrality debate is nothing new; rather it is a new application for long-standing economic and political tensions about the appropriate use of networks such as roads and telephones. The Internet is not separate from society but a part of it. Historically, freedom of access has been an important element of Internet use, but the commercialization of the system and the demands placed on it for use have strained this practice. Robin Lee and Tim Wu note that currently content providers do not pay any extra fees to reach users.[6] This "zero-price" rule is at the core of the net neutrality debate. Zero pricing maintains free access by users and content providers but limits the commercial return for network operators. The net neutrality issue shows how culture and governance assert power over technology as supporters and opponent seek legislation or use the courts to influence how the Internet is used. An additional challenge common to information technology issues is that the technology changes so quickly that the governance system is unable to keep up.[7] The regulatory system dealing with net neutrality dates back to 1996 when the scale and scope of ICT was far less developed.

The Caribbean

The Caribbean represents many countries spread across the tropical and subtropical latitudes of the Western Hemisphere. The countries generally have small populations, with Cuba the main exception, having more people than all other countries in the region combined. The economies are often dependent on natural resources, tourism, and agriculture and are dependent on external economic stimulus. The special features of information society addressed in this section include electronic back offices and the location of online gambling services.

Data on information society in the Caribbean are presented in table 7.2. The Human Development Index shows most Caribbean countries in the middle income range, although Haiti faces many economic challenges with the lowest level of development in the region, compounded by a devastating earthquake in 2011. Incomes in the region tend to be low, with the higher income for Trinidad and Tobago tied to its petroleum industry. Data on incomes are limited for this region, with high-income areas such as the Cayman Islands and Bermuda classified as colonies rather than countries.

Television infrastructure in the Caribbean is highest in Bermuda (100.1 televisions per 100 people), an affluent British colony, with other countries far lower, such as Antigua and Barbuda (45.1/100), Trinidad and Tobago (39.5/100), and Granada (36.9/100). In some countries, television ownership rates are among the lowest in the world, with Haiti averaging one television per two hundred people. Some distortion may be introduced for tourism-oriented countries having many hotels with televisions, which overestimates access to information from this medium for the general public.

The pattern of personal computer ownership differs from television ownership, with Anguilla, Dominica, and Haiti having more PCs than TVs per one hundred people. The highest ownership of PCs occurs in Bermuda (22.3/100) and Antigua (20.7/100), with the lowest rate in the Dominican Republic (2.1/100). The Digital Opportunity Index reflects the early stages of information society in the region, from advanced countries such as Barbados (0.64) and the Bahamas (0.63) to Cuba (0.28) and Haiti (0.15). In terms of population, Cuba and the Dominican Republic represent more than 20 million people with low levels of information access. As the largest Caribbean economy, Cuba is undertaking economic restructuring and focusing on tourism and health services. As Gabriele (2010) notes, the restructuring is developing new economic activities, but the U.S. embargo, which forces Cuba to use costly satellite communications, acts as a brake on its information development. For most countries in the region, digital infrastructure shows only moderate opportunity, with the implication of challenges for these countries as evolving information societies.

Telephone infrastructure shows the same patterns evident in other developing regions, with mobile phones outpacing landlines. Landlines range from high levels in financial centers such as Bermuda (89/100) and the Cayman Islands (68.28/100) to low levels in Haiti (1.09/100), Cuba (9.85/100), and the

TABLE 7.2
Information Society in the Caribbean

Country	Pop. Millions 2009	Income per Capita US$PPP US$ 2008	Human Devel. Index 2005	TVs per 100 2003	PCs per 100 2005-8	Digital Opp. Index 2005-6	Tel. Lines per 100 2008	Mobile Lines per 100 2008	Internet Subs. per 100 2008	Internet Users per 100 2008	B'band Subs. per 100 2008	Internet Cost US$ per Month 2005	Press Freedom Index 2009
Anguilla	0.14	—	—	7.5	18.3	—	39.1	95.56	11.91	30.34	16.23	—	—
Antigua and Barbuda	0.9	13,620	0.815	45.1	20.7	0.57	43.86	157.67	15.36	75.03	14.52	22.14	38
Aruba	0.1	—	—	27.9	9.7	—	36.47	114.56	17.44	22.76	17.44	—	—
Bahamas	0.3	—	0.845	22.2	12.3	0.63	39.32	106.04	10.51	31.54	10.08	25.00	20
Barbados	0.3	—	0.892	27.3	15.8	0.64	58.78	159.09	—	73.67	64.81	25.55	19
Bermuda	0.7	—	—	100.1	22.3	—	89.00	122.07	58.84	78.80	52.47	—	—
Cayman Islands	0.5	—	—	15.8	—	—	68.28	66.84	—	41.33	—	—	—
Cuba	11.5	—	0.838	23.3	5.6	0.28	9.85	2.96	0.30	12.94	0.02	30.00	94
Dominica	0.7	8,300	0.798	8.7	19.2	0.51	26.19	149.66	8.91	41.16	15.42	20.73	22
Dominican Republic	9.7	4,390	0.779	8.6	2.1	0.42	9.90	72.45	3.42	21.58	2.27	18.76	40
Grenada	0.9	5,710	0.777	36.9	15.7	0.47	27.60	57.97	10.50	23.18	9.79	22.14	24
Haiti	9	660	0.529	0.5	5.1	0.15	1.09	32.40	1.03	10.13	—	70.99	53
Jamaica	2.8	4,870	0.736	16.8	6.7	0.51	11.69	100.58	3.72	56.88	3.59	34.25	15
Montserrat	0.5	—	—	32.1	—	—	47.42	50.80	16.19	20.32	5.01	—	—
Puerto Rico	4	—	—	26.1	—	—	26.18	85.71	—	25.22	5.40	—	—
St. Lucia	0.2	5,530	0.795	19.2	15.9	0.46	24.02	99.53	9.08	58.68	9.10	22.14	15
St. Vincent	0.1	5,140	0.761	15.3	15.2	0.47	20.87	119.23	8.94	60.49	8.58	22.14	17
Trinidad and Tobago	1.2	16,540	0.814	39.5	13.2	0.5	23.02	112.87	6.15	17.02	4.58	13.41	23

Sources: See information society data discussion in chapter 6.

Dominican Republic (9.9/100). The availability of mobile service, however, shows eleven countries in the region having close to or more than one mobile phone per person. Of note are the high levels in Barbados (159.09/100), Antigua (157.67), and Dominica (149.66/100). Cuba has the lowest level of mobile phone access (2.96/100) and is the only country in the region with more landlines than mobile subscribers.

Internet access and use in the Caribbean reflects the development stage of the region. High levels of Internet subscription occur in Bermuda (58.84/100), reflecting its strong financial services economy, with a significant drop to the next level with Antigua, Aruba, and Montserrat at around 15/100 subscribers. Another measure is the number of users, with many information societies sharing Internet access through schools, cafés, and work. The highest levels of Internet use are found in Antigua (75.03/100), Barbados (73.67/100), St. Vincent (60.49/100), St. Lucia (58.68/100), and Jamaica (56.88). Low levels of use reflect the poverty of Haiti (10.13/100) and the constrained and costly access in Cuba (12.94/100). The pattern is reflected in broadband access as well, with Cuba noticeable for a subscription rate of 0.2/100.

Internet cost is also an important factor, especially when seen in terms of annual incomes. Monthly access costs of US$70.99 in Haiti compare to an annual income of US$660 per capita, which means that the Internet costs more than the average income in the country. While income data are not available, estimates show Cuba's cost of US$30 per month to be similar to the average monthly wage. With half of the region's population, Cuba lags in Internet access and use due to state control and the U.S. embargo that prevents submarine cable access.[8] Cuba relies upon satellite Internet access, which carries a high cost and slow speeds.

Moving from the technical side of access, which is highly influenced by economic and governmental decisions, we focus on the social context of use. As a communications system, the freedom to access and use information is shaped by government policy. The Press Freedom Index is used as a proxy for Internet freedom and shows that freedom is limited for most residents of the region, especially Cuba and Haiti. Countries with an index of 30 or lower are classified as free, which represents the former British colonies in the Caribbean. Partly free countries include Antigua, the Dominican Republic, and Haiti.

Caribbean Information Society: Back Offices and Online Industries

In terms of information society and its economy, the Caribbean represents two unique elements: first, the early opportunity and potential dependency of offshore back offices starting almost fifty years ago, and second, the recent development of a sophisticated online gambling industry.

Back offices undertake many straightforward tasks, such as the collection, generation, management, and processing of information as an intermediate input to the production of goods and services. Activities commonly undertaken by back offices include data entry and processing, call centers, database management, accounting and financial services, processing of magazine subscriptions and insurance claims, animation, and computer software development. These activities are noted in part I of this book in the discussion of information industries and production.

Back office tasks, by their very nature and name, are hidden from daily life and consumed in the production of other goods and services. As individuals, we frequently use back offices, often without knowing it, as we track down paperwork, place orders, make travel reservations, or battle the bureaucracies of our service providers. Historically, offshore offices started during the 1970s when U.S. firms sent occasional batch work to the Caribbean for processing.[9] This was a time-consuming method as documents were transported by sea, with a two-week journey in each direction. The industry remained quite small until the early 1980s when advances in telecommunications and transportation coincided with growing demands for clerical work and information processing. Back offices were popular as they offered significant cost savings over locations in advanced economies such as North America and Western Europe.

Offshore back offices reflect many dimensions of the globalization of production, with communications linking transnational corporations, offshore subsidiaries, and local firms electronically. Ruth Pearson notes the role of gender and Richard Metters the role of culture in back office development and how these social dimensions have shaped local societies and practices and are also affected by them.[10] The failure of one back office was traced to a lack of cultural understanding between an American employer and a Caribbean subsidiary.[11] Back offices evolve over time based on technology and work demands. Some activities are less needed today because the work no longer exists, such as basic data processed electronically or transferred directly from the source, like newspaper transcription. New activities emerge, such as managing databases or geographic information system files, that seek offshore locations, although they may not choose past back office countries if skill levels or costs are not competitive.

The Internet has also changed the way gambling takes place, with information society now offering many ways to spend money on games of chance. In the past, legal gambling was often regulated and limited to particular games, conditions of play, and locations. With the potential of the Internet to collapse time and space, people living distant from many forms of gambling are now able to participate electronically. It is not just the limit on location, but age limits on access to gambling can also be circumvented online. The impact of distance online and legal jurisdiction is shown by the legal issues faced by a New York resident gambling on a website located in Antigua where online gambling is legal. It is legal for the website to operate in Antigua, but it is not legal for the New York resident to gamble on the website.[12] The issue of jurisdiction clouds the issue and makes legal progress difficult; U.S. states have faced significant problems trying to bring offshore operators to trial because they operate in legal environments even if some users do so illegally. The issues of online gambling are not so much technological as social and legal, linking to our spectra of culture and governance.[13]

As a region, many countries in the Caribbean were quick to recognize the economic potential of online gambling, and several countries established a regulatory environment to attract this industry.[14] Leading locations in the Caribbean include Antigua, Haiti, the British Virgin Islands, and St. Kitts and Nevis, which have combined Internet access with a regulatory environment designed to attract online gambling firms.[15] Moving beyond basic hosting, countries like Antigua have attracted gambling software and financial service firms to support the basic hosting activities. As hosting became established, financial service firms were later attracted to manage the flow of funds associated with a popular online business. The success of online gambling in the Caribbean has opened new opportunities for other online industries. For example, online gambling expertise is also attracting online pharmacies to locations such as St. Kitts.[16]

Latin America

Latin America represents territory stretching from Mexico south to Chilean and Argentinian Antarctica. The region contains more than 500 million people and generally reflects information societies in the development stage. Data on Latin American information society are presented in table 7.3. Important elements of information society included in this section are e-commerce, the role of the state, and political voice.

The highest incomes are found in Chile (US$13,270) and Costa Rica (US$10,950), with incomes below US$5,000 per capita found in Belize, Bolivia, Colombia, Ecuador, El Salvador, Guyana, Honduras, Peru, and Suriname. The Human Development Index reflects the development stage for Latin America with a number of countries having DOIs (Digital Opportunity Indexes) greater than 0.8. It is significant that there are six countries at this level, yet their incomes range from US$6,180 to US$13,270, indicating that development accomplishments do not always have a direct association with

TABLE 7.3
Information Society in Latin America

Country	Pop. Millions 2009	Income per Capita US$PPP US$ 2008	Human Devel. Index 2005	TVs per 100 2003	PCs per 100 2005-8	Digital Opp. Index 2005-6	Tel. Lines per 100 2008	Mobile Lines per 100 2008	Internet Subs. per 100 2008	Internet Users per 100 2008	B'band Subs. per 100 2008	Internet Cost US$ per Month 2005	Press Freedom Index 2009
Argentina	40.9	7,200	0.869	20.1	9.0	0.51	24.43	116.61	9.37	28.11	7.99	14.37	49
Belize	0.3	3,820	0.778	14.6	15.3	0.42	10.35	53.23	2.60	11.31	2.56	45.67	21
Bolivia	9.8	1,460	0.695	10.2	2.4	0.33	7.12	49.82	2.08	10.83	0.68	12.26	42
Brazil	198.7	7,350	0.800	19.6	16.1	0.48	21.43	78.47	5.94	37.52	5.26	25.98	42
Chile	16.6	13,270	0.867	19.7	14.1	0.57	20.99	88.05	8.56	32.47	8.49	25.63	29
Colombia	43.7	4,660	0.791	10.7	11.3	0.45	17.89	91.90	4.50	38.50	4.23	7.78	59
Costa Rica	4.3	10,950	0.846	13.1	23.1	0.46	31.81	41.75	4.06	32.31	2.38	28.08	19
Ecuador	14.6	3,640	0.772	18.7	13.0	0.40	14.12	85.61	2.09	9.71	0.26	36.96	44
El Salvador	7.2	3,480	0.735	9.0	5.8	0.40	17.56	113.32	2.05	13.47	2.01	22.60	42
Guyana	0.75	1,420	0.750	6.0	3.8	0.33	16.37	36.84	6.28	26.85	0.26	12.52	30
Honduras	7.8	1,800	0.700	79.5	2.5	0.27	11.28	84.86	0.81	9.60	—	33.41	52
Mexico	111.2	9,980	0.829	24.1	14.1	0.47	19.04	69.37	7.62	21.71	7.00	20.05	55
Panama	3.4	6,180	0.812	16.2	6.3	0.41	15.42	115.19	6.11	27.49	5.76	38.45	44
Paraguay	7	5,430	0.755	15.6	7.8	0.35	7.87	95.46	1.69	14.34	0.61	11.70	59
Peru	29.5	3,990	0.773	11.0	10.1	0.40	9.98	72.66	3.65	24.72	2.52	23.56	44
Suriname	0.5	4,990	0.774	14.4	4.0	0.36	15.82	80.76	1.63	9.71	1.12	30.20	23
Uruguay	3.5	8,260	0.852	22.9	13.5	0.48	28.64	104.73	8.59	40.01	7.30	23.87	26
Venezuela	26.8	9,230	0.792	16.2	9.3	0.46	22.42	96.31	5.24	25.49	4.37	42.61	73

Sources: See information society data discussion in chapter 6.

income. The DOI is highest in Chile (0.57), Argentina (0.51), Brazil (0.48), and Uruguay (0.48) and lowest in Honduras (0.27), Bolivia (0.33), Guyana (0.33), and Paraguay (0.36).

Television ownership is very high in Honduras (79.5 TVs/100 population), with nine countries having fewer than 15 TVs/100. The lowest level of television access occurs in Guyana (6.0/100), El Salvador (9.0/100), Bolivia (10.2/100), Colombia (10.7/100), and Peru (10.0/100). This means that in most of Latin America, there are five to ten people per television. Personal computer ownership exists at low levels in Bolivia (2.4/100), Honduras (2.5/100), Guyana (3.8/100), Suriname (4.0/100), El Salvador (5.8/100), and Panama (6.3/100). The highest ownership rate is in Costa Rica with 23.1 PCs per one hundred residents. PC ownership levels are low, which suggests that access may be limited or a problem for many people in the region.

Landline access tends to be low, ranging from 7.12/100 in Bolivia, 7.87/100 in Paraguay, and 9.98/100 in Peru, to 31.81/100 in Costa Rica and 28.64/100 in Uruguay. Limited landline access contrasts with high levels of mobile phone subscriptions across Latin America. Four countries have more than one subscription per person: Argentina, El Salvador, Panama, and Uruguay. The lowest levels still exceed a third of the population, such as Guyana (36.84/100) and Costa Rica (41.75/100). Costa Rica is unusual in that it has high incomes and is relatively well developed; it also has an established landline system that may remain effective for many people.

Internet subscription in Latin America is heaviest in Argentina (9.37/100), Uruguay (8.59/100), and Chile (8.56/100), but by global standards these levels are low. The other end of the spectrum shows very low subscription rates in Honduras (0.81/100), with Belize, Bolivia, Ecuador, El Salvador, Paraguay, and Suriname at around two subscribers per one hundred population. Internet use is higher due to the number of shared subscriptions, with the highest level of use in Uruguay (40.01/100), Brazil (37.52/100), Chile (32.47/100), and Costa Rica (32.31/100). Internet use is approximately 10 percent in five countries representing the low end of use: Belize, Bolivia, Ecuador, Honduras, and Suriname. Broadband subscriptions mirror the low rates shown for other access methods, with countries such as Argentina and Chile leading and low levels in Bolivia, Ecuador, Guyana, Paraguay, and Suriname.

Internet cost varies across the region from a low of US$7.78 per month in Colombia to US$45.67 in Belize. The monthly rates are similar to those in advanced countries yet the disposable income available in Latin America is many times less than North America and Western Europe. In the poorer countries, Internet costs can exceed 10 percent of average income, and usage data for these countries show that many do not have any access.

As consumers of information, Latin America also has many constraints on free production and access to information. The Press Freedom Index shows six countries with press freedom: Belize, Chile, Costa Rica, Guyana, Suriname, and Uruguay. Partly free countries (scoring 31 to 60) include eleven countries, while Venezuela lacks any press freedom.

Overall, the development status of much of Latin America reveals an emerging information society with economic and governance issues. Rolando Pena-Sanchez analyzes teledensity indicators for Latin America and finds high teledensities for fixed, mobile, and Internet access in Argentina, Uruguay, Chile, Venezuela, and Colombia, with the lowest levels in Honduras, Peru, Nicaragua, and Bolivia.[17]

Latin American Information Society: The State, Voice, and E-Commerce

Several themes that relate to the four spectra used for our analysis can be seen in Latin America. In this section, discussion focuses on three topics: (1) the role of the state and governance in shaping the rollout of ICT, (2) ICT as a way to provide voice for grassroots and political organizations, and (3) e-commerce.

One theme arising throughout this book is the role of culture and governance as influences on information society behavior. For example, Marcos Maciel and colleagues show the complexity of the Brazilian market for the rollout of mobile services.[18] The Brazilian government structured a fragmented market to attract foreign investment, which resulted in four main operators with more than 90 percent of the market and more than forty regional operators. Initially, Telebras, the state monopoly, was unable to access the capital needed for mobile service expansion. The market was characterized by excess demand, high prices, and poor service. Market liberalization started in 1995 as a way to reform the telecom sector and improve service. With the decision to privatize, the Brazilian government fragmented the market in order to reverse the dramatic geographic inequality of service provision, limit monopoly potential of any one operator, and maximize the value of state assets sold in the process. In the three years prior to 2001, the market expanded from 5.6 million to 28.7 million subscribers. By 2005 there were 86.2 million subscribers. Fragmenting the market was successful in addressing inequality issues as it prevented a national operator from focusing solely on the most profitable urban areas and regions.

The political and grassroots opportunities afforded by growing communications and Internet access provide ways for groups to organize as well as for government to control. Kristy Belton notes how indigenous societies have been able to use ICTs that access global resources and influence or promote their needs.[19] For example, in the Mexican state of Chiapas, the revolutionary

Zapatistas used the Internet to turn an internal issue in Mexico into a global cause through effective information dissemination.

A number of Latin American indigenous organizations link together for information sharing and solidarity building. They identify the main uses of cyberspace in Latin America as focusing on local rights, land use, and developing businesses based on craft and cultural products. John Cameron notes the growth of participatory groups and actions by government in Latin America and the need to be more inclusive in decision making.[20] Political leaders see new media as a way to link closely with the public. In Venezuela and Ecuador, these actions by leaders cause tensions with established media who feel bypassed by these actions, while the appearance of direct democracy is not always fulfilled.

Access alone does not necessarily mean progress or automatically guarantee a political or social voice. Elisabeth Friedman challenges the idea that ICT always plays a positive role in gender equality advocacy in Latin America.[21] Despite a recent history of opposition to authoritarian regimes and the promotion of civil society, women's movements remain concerned about the progress of gender equality. Information technology is a means, not an end, and the use of ICT must be addressed in terms of its cultural context. As Friedman noted, there are examples where access to technology does not always allow a cause to advance, especially when social and cultural views are difficult or slow to change.

The state can also promote technology use, or shape its development. Brazil's efforts to promote domestic software development by limiting the use of imported software was an experiment that served the interests of one sector but also harmed the advancement of overall ICT use. In 1987, Brazil passed legislation that banned imported software, such as Microsoft's MS-DOS, as a way to support the domestic software sector. The United States threatened trade retaliation against Brazil's exports, and over time the law was relaxed. In 2000, Colombia started a policy to introduce ICT into daily life and government and to foster greater participation in government and decision making. Despite the vision, it is also important to understand the implementation of e-government and whether it will be a positive force on current power relationships between citizens and government.[22] Stating the existence of e-government does not automatically translate into greater voice or access to power.

The emergence of a viable e-commerce sector is also challenging in developing economies. Okoli and colleagues found that small/medium enterprises (SMEs) in Latin America were excluded from the information flows about e-commerce that they needed.[23] Policies tend to favor large firms that use ICT. This may well mean that small innovative organizations are unable to access the information and resources they need to expand, while large firms exert more control. The researchers also note how Brazil uses protectionist and paternalistic policies that severely limit the ability of SMEs to innovate in e-business. Also hindering e-business was the cost and monopoly mind-set of communications services that do not have the necessary customer service mentality.

Another example of introducing e-commerce into a developing economy is mobile banking in Brazil, with the cost, risk, and complexity of operating acting as significant barriers to the use of mobile banking.[24] With 40 percent of Brazilians lacking a bank account, the market has a lot of potential, especially with an 80 percent penetration rate for mobile phones. One challenge is technology, as very few people have 3G handsets. High Internet and mobile access fees limited interest in mobile banking even though banks did not charge for the service. The cost of mobile access currently limits the ability of Brazilian banks to offer mobile services.

Conclusion

Information society in the Americas ranges from the largest information market in the world in the United States to small, developing economies just starting to establish an information infrastructure. Themes include equity issues, both within countries but also between countries in the same hemisphere. Tensions are also evident, illustrated by the culture of work and use of power to manage information and to try to control access to, and use of, the assets of information society. Finally, the experience of the Americas can also apply in other world regions, which try to balance the benefits of new opportunities and employment in information industries against ongoing social battles over the roles of the state and the citizen.

Notes

1. Pew Internet and American Life (2012)
2. NTIA (1999)
3. Pew Internet and American Life (2012)
4. Howard et al. (2010)
5. Quail and Larabie (2010)
6. Lee and Wu (2009)
7. Selwyn and Golding (2010)
8. Mohr (2007)
9. Woodward (1990); Wilson (1995)

10. Pearson (1993); Metters (2008)
11. Metters (2008)
12. Rose and Owens (2005)
13. Fidelie (2007); Laffey and Laffey (2010)
14. Wilson (2003)
15. Patterson et al. (2010)
16. Liang and McKay (2009)
17. Pena-Sanchez (2010)
18. Maciel et al. (2006)
19. Belton (2010)
20. Cameron (2010)
21. Friedman (2005)
22. Cordoba-Pachon and Orr (2009)
23. Okoli et al. (2010)
24. Cruz and Laukkanen (2010)

8

Europe

A NALYSIS OF THE SCALE and scope of information society in Europe includes many languages, cultures, and interests. Europe can be divided in many ways, but for this chapter the more advanced Western European countries are contrasted with Eastern Europe and Russia. Eastern Europe is defined both geographically but also with reference to the former Soviet bloc of countries. The focus for Europe is on social media and the relationship between ICT and the transition to development for Eastern Europe.

Western Europe

Western Europe represents one of the most advanced information regions in the world, with heavy concentrations of knowledge production and consumption. The countries in this section of the continent tend to be affluent, with well-educated citizens and a well-established information and communications technology infrastructure, as shown in table 8.1. Many of these countries were early members of the European Union and represent considerable economic power.

The countries in this analysis represent over 400 million people, who earn high incomes by global standards. Only Malta averages less than US$20,000 in per capita income, with most countries having annual incomes exceeding US$30,000, with a high of almost US$65,000 in Luxembourg. The Human Development Index reinforces the affluence and quality of life of Western

TABLE 8.1
Information Society in Western Europe

Country	Pop. Millions 2009	Income per Capita US$PPP US$ 2008	Human Devel. Index 2005	TVs per 100 2003	PCs per 100 2003-7	Digital Opp. Index 2005-6	Tel. Lines per 100 2008	Mobile Lines per 100 2008	Internet Subs. per 100 2008	Internet Users per 100 2008	B'band Subs. per 100 2008	Internet Cost US$ per Month	Press Freedom Index
Austria	8.2	37,680	0.948	53.3	61.01	0.67	39.40	129.73	24.55	71.21	20.74	15.52	21
Belgium	10.4	34,760	0.946	46.4	42.16	0.65	42.08	111.63	28.85	68.86	27.97	37.23	12
Denmark	5.5	37,280	0.949	59.1	55.13	0.76	45.56	125.72	39.14	83.89	37.12	23.18	13
Finland	5.3	35,660	0.952	62.3	50.01	0.69	31.11	128.76	26.78	82.62	30.50	22.25	10
France	64.4	42,250	0.952	59.8	65.87	0.64	56.42	93.45	30.14	68.21	28.52	12.43	23
Germany	82.3	42,440	0.935	56.7	65.28	0.66	62.48	128.27	24.27	75.33	27.47	7.40	17
Greece	10.7	28,650	0.926	23.6	9.38	0.53	53.65	123.90	15.66	43.50	13.53	16.35	30
Iceland	0.3	25,220	0.968	36.0	53.85	0.74	61.34	108.64	35.07	90.56	32.87	59.60	12
Ireland	4.2	37,350	0.959	40.0	58.91	0.61	49.66	120.74	25.44	62.54	20.09	31.06	16
Italy	58.1	35,240	0.941	53.3	36.99	0.63	35.65	151.57	34.39	41.93	18.93	24.80	34
Liechtenstein	0.4	—	—	—	—	—	55.01	95.43	47.25	65.96	55.01	—	14
Luxembourg	0.5	64,320	0.944	38.7	67.54	0.69	54.22	147.11	32.48	80.53	29.80	27.35	12
Malta	0.4	16,680	0.878	73.1	—	0.60	59.18	94.64	25.26	48.79	24.77	8.67	22
Netherlands	16.7	50,150	0.953	51.9	91.22	0.71	44.27	124.80	34.13	86.55	35.14	12.37	14
Norway	4.7	58,500	0.968	46.1	63.13	0.69	39.78	110.62	35.87	82.55	33.27	29.76	11
Portugal	10.7	20,560	0.897	32.8	17.22	0.61	38.50	139.64	15.69	41.92	15.31	37.76	17
Spain	40.5	31,960	0.949	40.9	39.84	0.65	45.41	111.67	20.54	54.74	20.22	31.72	23
Sweden	9.1	38,180	0.956	52.0	88.20	0.70	57.83	118.33	44.26	87.84	41.19	19.23	11
Switzerland	7.6	46,460	0.955	46.7	92.60	0.69	64.11	117.97	36.86	77.00	32.89	7.95	13
United Kingdom	61.1	45,390	0.946	52.2	81.21	0.69	54.24	126.34	31.65	76.24	28.21	27.25	19

Sources: See information society data discussion in chapter 6.

Europe, with all countries exceeding 0.9 on the index, with the exceptions of Portugal and Malta.

The basic information infrastructure across Western Europe is well developed. Television ownership ranges from lows in Greece (23.6 TVs per 100 population), Portugal (32.8/100), Iceland (36.0/100), and Luxembourg (38.7) to high levels in Malta (73.1/100) and Finland (62.3/100). It is worth noting that some of the highest ownership rates occur in lower-income countries, and the most affluent country, Luxembourg, has a low television ownership rate. Access to personal computers in the region is very high, in some countries close to one PC per person. The highest levels of PC ownership occur in Switzerland (92.6/100) and the Netherlands (91.22/100), followed by Sweden (88.2/100) and the United Kingdom (81.21/100). Lower levels are found in Greece (9.38/100) and Portugal (17.22/100). It is important to note that levels of ownership are subjective; what is considered a low level of PC use in Western Europe would be considered high in many countries across Africa, Latin America, and Asia.

Measures of digital opportunity across Western Europe are very high in the Nordic countries of Denmark (0.76), Iceland (0.74), Sweden (0.7), Norway (0.69), and Finland (0.69). At an equal level are Switzerland, the Netherlands, and the United Kingdom. The DOI (Digital Opportunity Index) is lowest for Greece (0.53), Malta (0.60), Ireland (0.61), and Portugal (0.61).

As developed economies, the landline infrastructure of Western Europe is extensive. Germany, Iceland, and Switzerland all report more than sixty lines per one hundred population, with the lowest levels in Finland (31.11), Italy (35.65), and Portugal (38.50). It is important to note that in the past the number of landlines was an indicator of development. With the growth of mobile telephony, however, some countries show a drop in landlines as residents favor mobile phones over landlines. In Western Europe the low level of landlines in Portugal reflects its development status, but the low level in Finland results from reliance on mobile phones as Finland was once a leader in landline infrastructure and now leads in mobile telephony.

The data for mobile phone subscriptions shows that there is more than one mobile phone for every person in most countries, with the lowest rate of 94.64 mobile phones per one hundred in Malta. In contrast, the highest rate is over 150 phones per one hundred residents in Italy. The density of mobile phone use suggests a ubiquity of access for residents of Western Europe, but we still need to be wary of assuming access for all just because data show one hundred mobile phones per one hundred population.

Internet subscriptions also reflect advanced information societies, with most countries having one subscription for every two to four people. The highest rates are in Liechtenstein (47.25) and Sweden (44.26), with the lowest rates in

Greece (15.66) and Portugal (15.69). With high rates of Internet subscription, the expectation is that use rates would also be high. In Western Europe, seven countries have Internet use rates exceeding 80 percent, and only Greece, Italy, Malta, and Portugal have use rates less than 50 percent. The ease of access to the Internet is reinforced by the high levels of broadband access, with Greece, Italy, and Portugal the only countries with fewer than twenty broadband subscriptions per one hundred population. The highest levels are for Liechtenstein (55.01/100) and Sweden (41.19/100).

Monthly Internet costs range from lows of US$7.40 in Germany, Switzerland (US$7.90), and Malta (US$8.67) to highs of US$59.60 in Iceland, Portugal (US$37.76), and Belgium (US$37.23). The variation in costs for similarly located countries using similar technology reveals the role of governance in shaping Internet use. For example, France and Germany have similar average incomes, yet the monthly Internet cost in France is 80 percent higher than in Germany. Costs in the United Kingdom are almost four times greater than in Germany and more than double the cost in France. In similar-population countries, the competitiveness of Internet service delivery is a product of market organization, which in turn is often influenced heavily by taxes and regulation.

Of the twenty countries in the region, all but one have a free press as determined by the Press Freedom Index, where a result of 30 or less indicates a free press. The one exception is Italy, with a score of 34, showing a partly free press.

Western European Information Society: Social Media

Europe has more than fifteen years' experience with social media, starting with LunarStorm in 2000, followed by MySpace, Facebook, YouTube, and Twitter.[1] As the United States has transitioned from social media services, so has Europe. In 2011, the most popular social media site for most European countries was Facebook, with Kontakte more popular in Russia, Belarus, and Ukraine. The dominance of Facebook globally is illustrated by more than 800 million users, of whom 350 million use mobile phones for access.

In September 2011, the leading Facebook countries in Western Europe were the United Kingdom (30.5 million, 48.9 percent penetration); France (923.3 million, 35.9 percent penetration); Germany (21.6 million, 26.3 percent penetration); Italy (20.6 million, 35.4 percent penetration); and Spain (15.3 million, 32.9 percent penetration).[2] In these countries, Facebook users are divided equally between men and women, with the most important demographic being twenty-five to thirty-four-year-olds in all countries except Germany, where it is eighteen- to twenty-four-year-olds. In terms of penetration, the leading countries are Iceland (67.7 percent), Norway (54.4 percent), and Denmark (50.5 percent). In 2010, European languages dominated Facebook, with English used by 52 percent of users. Other important languages included Spanish, French, Turkish, Italian, German, and Portuguese,[3] although the English market was increased with the United States, Canada, and Australia, and the Spanish/Portuguese market is also growing in Latin America.

One element of interest to many residents and policy makers in Europe is maintaining national identity given the closer ties afforded by the European Union and the integration of markets and education. France has long protected its language and through the Internet sought to preserve its cultural traditions. Hazel Warlaumont notes that social networking sites, such as Facebook and YouTube, are growing rapidly in Europe and that the French government has sought to limit the influence of sites such as Google to preserve national identity.[4] Just as the Paris suburbs became the physical location of riots by disaffected youth, online forums serve a virtual role in French society as a way to vent frustrations and protest government policies. The challenge for France and other countries in Europe is maintaining linguistic and cultural identity at a time of global interaction dominated by English.

Eastern Europe

Analysis of Eastern Europe shows greater variation in the technology and practice of information society. Western Europe is characterized by affluent economies with well-developed information infrastructure. Eastern Europe includes many countries recently emerged from the Soviet bloc and from the breakup of Yugoslavia, having experienced considerable political, social, and economic turbulence during the past twenty years. Eastern Europe represents a population over 400 million, which matches the population base in Western Europe. Of this population, one-third live in Russia and another third in Turkey and Ukraine. It is a region comprising a few very large countries and many small and emerging nations. Data for the information society of Eastern Europe are presented in table 8.2.

While sharing borders with Western European countries, and for many, membership in the European Union, incomes are lower in the east and represent considerable disparity across Europe. The highest incomes in Eastern Europe are found in Slovenia (US$26,910), Estonia (US$19,280), the Czech Republic (US$16,600), and Latvia (US$16,360), with six countries averaging incomes under US$6,000 and as low as US$1,680 in Moldova. Generally the Human Development Index is higher in the countries bordering Western Europe, with low levels of development in Moldova (0.708), Turkey (0.775), and Ukraine (0.788). It is important to note that some lower-income countries have achieved higher levels as measured by the HDI (Human Development

TABLE 8.2
Information Society in Eastern Europe

Country	Pop. Millions 2009	Income per Capita US$PPP US$ 2008	Human Devel. Index 2005	TVs per 100 2003	PCs per 100 2003–7	Digital Opp. Index 2005–6	Tel. Lines per 100 2008	Mobile Lines per 100 2008	Internet Subs. per 100 2008	Internet Users per 100 2008	B'band Subs. per 100 2008	Internet Cost US$ per Month	Press Freedom Index
Albania	3.6	3,840	0.801	13.1	3.81	0.37	10.63	99.93	1.91	23.86	2.04	16.32	50
Belarus	9.6	5,380	0.804	24.9	0.81	0.45	38.41	83.98	4.17	32.10	4.94	10.53	93
Bulgaria	7.2	5,490	0.824	39.8	8.91	0.54	28.84	138.30	10.94	34.86	11.11	7.32	35
Croatia	4.5	13,570	0.850	26.7	17.69	0.53	42.47	132.95	29.43	50.60	11.86	16.11	41
Czech Republic	10.2	16,600	0.891	53.1	27.40	0.57	21.94	133.54	17.39	58.41	17.05	18.76	19
Estonia	1.3	19,280	0.860	43.2	52.42	0.65	37.14	188.20	24.19	66.20	23.70	10.78	18
Hungary	9.9	12,810	0.874	43.0	25.64	0.59	30.90	122.09	17.73	58.66	17.48	11.04	30
Latvia	2.2	16,360	0.855	50.0	32.59	0.54	28.51	98.90	6.43	60.63	8.85	12.48	26
Lithuania	3.6	11,870	0.862	47.4	18.13	0.61	23.64	151.24	17.88	55.00	17.77	7.20	22
Macedonia	2.0	4,140	0.801	25.7	—	0.47	22.39	122.56	14.13	41.54	8.87	25.33	48
Moldova	4.3	1,680	0.708	29.3	—	0.35	30.68	66.70	4.29	23.39	3.17	24.13	55
Montenegro	0.7	6,440	—	—	—	0.49	58.17	118.10	14.27	47.24	9.99	—	37
Poland	38.5	11,880	0.870	33.8	16.77	0.51	25.49	115.28	13.57	49.02	12.58	11.27	25
Romania	22.2	7,930	0.813	23.3	19.33	0.52	23.58	114.54	11.80	29.00	11.73	16.96	42
Russia	140.0	9,620	0.802	41.1	13.33	0.52	31.75	141.11	21.49	32.00	6.56	12.72	81
Serbia	7.4	5,700	—	25.9	18.26	0.47	31.35	97.76	8.64	33.54	4.59	13.18	33
Slovak Republic	5.5	14,540	0.863	48.7	51.50	0.55	20.33	102.23	12.41	66.05	11.20	18.95	22
Slovenia	2.0	26,910	0.917	35.8	42.87	0.62	50.11	101.97	22.65	55.86	21.17	18.62	25
Turkey	76.8	9,340	0.775	32.6	5.93	0.52	23.68	89.05	7.89	34.37	7.78	11.61	54
Ukraine	45.7	3,210	0.788	35.7	4.61	0.41	28.65	121.09	4.14	10.60	3.38	7.67	56

Sources: See information society data discussion in chapter 6.

Index), such as Ukraine having a higher development level on a third of the income of lower-ranked Turkey.

Television is accessible, averaging two to four people per television across the region. The highest levels of ownership occur in the Czech Republic (53.1 TVs/100 population), Latvia (50/100), and the Slovak Republic (48.7/100), with low levels in Albania (13.1/100), Romania (23.3/100), and Belarus (24.9/100). Personal computer ownership shows far greater variation, from Estonia (52.42/100) to Belarus (0.81/100). Eastern Europe is placed in the middle of global digital opportunity, with the most advanced countries being Estonia (0.65), Slovenia (0.62), and Lithuania (0.61). Lagging countries include Moldova (0.35), Albania (0.37), and Ukraine (0.41).

Current infrastructure is most advanced for mobile phones, as most countries in Eastern Europe offered limited development of landlines and so lacked the inertia associated with heavy investments in an older technology. Wired infrastructure is most advanced in Montenegro (58.17/100) and Slovenia (50.11), with a gap until most other countries report twenty to thirty landlines per one hundred population. Mobile phone access is far greater, as countries with poor wired systems could leapfrog to new mobile technology. Seven countries have more than 120 mobile subscriptions per 100 population, noteworthy being Estonia (188.20/100) and Lithuania (151.24/100), which have the highest rates in Europe. The lowest rates are in Moldova (66.7/100) and Belarus (83.98/100). Overall, with the exception of Moldova, Eastern Europe has mobile phone rates that are close to or exceed one phone per person. Teledensities at this level suggest almost ubiquitous levels of connectivity.

Telephone connectivity does not translate to as high a density for Internet access. Subscriptions range from highs in Croatia (29.43/100) and Estonia (24.19/100) to low levels less than ten per one hundred in seven countries. In terms of access, the data show that more than half of the populations have access in Croatia, the Czech Republic, Estonia, Hungary, Latvia, Lithuania, the Slovak Republic, and Slovenia. Far less access is evident in Ukraine (10.60/100), Moldova (23.39/100), and Albania (23.86/100). Broadband is most common in Estonia (23.7/100), Slovenia (21.17/100), Lithuania (17.77/100), Hungary (17.48/100), and the Czech Republic (17.05/100). For ten countries, however, broadband is rare, with fewer than ten subscriptions per one hundred population, with the lowest rates in Albania (2.04/100), Moldova (3.17/100), and Ukraine (3.38/100).

Contributing to access levels is the cost of the Internet. Costs are generally low in Eastern Europe, although in most countries so are incomes. The lowest-cost Internet is in Lithuania (US$7.20), Bulgaria (US$7.32), and Ukraine (US$7.62), but while the monthly rates are similar, incomes across the three countries range from US$3,210 in Ukraine to US$11,870 in Lithuania, making Internet costs far from comparable. The highest rates are in Macedonia (US$25.33) and Moldova (US$24.13), which also have low incomes.

Freedom of expression in information society is curtailed in twelve of the twenty countries of Eastern Europe. Countries with a free press include the Czech Republic, Estonia, Hungary, Latvia, Lithuania, Poland, the Slovak Republic, and Slovenia. The least freedom is exercised in Belarus and Russia.

Eastern European Information Society: Transition and Development

The information infrastructure of Eastern Europe was poorly developed, both as a control mechanism of authoritarian governments and as a statement about the development status of the region. Throughout Eastern Europe, information access was tightly controlled until the fall of communist governments between 1989 and 1991. Rapid political change saw the remaking of the Eastern European map with the end of the Soviet Union in 1991 and the breakup of Yugoslavia in 1992. Until these changes, information was managed and disinformation was an art. The opening of Eastern Europe to Western markets and information coincided with the commercialization of the Internet in the early 1990s.[5]

Central European countries that bordered Western and northern Europe were faster to adopt new ICTs as they had more advanced economies; a history of limited, if illegal, access to Western information; and faster economic integration with the West.[6] In the absence of forums for public discourse, the Internet provided ways for civil society to develop and created diverse organizations that tended to focus on local political and social issues.[7] After twenty years of transition, Eastern Europe has a number of global leaders in the development of information society, such as Estonia, Lithuania, the Slovak Republic, and Slovenia, as well as lagging countries such as Belarus, Moldova, and Ukraine.

Estonia is a good example of a rapidly growing and innovative information society. As noted in the previous section, Estonia has high rates of mobile telephone and Internet use, which prompts the research question of why and how it reached that position. Contributing to its development were high levels of literacy and education by Eastern European standards, as well as expertise in electronics dating from its control by the USSR. Estonia's joining of the European Union formalized its shift from an Eastern to a Western market focus. Estonia was helped by the speed of its telecommunications upgrade and adoption of new technology,[8] an approach shared by the Baltic countries in general. In terms of e-commerce, Estonia rapidly moved from the limited range of Soviet-era retailers to online options, without the opportunity to develop brick-and-mortar facilities. In particular, Estonia became a leader in Internet banking because of the perceived and real ease of the Internet over real banking.[9]

Conclusion

Europe's development as an information society can be generally divided into the advanced information economies of Western Europe, with Eastern Europe showing both rapid attainment in areas such as the Baltic countries and lagging information development in countries such as Moldova, Ukraine, and Albania. The range of experience roughly tracks the economic development of each country, but the role of the state can also play an important role in allowing countries to catch up or advance their information sectors.

Notes

1. Edosomwan et al. (2011)
2. SocialBakers (2011)
3. InsideFacebook (2010)
4. Warlaumont (2010)
5. Sroka 1998)
6. James et al. (2008)
7. Bruszt et al. (2005)
8. Hans (2005)
9. Eriksson et al. (2008)

9

Asia-Pacific

A SIA IS THE MOST populous global region with almost 3.5 billion people, half of the world total. The region is diverse in its heritage, cultures, and economy and has some of the fastest-growing Internet- and information-using countries. This chapter divides Asia into three areas of analysis: East Asia, South and Central Asia, and Australia/Oceania.

East Asia

East Asia is positioned as the emergent if not leading Internet global region. With more than two billion people, it includes early technological leaders such as Japan, South Korea, Taiwan, Hong Kong, and Singapore, as well as the emerging Internet power of China. In addition to summary data presented in table 9.1, this section will focus on two dimensions of East Asia's information society: the development of knowledge and communication hubs as drivers of economic growth, and the production and use of video games as a signature of youth culture.

East Asia's economy is led by six middle- to high-income countries that average US$26,000–53,360 annually per capita (Brunei, Hong Kong, Japan, South Korea, Macau, and Singapore). In contrast, the remaining countries have low incomes under US$7,000, with very low incomes in Cambodia (US$600), Laos (US$740), Vietnam (US$890), Mongolia (US$1,680), the Philippines (US$1,890), Indonesia (US$2,010), Timor-Leste (US$2,460), and Thailand (US$2,840). This pattern is reflected in the Human Development

TABLE 9.1
Information Society in East Asia

Country	Pop. Millions 2009	Income per Capita US$PPP 2008	Human Devel. Index 2005	TVs per 100 2003	PCs per 100 2003–7	Digital Opp. Index 2005–6	Tel. Lines per 100 2008	Mobile Lines per 100 2008	Internet Subs. per 100 2008	Internet Users per 100 2008	B'band Subs. per 100 2008	Internet Cost US$ per Month 2005	Press Freedom Index 2009
Brunei	0.4	26,740	0.894	24.8	8.83	0.56	19.53	95.85	4.66	55.32	3.56	17.85	75
Cambodia	14.5	600	0.598	0.8	0.36	0.18	0.30	29.01	0.12	0.51	—	33.08	63
China	1,338.6	6,020	0.777	32.5	5.60	0.45	25.48	47.94	11.31	22.28	6.23	9.75	85
Hong Kong	7.1	43,960	0.937	28.4	—	0.70	58.72	165.85	42.00	67.00	28.11	3.86	32
Indonesia	240.3	2,010	0.728	6.9	2.00	0.34	13.36	61.83	1.39	7.92	0.18	17.26	53
Japan	127.1	35,220	0.953	68.6	40.72	0.77	38.04	86.73	—	75.40	23.65	13.79	21
Korea	48.5	28,120	0.921	34.6	57.63	0.80	44.29	94.71	32.14	76.50	32.14	32.62	32
Laos	6.8	740	0.601	1.1	1.69	0.18	2.06	32.59	0.09	8.50	0.10	27.60	85
Macau	0.6	53,360	—	11.5	—	0.69	—	—	—	—	—	11.77	
Malaysia	25.7	6,970	0.811	16.8	23.41	0.50	15.89	102.59	19.33	55.80	4.93	7.39	64
Mongolia	3.0	1,680	0.700	5.1	13.44	0.32	6.25	37.82	2.75	12.49	0.59	10.71	39
Myanmar	—	—	0.583	0.6	0.88	0.04	1.64	0.74	0.04	0.22	0.02	48.87	94
Philippines	98.0	1,890	0.771	5.2	7.46	0.38	4.51	75.39	3.32	6.22	1.16	1.81	46
Singapore	4.7	47,940	0.922	35.1	76.87	0.72	40.24	138.15	23.91	73.02	21.74	20.48	68
Taiwan	23.0	—	—	—	—	—	61.96	110.31	26.16	63.73	21.81	—	25
Thailand	66.0	2,840	0.781	25.5	6.86	0.43	10.42	92.01	—	23.89	1.14	6.95	62
Timor-Leste	1.1	2,460	0.514	—	—	0.11	0.22	9.20	0.07	0.16	—	93.80	35
Vietnam	88.6	890	0.733	4.7	9.51	0.29	44.60	80.37	6.09	23.92	2.35	10.66	83

Sources: See information society data discussion in chapter 6.

Index, with leading countries Hong Kong, Japan, South Korea, and Singapore, contrasting with low development levels in Cambodia, Laos, Myanmar, and Timor-Leste.

Television is widely available, especially in Japan (68.6/100), Singapore (35.1/100), South Korea (34.6/100), and China (32.5/100). In a number of East Asian countries, however, television ownership rates are low, in some cases lower than personal computer ownership rates. Televisions are owned by fewer than 10 percent of the population in Myanmar (0.6/100), Cambodia (0.8/100), Laos (1.1/100), Vietnam (4.7/100), Mongolia (5.1/100), the Philippines (5.2/100), and Indonesia (6.9/100). The ability of residents in these countries to access television broadcasts is limited, especially at a time when satellite access provides more information than sanctioned by the state.

Personal computers continue the pattern seen for other information technologies in the region, with Singapore leading with more than three-quarters of the population having a PC, followed by South Korea (57.63/100), Japan (40.72/100), and Malaysia (23.41). The data for Japan are somewhat surprising given the affluence and technological leadership of the country. One explanation may be the use of mobile phones as a substitute for computers, although Japan has a lower rate of mobile phone ownership than its peers.

Overall, the digital opportunity evident for East Asia starts with South Korea (0.80), Japan (0.77), Singapore (0.72), Taiwan (0.71), and Hong Kong (0.70). These five countries include the two technology leaders globally—South Korea and Japan—and represent five of the top eight countries worldwide. As a region, East Asia ties with Europe for high-ranking Digital Opportunity Index countries, as each has five countries in the top ten. It is important to note that the European leaders tend to be smaller (Denmark, Iceland, Sweden) than the Asian leaders.

East Asia has a well-developed landline infrastructure in Taiwan (61.96/100), Hong Kong (58.72/100), Vietnam (44.60/100), South Korea (44.29/100), and Singapore (40.29/100). These data show the development disconnect, with affluent countries like South Korea and Singapore moving away from landlines to mobile phones, and developing countries like Vietnam with higher levels of landline access. Vietnam is unique in landline access given its low average income, as its peer countries have far lower levels. For example, Timor-Leste (0.22/100), Cambodia (0.30/100), Myanmar (1.64/100), and Laos (2.06/100) have a 2 percent or less landline density. As noted in other world regions, the leapfrogging possible by mobile telephony has advanced countries scaling back landlines and developing countries skipping this stage of technology.

Mobile telephony is a significant technological force in East Asia, with both advanced and developing countries showing high subscription rates. Mobile phones exceed one per person in Hong Kong (165.85/100), Singapore

(138.15/100), Taiwan (110.31/100), and Malaysia (102.59/100), and even developing countries that have low scores in other technologies have a third of the population with mobile phones (Cambodia and Laos). Noteworthy in the data is the absence of mobile telephony in Myanmar (0.74/100), where the state exerts influence to limit access to information. The low level for Timor-Leste (9.20/100) reflects its recent emergence from war and instability.

Internet subscriptions in East Asia are highest in Hong Kong (42.00/100), South Korea (32.14/100), Taiwan (26.16/100), Singapore (23.91/100), and Malaysia (19.33/100) and lowest in Myanmar (0.04/100), Timor-Leste (0.07/100), Laos (0.09/100), Cambodia (0.12/100), and Indonesia (1.39/100). Internet use shows more than half of the population of seven countries to be online: Brunei, Hong Kong, Japan, South Korea, Malaysia, Singapore, and Taiwan. Comparing the number of subscribers with users shows how much sharing takes place. For example, Brunei has a moderate level of Internet subscription but high levels of use, suggesting that families share or the popularity of cafés, schools, and libraries as access points. Broadband use tends to be concentrating in Hong Kong, Japan, South Korea, Singapore, and Taiwan.

Internet costs have a major impact on access, especially in low-income countries. Low-income/high-cost countries in East Asia include Timor-Leste (US$93.80 per month), Myanmar (US$48.87), and Cambodia (US$33.08), which contrast with high-income/low-cost countries such as Hong Kong (US$3.86), Macau (US$11.77), and Singapore (US$20.48).

Of the eighteen countries reviewed in East Asia, all but two lack a free press, the exceptions being Japan and Taiwan. Most of the residents of this region have access to information technology, even if limited, but few can access a free local press. As information technology brings advantages, it can also been seen as a threat. As Jongpil Chung notes for China, "One view sees the Internet as crucial to economic modernization, while the other appraises it as a direct threat to the central government's control over the country."[1]

East Asia Information Society: Knowledge, Information, and Gaming

The explosion of information and development has been significant in Asia, where government and business are actively encouraging local scientific and technological advance. To illustrate trends in information society, this section shows three elements: the generation of knowledge, collaboration for research, and the economic and social role of gaming. The past decades have seen a development trajectory in Asia of countries importing technology in the early stages but later developing local capacity. This trend has been experienced to date in Japan, South Korea, Taiwan, Malaysia, and Singapore, and is evident in China. The importance of connectivity for science- and technology-based development is underscored by Poon, Hsu, and Suh:

Asian firms increasingly view the need to source and transform new knowledge from various cultural regions in the world as essential to making the transition from low cost suppliers to medium or even high technology producers. Over time, the ability to successfully integrate spatial scales of knowledge flows may well help firms from these countries to move from process to product innovation, and from learner to innovator status.[2]

Knowledge creation and management is very much a social act,[3] drawing attention to planning for the people who create networks.[4] This is especially the case with high-technology start-ups that need to spread risk and combine resources.[5] Even more than microelectronics firms, biotechnology-based organizations need information and resource flows through informal networks due to the very close nature of relations among universities and commercial firms, biotech firm founders with virtually no management or production experience, and strong reliance on licensing, partnering, and alliances to commercialize new technology.[6] Close interorganizational relations, especially through research collaboration, benefit from and in turn strengthen access to knowledge. Invention and subsequent innovation are dependent on a set of contextual factors,[7] similar to the way that scientific and technological progress are each dependent on societal norms and public policy.[8]

Scholars see access to the social networks of science and knowledge as critical to the processes of invention and innovation,[9] both at the level of individuals[10] and interacting organizations.[11] The International Association of Science Parks finds that 60 percent of science parks have five universities within 50 kilometers, but 21 percent have more than twenty universities around them.[12] Small businesses, in particular, are dependent on interorganizational resources, trust, obligation, and interdependency.[13] These interpersonal and interaction influences set the stage for the iterative, process-bound sharing of information and resources and reciprocal transfers of technology between the developers of technology and the scientists carrying out research.[14]

Growing globalization means that the local linkages that supported industrial districts thirty years ago now must incorporate a far wider range of participants. The interconnectivity of these sites at intercontinental and global scales is of particular interest for this research.[15] The economic benefits of technology concentration have long been recognized and have been a popular target for replication.[16]As Bernard Ganne and Yveline Lecler note concerning the establishment of knowledge centers,

At this stage the essential thing for enterprises, as for local and regional government is to coordinate with each other and reach agreement to set up, around specialised activities, powerful regional developments aiming to reach the world production chain of value, thus claiming global excellence by organising around a large local pole, all the various actors of a particular sector: firms, research organisations, teaching and training institutes, specialist management services and so on.[17]

Susan Walcott's analysis of Chinese and Indian high-tech clusters recognizes "the need to configure amenity-rich spaces in order to attract and employ young, highly skilled and internationally aware workers along with transnational investment."[18] She also notes the enclave character of these knowledge districts as they represent international design and structure in a local setting. Suburban technopoles and the creation of the international campus-garden-suburb for R&D link garden cities to university and research centers, combining quality of life and knowledge functions.[19] Regional variations in the location of science parks range from 62.5 percent of science parks in Asia/Oceania in cities, compared to 25 percent in North America and 72.55 percent in Europe.[20] The core attributes of a science park focus on global competitiveness, attractiveness, and governance as essential elements for a pole of competitiveness today.[21]

Interaction among scholars plays an important role in science and technology advancement, in particular the mobility of human capital and the opportunities scholars and researchers have to link people and places.[22] The value of integration for Asia is just emerging as scholars have opportunities to work together.[23] While authorship of scientific articles in North America and Europe seems to involve a web of interactions within and between the two continents, linkages among authors in different locations in Asia are far less common. One linkage is between Tokyo and Osaka, and another between Beijing, Shanghai, and Sydney, while Seoul shows little collaboration with scientists outside South Korea. Linkages vary by field, with Asia far better connected for research on ICT and nanotechnology than for biotechnology. Missing are strong links across the sciences between Asia and North America and Europe in the publication of scientific knowledge.

Video games have been an important part of electronic and online entertainment for the past twenty years. Online games are a significant economic force and are an important social phenomenon.[24] Japan has been a leader in video game development, with early collaboration between Nintendo and Sony launching a major industry. The partnership, since disbanded, merged the board game expertise of Nintendo with the electronic capacity of Sony.[25] Since then, South Korea and China have also emerged as important countries in game development. Nir Kshetri sees online gaming in China as the equivalent of television for young people, with over 120 million Chinese playing online games. The online game market in China exceeds US$3 billion.[26] Of note is the phenomenon of "gold farming" in China where online games are played to accumulate virtual goods that can be sold for hard currency through services such as eBay.

The social context of online gaming includes the replication of societal norms played out through online characters, as well as the creation of virtual communities. In South Korea, PC bangs (rooms) are facilities that serve real and virtual communities that meet to play video games. In countries where space is limited and the cost of equipment high, Internet cafés and gaming centers play an important role as access points to information.

South and Central Asia

South and Central Asia represent 1.5 billion people, with the subcontinent dominated by India. Our analysis considers eight countries that generally have low incomes of less than US$4,000 annually, with data presented in table 9.2. Reflecting income levels is the low result for the Human Development Index, with the most advanced countries in the region being Azerbaijan (0.746), Sri Lanka (0.743), and the Maldives (0.741). The region has limited access to information, with television access less than 10 percent; even India, which pioneered satellite access and use of television for development, can only claim 6.5 televisions per one hundred population. Access to personal computers shows some unexpected results, with Azerbaijan, Bangladesh, and the Maldives having more PCs than televisions. The Digital Opportunity Index shows low levels across the region, with the leading countries being the Maldives (0.46), Azerbaijan (0.38), and Sri Lanka (0.35).

Telephone infrastructure is strongest for landlines in Sri Lanka (17.18/100), the Maldives (15.39/100), and Azerbaijan (15.01/100) and weakest in Bangladesh (0.84/100). The generally low level of landline access is reversed in most countries by access to mobile telephones. The Maldives leads with more than 140 mobile phones per one hundred population, followed by Azerbaijan (75.00/100), Sri Lanka (55.24/100), and Bhutan (36.55/100). The lowest level in the region is in Nepal (14.58/100), which in 2011 obtained Internet access on Mount Everest, yet many remote areas of the country remain without mobile connectivity.

Internet access is limited in general, with the Maldives having the most subscribers in the region (5.86/100), although most people in South and Central Asia live in countries with approximately one subscriber per one hundred population. Access is approximately one-quarter of the population in Azerbaijan (28.00/100) and the Maldives (23.52/100), but for most of the other countries, access tends to be less than 6 percent of the population. With the exception of the Maldives (5.15/100), broadband access is very low; fewer than one in one hundred subscribe to a broadband service. Internet costs tend to be low by global standards (less than US$10 per month) but in terms of

TABLE 9.2
Information Society in South and Central Asia

Country	Pop. Millions 2009	Income per Capita US$PPP 2008	Human Devel. Index 2005	TVs per 100 2003	PCs per 100 2003–7	Digital Opp. Index 2005–6	Tel. Lines per 100 2008	Mobile Lines per 100 2008	Internet Subs. per 100 2008	Internet Users per 100 2008	B'band Subs. per 100 2008	Internet Cost US$ per Month 2005	Press Freedom Index 2009
Azerbaijan	8.2	3,830	0.746	2.2	2.43	0.38	15.01	75.00	4.70	28.00	0.69	9.99	—
Bangladesh	156.0	520	0.547	0.6	2.42	0.25	0.84	27.90	0.10	0.35	0.03	24.01	54
Bhutan	0.7	1,900	0.579	2.1	1.95	0.22	4.00	36.55	0.87	6.55	0.30	14.91	57
India	1,156.9	2,960	0.619	6.5	3.17	0.31	3.21	29.36	1.09	4.38	0.45	6.78	35
Maldives	0.4	3,630	0.741	2.6	20.08	0.46	15.39	142.82	5.86	23.52	5.15	51.24	50
Nepal	28.7	400	—	0.6	0.49	0.19	2.79	14.58	0.28	1.73	0.03	8.11	59
Pakistan	176.7	2,787	0.480	2.4	—	0.29	—	—	—	—	—	9.50	61
Sri Lanka	21.3	1,780	0.743	8.2	3.54	0.35	17.18	55.24	1.23	5.80	0.51	4.57	71

Sources: See information society data discussion in chapter 6.

incomes remain very high. Significant is the Internet cost of US$51.24 in the Maldives, which has low incomes but high rates of Internet use despite the cost. Finally, none of the countries sustain a free press, and the limited information access through the Internet and television suggests that this region faces many constraints as an information society.

South and Central Asian Information Society: Technology and Happiness

Among the characteristics of information society in South and Central Asia are the concentrations of offshore call centers and Bhutan's desire to link national happiness to technology. Call centers are part of the global business process outsourcing industry that uses telecommunications to access low-cost and often well-educated workers. India is a leader in this field due to its large English-speaking and educated workforce facing limited employment options, and the ability to save at least 50 percent over similar services in the United Kingdom.[27] Call centers offer services that range from airline reservations to software help desks to financial services. Call centers offer employment to college graduates in India that allow a middle-class lifestyle.[28]

As centers for global business and communications, call centers seek to mask location, accents, local culture, and time so that callers feel they are speaking to someone local.[29] At the same time, the professional veneer of call-center work can also obscure the stressful and monotonous nature of the work.[30] Also significant culturally is the need for Indian call-center workers to adopt personas appropriate to their client base, which includes adopting accents, new names, and backstories to support their position. This requirement, however, can cause psychological stress and identity issues for workers.[31] The psychological cost forces some call-center workers in India to live in two cultures, resulting in tensions caused by different patterns of behavior required for both work-based personas due to the cultural context of a joint operation.[32]

Another dimension of India's information society is the development of science parks and the clustering of advanced electronic and software functions in cities such as Bangalore and Hyderabad. Bangalore has a thirty-year history in electronics, but the arrival of Texas Instruments in 1984 raised awareness globally of India's technology sector.[33] Texas Instruments was followed by many transnational firms such as IBM, Motorola, HP, Intel, Nokia, and India's own Infosys. Elizabeth Chacko notes that India's high-tech centers are attracting return migrants and entrepreneurs now as they form global nodes in technology development,[34] while Indian centers today have advanced and are now cocreators of innovation using a global knowledge base rather than being used simply for outsourcing specific tasks.[35]

A different interpretation of information society is provided by Bhutan. Bhutan is a landlocked Himalayan country that did not allow television or the Internet until 1999. The late start to developing an information infrastructure was due to government actions designed to contribute to gross national happiness, which adopts a sustainable development approach, including ICT policy.[36] Concern about damaging external influences led Bhutan to control tourism and limit information flows until recently. Access to the Internet is limited by the need to use regional centers or Internet cafés for most people and the generally slow speed of access. Balancing concerns for the cultural impact of information and entertainment, there is the value of the Internet for distance education in Bhutan as well as the power of cultural norms. Even with this important contribution, Bhutan has concerns: "The use of ICT in education deviates from Bhutan's traditional modes of teaching and learning, and tends to undermine the traditional perception of the teacher as an authority figure."[37]

Australia/Oceania

This region contains fewer than 30 million people, most of whom live in Australia and New Zealand. The region has advanced diverse economies in the two leading countries, with the remaining island economies focusing on agriculture, fishing, and tourism. Information society data are presented in table 9.3. Most countries have annual incomes less than US$4,000, although many have human development indices higher than their incomes would predict. Besides Australia and New Zealand, television ownership is low, fewer than six per one hundred residents, with a similar pattern for personal computers. Overall, digital opportunity is low across the islands. One important difference emerges for Tonga and Vanuatu, which have similar incomes, but Tonga has far higher levels of development and information access.

In addition to their development status, many countries in Oceania are islands spread across distances lacking electronic infrastructure, making telephone and Internet access costly and difficult. Landline infrastructure is high in Australia (44.16/100), New Zealand (41.37/100), and Tonga (24.66/100) and lowest in the Solomon Islands (1.57/100) and Vanuatu (4.45/100). Mobile phone ownership mirrors landlines, with the leaders being Australia, New Zealand, and Tonga. Unusual for the developing world, low mobile phone rates apply for Samoa (3.65/100) and the Solomon Islands (5.87/100).

Outside Australia and New Zealand, Internet subscriptions are four or fewer per one hundred, while Internet use is approximately 12 percent or less for island countries. The pattern for broadband reinforces the low levels of access and use outside Australia and New Zealand. The Solomon Islands

TABLE 9.3
Information Society in Australia/Oceania

Country	Pop. Millions 2009	Income per Capita US$PPP 2008	Human Devel. Index 2005	TVs per 100 2003	PCs per 100 2003-7	Digital Opp. Index 2005-6	Tel. Lines per 100 2008	Mobile Lines per 100 2008	Internet Subs. per 100 2008	Internet Users per 100 2008	B'band Subs. per 100 2008	Internet Cost US$ per Month 2005	Press Freedom Index 2009
Australia	21.3	40350	0.968	54.8	60.83	0.65	44.46	104.96	37.94	71.98	24.39	22.82	21
Fiji	0.9	3,930	0.762	2.7	5.90	0.39	15.30	71.09	1.65	12.20	1.85	22.76	57
New Zealand	4.2	25,090	0.943	50.9	54.15	0.65	41.37	109.22	35.56	72.03	21.63	11.93	15
Samoa	0.2	2,780	0.785	6.4	2.34	0.29	16.10	3.65	—	5.03	0.09	11.37	30
Solomon Islands	0.6	1,180	0.602	0.8	4.60	0.13	1.57	5.87	0.40	1.96	0.29	101.65	29
Tonga	0.1	2,560	0.819	2.0	5.86	0.41	24.66	48.73	4.30	8.11	0.70	45.45	31
Vanuatu	0.2	2,330	0.674	1.1	1.42	0.21	4.45	15.39	0.74	7.27	0.07	58.22	25

Sources: See information society data discussion in chapter 6.

reports low levels of access, and with a monthly cost of US$101.65, an Internet subscription would exceed annual income. Internet costs in Vanuatu (US$58.22) and Tonga (US$45.45) are also very high given average incomes. With the exception of Fiji (51) and Tonga (31), all countries studied are considered to have a free press.

Australia/Oceania Information Society: Culture and Control

Many people indigenous to the Pacific islands are unable to find jobs at home and leave to find work in New Zealand, Australia, and the United States. One concern of both residents and migrants is retaining local culture and language, as Yuko Otsuka notes interest among many Tongans of preserving their language using the Internet even while the same technology introduces more English into their society.[38] Another dimension of Pacific island culture is the cultural value of information and the way that residents of many Pacific islands see their personal information as treasured and are reluctant to part with it, especially using e-government and online systems. In both cases, the Internet and telecommunications plays a role in defining culture, and can be seen as both a force to erode it as well as be sustaining.[39]

A major issue referenced in chapter 7 was net neutrality in the United States. A related issue has been significant in Australia since plans were announced in 2010 to filter the Internet. The rationale was to block access to some websites to protect children, but in so doing the filter would have also blocked access to innocent websites and expanded the role of government in determining acceptable online content.[40] As Internet access and information flows expand, so do calls to control and regulate content.[41] Unique in the Australian policy is that an advanced economy with a free press was proposing filtering that would have placed it globally with restrictive governments such as China. The public outcry against the policy has delayed its implementation, but it remains an interest of the government. Filtering and censorship of the Internet in Australia is seen as a threat to open society,[42] ironically by the same government that is promoting a national broadband policy at the same time.

Conclusion

The Asia/Pacific region is the most populous in the world with half of global population. In this region is the source and a major market for online gaming content, along with emerging technology clusters that make many Asian cities highly competitive innovation centers with North America and Europe. Perpetual human issues, ranging from happiness to power, are also played out socially and politically as part of the Asia/Pacific information society.

Notes

1. Chung (2008)
2. Poon et al. (2006: 557–558)
3. Ganne and Lecler (2009)
4. Tornatzky and Fleischer (1990)
5. Saxenian (1994)
6. Powell and Brantley (1992)
7. Monck et al. (1988)
8. Merton (1968); Hall (1986)
9. Shrum (1985)
10. Von Hippel (1987); Carter (1989); Bouty (2000)
11. Auster (1990)
12. IASP (2007)
13. Powell (1990)
14. Bouty (2000); Rogers (1995)
15. Corey (2000); Corey and Wilson (2006)
16. Castells and Hall (1994); Storper (1993)
17. Ganne and Lecler (2009: 7)
18. Walcott (2006)
19. Forsyth and Crewe (2010)
20. IASP (2007)
21. Ganne and Lecler (2009)
22. Woolley et al. (2008)
23. Matthiessen et al. (2006)
24. Zackariasson and Wilson (2010)
25. Cox (2006)
26. Kshetri (2009)
27. Knights and Jones (2007)
28. Sheth (2009)
29. Hudson (2009)
30. Budhwar et al. (2009)
31. Budhwar et al. (2009)
32. Cohen and El-Sawad (2007)
33. Collato (2010)
34. Chacko (2007)
35. Rai et al. (2010)
36. Dhakal et al. 2009)
37. Jamtsho and Bullen (2007)
38. Otsuka (2007)
39. Cullen (2009)
40. Stover (2010)
41. Palfrey (2010)
42. Hartley et al. (2010)

10

Africa and the Middle East

INFORMATION AND communications technologies are approaching ubiquity, evidenced by their presence in remote regions and often very poor countries. The experience of Africa and the Middle East contrasts the affluence of the Gulf States against the enduring poverty of sub-Saharan Africa, as well as the relative wealth of cities against the struggles of subsistence in rural life. Analysis of the scale and scope of information society in the Middle East and Africa illustrates emerging information society development along with innovative applications of ICT and different interpretations of information society. The following modules will specifically address information society in the Middle East, North Africa, and sub-Saharan Africa.

The Middle East

The Middle East for this analysis comprises countries around the Arabian Peninsula, Persian Gulf, and Red Sea. Of the twelve countries referenced in table 10.1, populations range from fewer than 1 million in Bahrain and Qatar to more than 20 million in Iraq, Saudi Arabia, Syria, and Yemen. Most dramatic is the range of wealth, from oil-rich states such as Kuwait and the United Arab Emirates (UAE, including Dubai and Abu Dhabi) to Jordan, Syria, and Yemen, where average incomes are one-tenth the levels of the most affluent Middle Eastern countries. In terms of the United Nations Human Development Index, advanced countries include Israel, the United Arab

TABLE 10.1

Information Society in the Middle East

Country	Pop. Millions 2009	Income per Capita US$PPP 2008	Human Devel. Index 2005	TVs per 100 2003	PCs per 100 2003–7	Digital Opp. Index 2005–6	Tel. Lines per 100 2008	Mobile Lines per 100 2008	Internet Subs. per 100 2008	Internet Users per 100 2008	B'band Subs. per 100 2008	Internet Cost US$ per Month 2005	Press Freedom Index 2009
Bahrain	0.7	—	0.866	40.0	18.28	0.60	28.42	185.77	14.76	51.95	14.18	30.23	71
Iraq	28.9	—	—	6.7	—	—	3.60	58.24	0.01	1.00	—	—	67
Israel	7.2	27,450	0.932	26.9	25.02	0.69	41.13	127.38	24.32	29.87	23.88	22.02	31
Jordan	6.3	5,530	0.773	8.7	6.34	0.45	8.46	86.60	3.73	26.00	2.24	11.14	64
Kuwait	2.7	52,610	0.891	37.5	22.33	0.50	18.53	99.59	10.49	34.26	1.37	22.22	55
Lebanon	4.0	10,880	0.772	30.8	11.62	0.40	17.03	34.10	6.25	52.22	5.03	10.00	71
Oman	3.4	20,650	0.814	53.3	6.89	0.44	9.84	115.58	2.88	20.00	1.15	14.53	65
Qatar	0.8	—	0.875	26.7	18.71	0.58	20.56	131.39	9.05	34.04	8.07	16.48	65
Saudi Arabia	28.7	22,950	0.812	19.3	13.89	0.46	16.27	142.85	7.27	30.80	4.16	21.33	82
Syria	21.8	4,350	0.724	5.7	9.03	0.37	17.12	33.24	3.36	16.79	0.05	13.97	83
UAE	4.8	—	0.868	12.1	30.06	0.59	33.63	208.65	26.06	65.15	12.43	13.07	69
Yemen	22.9	2,210	0.508	2.3	2.77	0.28	4.87	16.14	1.29	1.61	—	10.93	79

Sources: See information society data discussion in chapter 6.

Emirates, Kuwait, and Bahrain, in contrast to the remaining countries, which are classified as medium development.

The range of devices in the Middle East varies greatly, but it can be seen in many cases as a mobile telephone–led information society, with some countries having fully advanced ICT infrastructures. As a source of information, television is widely used, especially now that satellite TV offers a wide range of channels and the potential to access broadcasts that governments may otherwise prefer to limit. As the preeminent information source, access to TV varies from 2.3 sets per one hundred residents in Yemen to 53.3/100 in Oman. The range is influenced by development stage, although some middle-income countries have far more televisions than advanced countries such as Israel, the UAE, and Kuwait. Access to personal computers also varies, from 2.77/100 in Yemen to 30.06/100 in the UAE, with PC ownership associated with development. In most countries in the region, TV ownership exceeds PC ownership, often at double the rate, but in some cases the rates are close (Israel and Saudi Arabia), while in the UAE PC ownership is almost triple the TV ownership rate.

In most countries telephony is a necessity, and access to land or mobile phones is an important element of day-to-day life. In the region, landline subscriptions range from 3.6/100 in Iraq and 4.87/100 in Yemen to 41.13/100 in Israel. The range for landlines is of the magnitude of ten, and a similar range applies to mobile phone rates that extend from 16.14/100 in Yemen to 208.65/100 in the UAE. The result for seven of the twelve countries shows an average of one mobile phone per person, with two per person in the UAE. The ability of mobile infrastructure to be established quickly and competitively clearly shows, with mobile phones especially prevalent in developing countries.

Internet access and use in the Middle East is growing rapidly. Internet subscriptions ranged from 0.01/100 in war-torn Iraq and 1.29/100 in Yemen to 24.32/100 in Israel and 26.06/100 in the UAE. The ability to access the Internet does not depend on being a subscriber, as many may access content through shared computers in families, through schools and work, or via public access in cafés and libraries. When the number of Internet users is considered, the accessibility is far higher than subscriptions alone. User rates range from less than two per hundred in Iraq and Yemen to more than fifty in Bahrain, Lebanon, and the UAE. The numbers of subscriptions and users suggest a measure of sharing, with one or two users per subscription in Israel and the UAE, contrasting with more than seven sharing in Jordan and Lebanon, and one hundred sharing in Iraq.

The quality of access depends on Internet connections, with broadband offering a full range of information and entertainment possibilities. Data on broadband subscriptions range from essentially zero in Syria to 23.88/100 in Israel. Also revealing is the comparison with Internet subscriptions in general, as the access used in a number of countries is predominantly broadband (such as Bahrain, Israel, and Qatar), while for other countries, such as the UAE and Syria, much access remains slower than broadband. One anomaly is that wealthy Kuwait generally has a low rate of access and a low rate of broadband use.

Part of the access formula is cost, with a bundle of Internet services ranging from US$10 a month in Lebanon to more than US$30 in Bahrain, but what these cost data do not show is the income available for Internet. One year of Internet access in Yemen is more than half the average income, while in Kuwait, Internet costs less than a half percent of income. Given uneven income distributions and the cost of access, many residents of the Middle East do not have easy access to the Internet, although cafés and other public venues may provide a way to gain access affordably.

Middle East Information Society: Expression, E-Commerce, and Knowledge Production

One dimension of the Internet is its role as a vehicle for expression, making access important, as well as the ability to post and view content that may not serve the interests of the state or public authorities. In the absence of an Internet freedom index for this world region, the Press Freedom Index is used as a surrogate. The index shows that Israel has the only free press, with Lebanon and Kuwait rated as partly free, and the remaining countries as not having any press freedom. This suggests that while the Internet may establish a place or role within these countries, its ability to be a vehicle for expression may be significantly limited.

The findings of the Press Freedom Index are reinforced by data from the OpenNet Initiative that show a general absence of Internet filtering in Israel and Iraq, but sometimes pervasive filtering of content in Bahrain, Kuwait, Qatar, Oman, Saudi Arabia, Syria, and Yemen, with some political filtering in Jordan.[1] In these societies, users may or may not be aware of the extent of filtering or be able to find ways around the filtering systems. The combination of press freedom and filtering measures suggests that Internet users in most countries of the Middle East do not have the same range of information choices or access to opposing viewpoints as in other societies.

The combination of all ICT determinants culminates in the Digital Opportunity Index (DOI), which measures eleven indicators addressing opportunity, infrastructure, and utilization. The highest-ranked country in the Middle East is Israel, with a result of 0.69, which places it in the company of

Switzerland, Canada, and the United States. Next ranked would be Bahrain, the UAE, and Qatar, which rank with Ireland, Portugal, and Eastern Europe in having a well-established ICT sector. The result for Yemen (.28) captures its limited development and low income, with the DOI primarily due to the growth of mobile telephony rather than Internet. Telephony brings convenience and opportunity, but not to the same extent as a well-developed information system delivered via the Internet.

After a slow start, the region quickly adopted the Internet, with preferences for entertainment and news rather than commerce.[2] Essentially, the Internet serves as an extension of television or the telephone rather than as a business opportunity. Walter Armbrust sees ICT as part of a generational challenge over authority in Middle Eastern society:

> At a minimum the Internet in the Middle East can be seen as a new phase in a long evolution in hierarchies of authority. Blogs are one manifestation of this evolution, but so are mushrooming computer malls and Internet cafes, adaptations of digital technology to music and video making, and tensions between generations not accustomed to seeing youth empowered over their elders.[3]

As a social phenomenon in the region, social networking is one of the fastest-growing applications of ICT during the past five years. In the Middle East, social networking is popular, although there are geographic differences in the systems used. One factor affecting use is language, with Facebook offering Arabic and Hebrew languages starting only in early 2009.[4] Another factor is government control, such as Syria blocking Facebook in 2007 to limit online activism,[5] while the UAE bans Orkut, Flickr, and Hi5, as they host material objectionable to the telecommunications authority.[6] Of the major sites for networking, Facebook leads in Jordan, Lebanon, and the UAE, while Hi6 is popular in Kuwait.[7] In Israel, Qatar, and the UAE, Facebook penetration exceeds 20 percent of the population.[8]

As much of the Middle East's population falls into a developing and low-income category, the opportunities for e-commerce remain limited outside affluent areas such as the UAE and Israel. In addition to Internet or telephone access, there also need to be in place an electronic financial system and an efficient delivery system. Until all three factors are possible, along with demand, a growing e-business sector is unlikely. In their study of Saudi Arabia, Ahmed, Zairi, and Alwabel found limitations in terms of the cost of e-commerce, management commitment, reluctance of consumers to use e-commerce, and traditional business practices that depend on face-to-face meetings.[9] For many countries in the region, there is also the need for e-business systems respectful of Islamic tradition that takes into account Sharia-compliant transactions.[10]

While e-commerce requires purchasing power and access to the financial mechanisms of banking, delivery, and the Internet, e-government can serve as an information source and facilitator of public transactions that do not necessarily need all the preconditions of e-commerce. Information delivery can be electronic, and many transactions do not need a banking system for support. Jordan recognizes four elements of e-government in its strategic plan: an institutional framework, a legal framework, ICT infrastructure, and government business development. Jordan plans e-government around core services including citizen and business services, information, and government management.[11]

Implementing a successful e-government strategy can also create problems, as Al-Fakhri and colleagues found in their study of Saudi Arabia. Most of the problems identified were not specific to the region or country so much as to using a poorly designed system. In particular, the study notes the need to promote e-government services and raise awareness of the system, improve access to Internet services, establish a legal framework for e-services, and make content citizen oriented.[12]

Having noted that ICT access and use are limited in many countries in the Middle East, these technologies are also a growing force that governments and societies will find difficult to ignore. The decision to filter rather than ban access to the Internet is one sign of the need to acknowledge the Internet while also exercising control. For example, Hot Telecom references some deregulation and loosening of controls on ICT in Saudi Arabia as well as opening up to international service providers.[13] As in many countries, the Internet has become a force too large to be stopped, with governments seeking to control content and access rather than institute an outright ban.

Another dimension of information society is the production of technology and content. In this regard, Israel holds a globally competitive position for its production of ICT materials and in the conduct of ICT-related research and development.[14] No other country in the region serves as a technology exporter or R&D center at a global scale.

Currently, the Middle East's experience of information society is divided between affluent countries with developed infrastructure and developing economies. The structure of ICT favors mobile telephony, which dominates access forms across the region and far exceeds Internet use, which is growing rapidly but faces constraints in terms of cost, lack of Arabic content, and social limits on female participation.[15] A further dimension is the role of the state in filtering and banning access to some sites, or in the slow rollout of ICT in general.

North Africa

In the early years of the millennium, North Africa was a slowly evolving ICT region, with generally low levels of access and use. Countries in the region include Morocco, Algeria, Tunisia, Libya, and Egypt. The potential of ICT to expand rapidly and contribute to social change was dramatically shown during the Arab Spring of 2011. This season of protests and democracy movements in several countries continues as this book is being completed.

To start, summary data for North Africa are presented in table 10.2. With the exception of Libya's oil-based economy, the region lags behind the Middle East in terms of wealth and access to ICT, but it is far more developed than sub-Saharan Africa, which it borders. Populations range from 6 million people in Libya to almost 80 million people in Egypt. Incomes tend to be low, as is the state of human development. Even the most common medium, television, has limited distribution, averaging around ten TVs per one hundred population. Access to personal computers is also limited, ranging from one per one hundred in Algeria to more than seven in Tunisia. The low Digital Opportunity Index results reflect the development status of North Africa as well as its limited access to information. This is reinforced in data about landline telephones, ranging from 9.46 lines per one hundred people in Morocco to 16.41 lines in Libya.

Internet access tends to be limited, with subscribers per one hundred population ranging from 0.58 in Algeria to 3.07 in Egypt. In each country less than a handful of people have Internet subscriptions, with even lower levels of broadband access. Unlike many regions with developing economies, in North Africa Internet costs are commensurate with local incomes. Internet costs range from about 1 percent of per capita income in Egypt to almost 5 percent in Morocco. With costly, limited, and slow access to the Internet, development and educational opportunities cannot grow or serve the needs and interests of residents in the region.

Up to this point, the information infrastructure of North Africa suggests a region with little access to information and lacking the ability to disseminate information. Where North Africa, and many other developing regions, surprise is in the rapid rollout of mobile telephony. The significance of mobile phone ownership is evident from data showing from 50 percent mobile phone penetration in Egypt to more than 90 percent in Algeria. A region with little television, few landline phones, and generally low levels of Internet subscriptions has a well-developed infrastructure of mobile phones that has emerged rapidly over the past five years.

TABLE 10.2
Information Society in North Africa

Country	Pop. Millions 2009	Income per Capita US$PPP 2008	Human Devel. Index 2005	TVs per 100 2003	PCs per 100 2003-7	Digital Opp. Index 2005-6	Tel. Lines per 100 2008	Mobile Lines per 100 2008	Internet Subs. per 100 2008	Internet Users per 100 2008	B'band Subs. per 100 2008	Internet Cost US$ per Month 2005	Press Freedom Index 2009
Algeria	34.2	7,940	0.733	9.5	1.07	0.42	9.64	92.72	0.58	11.93	0.41	9.41	62
Egypt	78.9	5,460	0.708	9.9	4.87	0.41	14.64	50.62	3.07	16.65	0.94	4.97	60
Libya	6.3	15,630	0.818	12.7	2.22	0.36	16.41	76.71	1.36	5.13	0.16	21.98	94
Morocco	31.3	4,330	0.646	9.5	3.52	0.47	9.46	72.19	1.55	32.59	1.53	26.80	64
Tunisia	10.5	7,070	0.766	9.1	7.43	0.41	12.18	84.27	2.77	27.53	2.24	12.38	82

Sources: See information society data discussion in chapter 6.

As shown by the Arab Spring protests, a factor important in the region is evident in data on press freedom. With access to information and diverse political perspectives controlled, regimes seek to manage information to reinforce their own power. None of the countries in North Africa has press freedom, used as a proxy for Internet and information freedom in general. Press freedom rankings show the highest levels of freedom with the lowest index. Countries in North Africa start at an index of 60 (Egypt), which is classified as partly free, although for Egypt it is important to note that an index of 61 represents no press freedom. Indices of 82 in Tunisia and 94 in Libya underscore the lack of information available to residents of the region. Given the events of the Arab Spring, these 2009 data may well change depending on the pace of regime change.

North African Information Society: The Arab Spring

While the Middle East and North Africa (MENA) region contains few affluent economies, the growth of ICT, especially mobile phones, provides an important vehicle for communication and interaction. ICT can be seen as a technological and generational challenge to the hierarchical social order of many MENA societies. The growth of social networking, such as the 2009 introduction of Facebook in Arabic, confronts governments trying to restrict networking activities. The recent experience of democracy movements in a number of MENA countries shows how communications during times of social protest and unrest can be significant forces for organization and mobilization. The Arab Spring also serves as an example of the Internet evolving to a phase of contested access after less scrutiny in the past.[16]

The rapid expansion of mobile service in North Africa in the past five years seems to have taken authorities by surprise, moving from 2003–2005, when state control of most media limited the transmission and exchange of information in the region, to today when mobile phone penetration rates provide easy information access. The speed of mobile phone uptake is evident in figure 10.1, which shows penetration rates for five North African and Middle Eastern countries. The role of ICT in the democracy protests that started in Tunisia and moved to Egypt, Syria, Libya, and Yemen remains unclear. In the early stages of the protest movements, mobile phones and the Internet were often cited in the press, yet as protests continued, their role was less evident. A valid question can be asked whether ICT made a major difference, as protests in the past proceeded using telephones and word of mouth.

The Arab Spring represents a series of protests across the Middle East and North Africa that started in early 2011. In the region, the context of the protests was dissatisfaction with high rates of unemployment, especially for

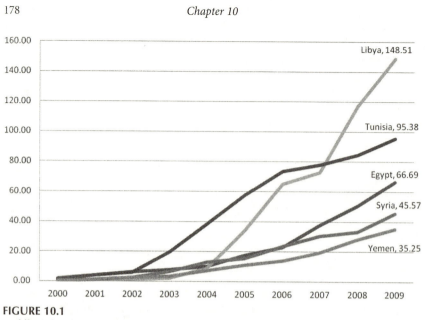

FIGURE 10.1
Mobile Subscriptions per 100 Residents, 2000–2009 (ITU 2012).

the educated young; government corruption; and media censorship. In Tunisia where the movement started, Internet censorship was a growing issue. The initiating event was the suicide death in December 2010 of Mohamed Bouazizi in protest of local government corruption. His death prompted protests aided by social media. Even with low Internet subscription rates, one-quarter of the population is estimated to be online. Access, however, was limited by censorship and the Tunisian government's decision to block YouTube, a decision that became a cause of protest as well as a constraint on the movement. What Tunisia did have was almost 85 percent penetration of mobile phones, which provided an effective organizational network.

News of successful protests in Tunisia spread to other countries in North Africa and showed the potential for public action to prompt change. One outcome was a series of demonstrations in Tahrir Square, Cairo, starting on January 25, 2011. Twitter and Facebook were used to facilitate protests, although the Egyptian government tried to block access to these services. For several days all Internet and most communication access between Egypt and the rest of the world were cut. International media coverage of the protests provided traditional press reporting so that the events were well documented, and media access to direct satellite connections also provided visibility.

Did ICT make a major difference? Protests in the past have proceeded using just telephones and word of mouth. Did ICT play a major or secondary role in the Arab Spring protest movements? There is some evidence that new technologies were a factor. As blogger Ethan Zuckerman noted,

Facebook became central to the Tunisian media ecosystem because all other sites that allowed video sharing—YouTube, Daily Motion, Vimeo, and others—were blocked by the Tunisian government, along with hundreds of blogs and dozens of key twitter accounts. This censorship, Sami argues, drove Tunisian users towards Facebook, and made it hard for the government to block it. The government tried in 2008, but the outcry was so huge, they reversed course. The main reason—usage of Facebook more than doubled during the 10 days of blockage as Tunisians found ways around the national firewall and onto the service.[17]

The events of the Arab Spring continue to unfold, but they also produced a number of unintended or unforeseen consequences. Closing or limiting ICT access may stifle dissent, but it can also limit business interaction and commerce. One constraint on Mubarak's control of the Internet was that to stop dissent also meant to stop service to the Egyptian Stock Exchange;[18] ISP Noor tried to close down all access except to aviation, banking, and finance services.

Cutting access to the Internet and mobile phones to limit expression can also lead to public protests. Tunisia and Egypt cut access through mobile service and the Internet, but in some cases that action encouraged people to leave home and seek information and join protests. Arab Media notes that when young people lost access in Cairo they left home to find more information, followed by parents trying to find their children when mobile phone service was cut.[19] The online and virtual protests taking place were stopped by government action, but that only served to move people outside and into public places where protests continued in real space.

Also, the belief that uploading video to YouTube and related sites directly influences opinion may be tempered with the realization that regimes will do all they can to limit access within a country. The power of uploaded images is not so much the internal audience but the international audience that reacts to the images. For example, YouTube was blocked in Tunisia but could be accessed externally. Protest images uploaded from Tunisia to YouTube through external links could be accessed outside the country. News broadcaster Al Jazeera, among others, was able to access footage of Tunisian protests and reach a wide audience through satellite television. Tunisians saw images of local protests relayed via YouTube and then satellite television. The power of the Internet in this case was relaying protest information to news media rather than directly influencing events.

As protest movements gained momentum, they gained a lot of support from Western democracies wanting to support regime change. As new initiatives to promote ICT access and provide covert access were established by the major powers, questions were raised about the true intent of their actions. Sami Ben Gharbia reports that Western support for Internet freedom and activism could mask strategic geopolitics and harm local activism.[20] Digital activism fills a gap left by the absence of other media and opportunities for expression. Internet freedom as a movement from the United States has ICT corporate support, with firms such as Yahoo! and Google aligning their interests in global market and information access with U.S. foreign policy.

Analysis of the Arab Spring is useful for a number of reasons. First, it exemplifies how new technologies can be used unexpectedly or with more power than anticipated. The cultural context of ICT in this case saw it used to facilitate protests. Second, the speed of events and lack of a social science research environment makes it difficult to ascribe shares to the role of different media and technologies. Third, the unintended consequences show how different societies use and react to new information technologies. Finally, it serves as a reminder that ICT is part of a larger, ongoing tension over control of ideas and space. Barney Warf reminds us that ICT is just a new element in the battle over contested spaces.[21]

Sub-Saharan Africa

The many countries in Africa south of the Sahara Desert reflect low levels of information society as defined through technology and media. The region has some of the world's lowest incomes, literacy rates, ICT access, and press freedom. A summary of sub Saharan information society is presented in table 10.3.

Many of the countries are small, with eighteen having populations of fewer than 5 million people, which is significant given the challenges of managing national infrastructures with low base populations. The largest countries include Nigeria (140.2 million), Ethiopia (85.2 million), and the Democratic Republic of the Congo (68.7 million). The region is characterized by low incomes. Only Equatorial Guinea and the Seychelles approximate US$20,000 per capita annually, with twelve countries averaging less than US$1,000 in annual per capita income. A similar pattern emerges for the Human Development Index (HDI): nineteen of the twenty lowest-ranked countries are in Africa, and only the most advanced sub-Saharan countries reach the medium development level (Gabon, Botswana, South Africa, Equatorial Guinea, Cape Verde, Swaziland, and the Democratic Republic of the Congo).

Television is perhaps the most universal medium globally, yet in Africa access to television is very low. Almost all sub-Saharan countries report rates of fewer than five TVs per one hundred population. Access would depend on how television is used, and one television could provide information access to a small village. However, it shows the challenge of information dissemination in the region. Personal computers are similarly sparse, although for a number

TABLE 10.3
Information Society in sub-Saharan Africa

Country	Pop. Millions 2009	Income per Capita US$PPP 2008	Human Devel. Index 2005	TVs per 100 2003	PCs per 100 2003–7	Digital Opp. Index 2005–6	Tel. Lines per 100 2008	Mobile Lines per 100 2008	Internet Subs. per 100 2008	Internet Users per 100 2008	B'band Subs. per 100 2008	Internet Cost US$ per Month 2005	Press Freedom Index 2009
Angola	12.8	5,020	0.446	1.7	0.70	0.23	0.63	37.59	0.59	3.05	0.09	34.28	61
Benin	8.8	1,460	0.437	0.9	0.66	0.19	1.84	39.66	0.10	1.85	0.03	20.73	31
Botswana	2.0	13,100	0.654	1.9	5.11	0.38	7.41	77.34	0.52	6.25	0.46	21.28	37
Burkina Faso	15.7	1,160	0.370	1.0	0.66	0.14	0.95	16.76	0.11	0.92	0.03	90.56	41
Burundi	9.5	380	0.413	0.3	0.83	0.09	0.38	5.95	0.06	0.81	—	52.00	75
Cameroon	18.9	2,180	0.532	2.6	1.23	0.24	1.04	32.28	0.14	3.80	—	44.56	65
Cape Verde	0.4	3,450	0.736	3.6	10.85	0.34	14.41	55.68	1.85	20.61	1.48	40.34	28
Central African Rep.	4.5	730	0.384	0.4	0.30	0.09	0.28	3.55	0.06	0.44	—	147.80	61
Chad	10.3	1,160	0.388	0.1	0.16	0.04	0.12	16.58	0.03	1.19	—	86.35	76
Comoros	0.8	1,170	0.561	0.1	0.68	0.17	3.53	14.90	0.18	3.48	—	37.92	50
Congo	4.0	3,090	0.548	—	0.48	0.17	0.61	49.98	0.03	4.29	—	84.51	53
Côte d'Ivoire	20.6	1,580	0.432	6.3	1.78	0.20	1.73	50.74	0.09	3.21	0.05	67.08	67
Dem Rep Congo	68.7	290	0.411	10.7	0.02	0.08	0.06	14.42	0.10	0.45	—	93.24	81
Djibouti	0.7	2,330	0.516	5.9	2.40	0.26	1.76	13.29	0.74	2.26	—	41.11	73

(continued)

TABLE 10.3
(continued)

Country	Pop. Millions 2009	Income per Capita US$PPP 2008	Human Devel. Index 2005	TVs per 100 2003	PCs per 100 2003–7	Digital Opp. Index 2005–6	Tel. Lines per 100 2008	Mobile Lines per 100 2008	Internet Subs. per 100 2008	Internet Users per 100 2008	B'band Subs. per 100 2008	Internet Cost US$ per Month 2005	Press Freedom Index 2009
Equatorial Guinea	0.6	21,700	0.642	0.8	1.79	0.27	1.52	52.49	0.20	1.82	0.03	32.74	90
Eritrea	5.6	630	0.483	0.0	0.78	0.07	0.82	2.20	0.13	4.06	—	28.63	94
Ethiopia	85.2	870	0.406	0.9	0.64	0.10	1.11	2.42	0.04	0.45	—	23.32	76
Gabon	1.5	12,270	0.677	4.5	3.34	0.37	1.83	89.77	0.76	6.21	0.15	40.08	69
Gambia	1.8	1,280	0.502	0.3	3.34	0.21	2.94	70.24	0.22	6.88	0.02	17.78	79
Ghana	23.4	1,430	0.553	8.7	0.58	0.21	0.62	49.55	0.12	4.27	0.10	23.56	26
Guinea	10.1	1,190	0.456	0.9	0.48	0.15	0.21	39.06	—	0.92	—	24.72	66
Guinea-Bissau	1.5	530	0.374	—	0.19	0.04	0.29	31.75	0.04	2.35	—	74.95	52
Kenya	39.0	1,580	0.521	2.2	1.03	0.17	0.63	42.06	1.05	8.67	0.01	75.93	60
Lesotho	2.1	2,000	0.549	—	0.28	0.26	3.18	28.35	0.13	3.58	0.01	38.55	48
Liberia	3.4	300	—	2.4	—	—	0.05	19.30	0.41	0.53	—	—	63
Madagascar	20.7	1,040	0.533	1.8	0.55	0.12	0.86	25.30	0.06	1.65	0.02	45.94	51
Malawi	15.0	830	0.437	—	0.19	0.09	1.18	12.00	0.71	2.13	0.02	41.92	56
Mali	13.4	1,090	0.380	0.4	0.44	0.12	0.64	27.07	0.08	1.57	0.04	28.42	26

Mauritania	3.1	2,000	0.550	3.2	4.40	0.17	2.37	65.07	0.30	1.87	0.18	54.25	58
Mauritius	1.3	12,480	0.804	21.0	17.52	0.50	28.48	80.74	14.46	29.69	7.17	17.46	26
Mozambique	21.7	770	0.384	0.3	1.43	0.12	0.35	19.68	—	1.56	0.05	32.87	41
Namibia	2.1	6,270	0.650	3.0	24.11	0.35	6.57	49.39	4.31	5.33	0.02	48.70	30
Niger	15.3	680	0.374	1.0	0.07	0.03	0.44	12.91	0.03	0.54	—	101.82	64
Nigeria	149.2	1,940	0.470	5.4	0.91	0.17	0.86	41.66	0.08	15.86	0.04	50.42	54
Rwanda	10.7	1,010	0.452	—	0.30	0.14	0.17	13.61	0.09	3.09	0.04	30.13	85
São Tomé & Príncipe	0.2	1,780	0.654	12.3	3.83	0.15	4.81	30.59	1.60	15.48	0.47	—	28
Senegal	13.7	1,760	0.499	3.1	2.14	0.37	1.95	44.13	0.39	8.35	0.39	25.58	53
Seychelles	0.1	19,770	0.843	13.5	20.78	0.48	27.70	101.78	6.75	38.17	4.08	31.45	59
Sierra Leone	5.1	750	0.336	0.9	—	0.11	0.57	18.14	—	0.25	—	10.56	56
Somalia	9.8	—	—	1.6	0.91	—	1.12	7.02	0.11	1.14	—	—	84
South Africa	49.0	9,780	0.674	13.5	8.36	0.42	8.91	90.60	7.51	8.43	0.86	63.21	30
Sudan	41.1	1,930	0.526	5.9	11.45	0.24	0.89	29.00	0.11	10.16	0.11	65.51	78
Swaziland	1.3	5,010	0.547	2.0	4.08	0.32	3.77	45.52	1.71	6.85	0.07	51.74	76
Tanzania	41.0	1,230	0.467	0.3	0.93	0.15	0.29	30.62	—	1.22	0.02	93.60	50
Togo	6.0	820	0.512	1.4	3.01	0.17	2.18	23.99	0.98	5.42	0.03	44.69	72
Uganda	32.4	1,140	0.505	1.8	1.67	0.16	0.53	27.02	0.07	7.90	0.02	99.59	53
Zambia	11.7	1,230	0.434	2.5	1.12	0.14	0.72	28.04	0.10	5.55	0.04	68.43	65
Zimbabwe	11.4	—	0.513	3.0	6.61	0.16	2.79	13.28	0.80	11.40	0.14	24.58	88

Sources: See information society data discussion in chapter 6.

of countries there are more PCs than TVs per capita. For example, in Botswana there are 1.9 TVs/100 but 5.11 PCs/100. The TV and PC relationship is not always income based; there are poorer countries that have much higher rates of PC ownership than more affluent countries in the region. Namibia, with an average income of $6,270, has 24.11 PCs/100, while neighboring South Africa, with incomes 50 percent higher, has 8.36 PCs/100. In examining ICT data and trends, it is valuable to remember that ICT use is a mix of forces: devices, access, culture, and governance.

The Digital Opportunity Index reflects the generally low income and information access levels evident in sub-Saharan Africa. As ICT access becomes mainstream globally for information, commerce, and education, Africa faces many challenges to participate. The highest DOI levels are in Mauritius (0.50), Seychelles (0.48), and South Africa (0.42), but there are also twenty-eight countries with DOIs less than 0.2.

Telephone access by landline is low across the region, with the exception of Mauritius and the Seychelles. What is significant is the use of mobile phone technology, with many countries reporting high subscription levels. In many countries, mobile subscriptions are ten, twenty, or thirty times greater than access rates by landline. The delay in wiring Africa allowed the newer and easier-to-provide mobile technology to leapfrog a telecommunications development stage. Leading mobile phone nations include Botswana (77.34/100), Gabon (89.77/100), Mauritius (80.74/100), Seychelles (101.78/100), and South Africa (90.6/100). The recent and rapid uptake of mobile technology has provided levels of access not possible before, taking Africa's telephone infrastructure to the level of many developed economies.

In contrast to mobile phone infrastructure, Africa's Internet access remains limited. Only eight out of forty-four countries average more than one subscriber per one hundred residents. The highest levels are in Mauritius (14.46/100), South Africa (7.51/100), and Namibia (4.31/100). Another measure of access is the number of users, which shows greater access, suggesting the use of Internet cafés, libraries, schools, and shared computers in many cases. Some countries with very few subscribers have many more users, such as Nigeria, with less than one subscriber but more than fifteen users per one hundred residents. The digital divide is not defined by access, but as effective Internet use requires broadband, this infrastructure becomes important. By this measure, Africa also lags, with less than one subscriber per one hundred people for almost every country, with the exception of Cape Verde, Mauritius, and the Seychelles.

As noted in chapter 6, access is not just physical but the cost of access, which in low-income regions can be very high. Across sub-Saharan Africa, Internet costs equal or far exceed that of countries with far higher incomes.

A common Internet bundle in the Central African Republic costs $147.80 per month in a country with an average annual income of $730. In this country, Internet access alone is double the average income. In Niger the Internet costs $101.82 per month with an annual income of $680. Even in countries with low Internet costs, such as Sierra Leone ($10.56), the annual cost is almost a fifth of average income. In a large developing economy such as South Africa, Internet costs are more reasonable and approach 7 percent of the annual income.

In addition to challenges of infrastructure and cost, sub-Saharan Africa also faces severe limits on information dissemination and use. Using press freedom as a proxy for information freedom, no country would be considered to have a free press. The most freedom is found in Benin, South Africa, and Namibia, but there are also nineteen countries with no freedom. The least free press globally is found in Eritrea. One of the values of telecommunications and the Internet is access to information, yet even with a developed infrastructure, the inability to access information diminishes the opportunities available and the quality of life in an information society.

Sub-Saharan Information Society: Infrastructure, Human Capital, and Education

Among the many challenges facing Africa in the development of information society are (1) infrastructure development, (2) professional ICT workers, and (3) distance education. Farrokh Mamaghani points to the need for developing countries to be able to build and maintain ICT infrastructure and to have the human capital necessary to gain the most from ICT.[22] Infrastructure challenges also apply to Nigeria, where the uptake of ICT is not so much an issue of the technology within the firm but the need for consistent sources of electricity and effective networks.[23] Other barriers to the advancement of African information society include restrictive regulations, high costs of access, and a shortage of IT professionals.[24] Infrastructure development is often tied to regulations, especially when there are so many small countries, each with specific conditions and policies. The problems of regulation fall into the social or governance sphere rather than being technical in nature. These barriers include high tariffs, lack of competition, and a need for investment.[25] All are affected by the regulatory environment that protects incumbent firms and political interests.

Two education-related themes in sub-Saharan Africa are the needs for education and skilled ICT professionals.[26] ICT plays many roles in education, from distance learning in remote locations to access to information and research collaboration.[27] Lack of infrastructure and resources for ICT is part of the problem, but so is organizational culture in many cases, where schools or universities need capacity building and training to advance. In case studies of Cape Verde and Mozambique distance education, users face the challenge of mind-set and attitude to the adoption of distance education methods, with conservative thinking being a major barrier to innovation.[28]

Conclusion

The experiences of the Middle East and Africa show the promise of information and communication technologies for development and at the same time reveal how its power can be used for expression as well as repression. As residents of the developed world take information access for granted, with some places having multiple devices per person, the developing information societies in Africa lack affordable access to even the most basic communications systems. With the better economics and coverage provided by mobile phones, this may change, but challenges remain to freely accessing and using information once it is available.

Notes

1. OpenNet Initiative (2009)
2. Al-Nuaim (2009)
3. Armbrust (2007: 533)
4. Eldon (2009)
5. Reuters (2007)
6. Rahimi and Bowman (2007)
7. Valleywag (2007)
8. Eldon (2009)
9. Ahmed et al. (2006)
10. Amin (2008)
11. Jordan Ministry of Information and Communications Technology (2006)
12. Al-Fakhri et al. (2008)
13. Hot Telecom (2009)
14. Kellerman (2002a; 2002b); Ein-Dor (2008)
15. Warf and Vincent (2007)
16. Palfrey (2010)
17. Zuckerman (2011)
18. Tsotsis (2011)
19. Arab Media (2011)
20. Gharbia (2011)

21. Warf (1997)
22. Mamaghani (2010)
23. Apulu and Ige (2011)
24. Alemneh and Hastings (2006)
25. Avila (2009)
26. Mutula and Van Brakel (2006)
27. Butcher et al. (2011)
28. Ramos et al. (2011)

III

POLICY AND ACTION FOR THE
GLOBAL INFORMATION SOCIETY

11

Policy

To this stage, we have introduced the foundational elements of the global information society by showing the importance of technologies, infrastructure, society, and the roles played by individuals and institutions in society. The social and technical context was discussed in part I, and the evolution of spatial patterns of ICT use was explored in Part II. Having laid this groundwork, this section addresses the use of policy and the importance of regions and places in framing development actions. The theme of this chapter, therefore, is policy for information society, or more accurately, policy for the many different information societies that have evolved globally.

Governance was emphasized in chapter 6 as a significant and growing spectrum of influences on information society. As economy and society change, the governance mechanisms used to shape or manage desired outcomes must also change. Technology is produced and shaped by societies globally, and it is important to remember that people should drive the technology and not be driven by it. Commonly, *policy is taken to mean a plan of action*; it is seen routinely as an intervention in an existing context, as a process or trajectory of development. Such an intervention is conventionally intended to change the present situation along a pathway that has a stated goal as the policy's planned destination or outcome. Such plans of action may apply to trading blocs (the European Union, ASEAN, NAFTA), countries, communities, firms and corporations, or other organizations and institutions.

The purpose of this chapter is to empower students, policy makers, practitioners, and other local and regional stakeholders to understand the concept of the *comprehensive intelligent development strategy* and to use that

understanding to create policies to develop localities and their regions intelligently—that is, to be able to live, work, function, and compete successfully
in the context of the global information society.

One of the challenges of information society is that there may be *too much
information*, which should require us to understand potential impacts in
order to mobilize local civil society to engage in intelligent development. Informed policy and resulting action are at the core of *intelligent development*.
It is intended here that the reader should be motivated to initiate, experiment
with, and practice the tasks and follow the development pathways that are
offered in this chapter. The ultimate intended result is *empowerment of the
reader* to be able to know about and to engage in the intelligent development
of city-regions in concert with other stakeholders. The sections that follow in
the first part of this chapter provide an operational and working definition
of intelligent development. This definition is couched within the context of
the global information society and the issues that arise at the scale of the city-
region, including localities of rural and small-town environments.

Framing for Understanding and
Creating Intelligent Development Policies Planning

On the one hand, collectively we are blessed today with copious amounts
of useful information. Unfortunately, we also are inundated with copious
amounts of information that we neither need nor want. This overabundance
of information can be managed and steered, however, if one operates from
frameworks that are designed to channel and direct selected information to
the advancement of social, economic, and other developmental purposes.

In addition to generating too much information in general, the global information society is highly complex, uncertain, and interconnected. In order
to make these complexities understandable and manageable, framing is recommended as a practical means for creating intelligent development policy.
This involves using frames, which are

> mental constructs that shape the way we see the world. As a result, they shape
> the goals we seek, the plans we make, the way we act, and what counts as a good
> or bad outcome of our actions.[1]

The core focus of attention that is framed here is *development*. Everett Rogers has offered an operational definition of development. It is

> a widely participatory process of social change in a society intended to bring
> about both social and material advancement (including greater equality, free-

dom, and other valued qualities) for the majority of the people through their gaining greater control over their environment.[2]

For planning intelligent development policies for city-regions in the global information society, some of the principal actors that need to be taken into account to engage in policy creation include stakeholders, strategic planners, practitioners, researcher-scholars, and co-learners, among others. Co-learners are emphasized here because understanding in order to take informed decisions and to create widely supported effective policy requires shared knowledge utilization beyond a single individual person. Collective engagement can also create and host innovative environments that can stimulate synergies that may exceed the sum of their parts.

In the context of the global information and network society and the global knowledge economy, it is important to draw explicit attention to *digital development* and its role in supporting policy analysis and policy planning that is informed and intelligently formulated. Digital development is the information and communications technologies (ICTs) infrastructure that operates to facilitate, enable, and transform our old-economy world to the new-economy world. Digital development has spawned dramatic change locally and globally, and over a remarkably brief time span.

Digital development is perceived as having been instrumental in producing both good news and bad news. Digital development has created jobs; it has lost jobs. It has enhanced productivity and reduced the costs of doing business in every sense of the word, and its informatization powers of automation, networking, instantaneous movements of capital flows, and resulting uses such as outsourcing and offshoring have generated profound dislocations and disparities for local and regional societies and economies. Digital development is composed of such technological platforms and applications as computers of all kinds, sizes, hybrids, and mobilities, with myriad communication options from data to voice to text to characters, ad infinitum. In addition to computers per se, a diverse range of computerized devices are routinely embedded in today's work, education, entertainment, and living. Digital development has become so pervasive in the global society and economy, one increasingly is more aware of the word *ubiquity* than ever before. In South Korea, for example, ubiquitous cities, or the U-city concept, have become part of daily parlance as shorthand for the incorporation of digital development throughout and routinely into city and regional development.

Lastly, one should keep in mind the concepts of development and digital development when engaging in the construction and creation of strategies for intelligent development. In this context, digital development is seen as a means to enhancing development and transforming digital development and development into the integrative social construct of intelligent development.

The discussion that follows offers an elaboration of those elements that can be used to frame an operating definition of intelligent development.

Branding for Creating Intelligent Development

When moving from *understanding* the development and digital development of city-regions to the *creation* and planning of intelligent development of places and regions, the function of branding should be noted. In the development frame adopted for this book, branding is a framing-related activity in that it seeks to convey an intended image or concept. In this era of a global information society, branding has become a critical component of Internet commerce and business.

For a region, a city, or a place, branding can confer coherence. For an area that is seen as one that is without a core identity and seems to behave like a collection of molecules, one can envisage investing in policies that enable aspiring toward a perception of a city-region that functions holistically, efficiently, and seamlessly.[3] For example, this may be a desired end state for a future planning strategy, and as such a reality begins to be set in motion, leaders may be positioned to be able to brand a city-region as one that works well for residents, for business, for learning, and for living. Branding can communicate tones of attractiveness, openness, and a welcoming environment, both for the consumption of insiders and outsiders alike. Branding cases may be studied for large city-regions such as Singapore for and rural and small-town regions such as remote Northwest Minnesota.[4] Malaysia has branded an ICT-based development region about the size of Singapore as the "Multimedia Super Corridor"; it includes the two intelligent cities of Cyberjaya and Putrajaya.[5]

The City-Region: Large Metropolitan Environments and Small-Town Rural Environments

In the context of the global information society, today's dominant geographical unit of observation is the city-region. The meaning of such territorial entities has evolved to cover a range of scales and sizes. Allen Scott refers to "a concept of the cosmopolitan metropolis as a command post for the operations of multinational corporations, as a centre of advanced services and information-processing activities."[6] He further extended the concept's "range of meaning so as to incorporate the notion of the wider region as an emerging political unit with increasing autonomy of action on the national and world stages."[7] This expansion of meaning is an overt incorporation of the influential roles played by large city-regions in the context of globalization.

Rural and small-town environments also demonstrate city-region characteristics. However, the density and spatially dispersed development patterns are much more extensive and sparse than the typical large metropolis case. In both the small- and large-scale cases, city-regions are the functional entities

> within which business and services operate. City-regional economies play a strong role in driving forward the economies of their region. The city-regional scale reflects the "geography of everyday life" rather than administrative boundaries and presents us with opportunities to develop policies that reflect and support the functioning of that city-region.[8]

In the context of globalization forces changing the role of the nation-state, Kenichi Ohmae has been exploring the role of the region-state as the older functions of the industrial age have seen the rise of the newer function of the global information age. In 1996, some of his information age functions could be characterized as

- driven by private capital;
- autonomous networks of independent private enterprises and regional entities;
- inherently borderless;
- welcoming of foreign capital and world-class companies/expertise, creating high-quality jobs;
- aiming for harmonious regional prosperity based on interdependent, network-centric companies creating information-intensive services to capture value from customers;
- entrepreneurial initiatives;
- good government nurturing regional development, not focused on a specific industry; and
- change occurring suddenly in months to years.[9]

After his region-state concept had evolved further, Ohmae observed that "the most essential element of any successful region must be openness to the outside world. The rest of the world must be viewed positively, as the source of prosperity."[10] He has defined the region-state as "a unit for creating a positive virtual cycle. The more people who come in, and the more varied their backgrounds and skills are, the more varied the region becomes over time."[11] This cycle generates spillovers of new services to support the region's core economic activities, such as financial services; these economic activities may deepen and widen the regional economy, and in turn, nonbusiness services, such as schools, health care, and businesses providing retail goods and services may expand. The scale and size of Ohmae's evolving region-state concept have become more diverse and include microregions as well as larger megalopolitan-scaled regions with millions of people. Examples include Lombardia, Italy, and Southern India, Bangalore. His recommendations for what a "successful region has to do" are worth exploring for both pragmatic and imaginative stimulation.[12]

In the global information society, so much of the development practice experience and literature to date have been influenced by analysis and action in the larger metropolitan city-region. As a consequence, care should be taken to be sensitive to the unique and particular characteristics of the smaller rural city-region. This is important because many lessons from the larger city-regions do not transfer well to the environment of the rural and small-town region. In part, this is the case because much of the benefits of broadband and most other modern media and information technologies have not reached fully into these much more dispersed and remote rural settlement areas.

The Big Ten Criteria of Intelligent Development Behavior

Definitions and Their Derivation

Understanding begins with acquiring knowledge about the object of planned action. In this case, the object is local and regional policy planning in the context of the global information society. A revealing approach to this knowledge acquisition is to trace the evolution of the concepts of global information society and the new economy. Often used interchangeably, these related concepts may be grasped best by *deriving a working definition* of the information society and new economy that have developed over the last several generations. Variously, these new social and economic conceptual constructs have been labeled *information society, postindustrial society, network society*, the *knowledge economy*, and the *new economy*.

Those who have interests in these topics often take it for granted that they know their meanings. However, when we try to operationalize such concepts locally for our own communities, we begin to realize that our understanding is anything but concrete and functional. This has been characterized as *fuzzy planning*.

"Fuzzy planning" tells us to understand that we are not as sure of anything as we think we are. That applies not only to planning but also to our individual lives. Real life is fuzzy, full of the unexpected![13]

New-economy concepts had their modern origins from structural shifts in occupations from blue-collar to white-collar occupations and from growth in the agricultural and industrial economic sectors to growth in the service sectors, especially advanced services such as law, accounting, advertising, insurance, banking and finance, and management consultancy. The core message of this criterion is that intelligent development begins by the practitioner understanding the context and evolution of the development issue so that local-area co-learners and stakeholders are positioned to define the strategic future direction of their city-region. The scholar's role is to consult and provide external support in operationalizing this criterion. Professional development planners and their citizen stakeholders, in turn, have the role of putting forward their visions and aspirations for the future of their communities.

Globalization and Digital Development

This is a dual factor that recognizes both *globalization* and *digital development*, and how the infrastructure of ICTs drives the new economy. It is characterized by a local economy that relies increasingly on technology, especially ICTs; modern physical infrastructure; and knowledge as the principal factors of today's economic production. The core message of this criterion is to ensure that the mind-sets of the students, practitioners, and scholars of intelligent development are focused on the strategic importance of these new-economy drivers. This awareness stems from recognition of shifts in the relative importance of the *content* of economies from muscle to more mind power, from local and regional to more global influence, and from self-containment and compartmentalization of economic functions to more interconnected and networked ones. Such shifts in perspectives are needed to see the new global information society through the lenses of changed geographies, changed time frames, and shifts in the economic and societal functions of production, consumption, and amenities quality of life.

Research and Theory

In an age when information and knowledge increasingly have taken center stage, *ideas and conceptions* have assumed more importance in local development than ever before. As noted above, framing and conceptualizing enable one to organize and make operational the complexities revealed due to the explosion and easy accessibility of information nowadays. Consequently, one should make a point of drawing on contemporary *research and theory*, concepts, paradigms, and models. This recognizes the complexities, uncertainties, multilayered and nonlinear functions, dynamic networks, and flows of the new global information society and knowledge economy. Many of the dominant theories of the near past continue to have relevance in the information age. For example, Plummer and Taylor's theories of local economic growth offer a helpful synthesis of some of these constructs,[14] such as

- growth poles and growth centers,
- the product-cycle model (industry life cycle),
- flexible production and flexible specialization,
- learning regions and innovative milieus,
- competitive advantage, and
- enterprise segmentation and unequal power relations.

These are illustrations of just some *substantive or thematic* concepts. There are many other such models; for example, core-periphery or basic–non-basic constructs are useful in both understanding development and creating development strategies. There are also *process or procedural* constructs that are helpful in both analysis and action. For example, concepts such as SWOT (strengths, weaknesses, opportunities, and threats) analysis and force field analysis enable one to dissect the various influences, drivers, and impediments to planned change.

Intelligent development implies that the dominant theoretical mind-set must go beyond traditional old-economy neoclassical positivistic theory by increasingly adopting relational theory.[15] The core message here is to make an early connection in mastering any planned change process between the particular empirical development issue being targeted and all applicable theory—informed especially by relational theory, thinking, and behavior. About this, Patsy Healey has written of the importance of using "an interpretive and relational intellectual lens to develop a way of thinking about this complexity" of the new information society and economy, thereby providing "a more systematic academic treatment so that practices can be better understood, developed and changed."[16] Relational thinking and behavior are elaborated below in the discussion of the criteria for continuous improvement of intelligent development practice.

Comparative Methods

Understanding today's more information-centric and knowledge-based world can be advanced by the use of *comparative methods*. These include benchmarking and identification of good practices or best practices for regional development. Simply put, such methods address the need to have *context* that is relevant, systematic, measurable, and critical to the monitoring and assessment of planned action on targeted development issues; this is the core purpose of this criterion. Benchmarking here involves setting a baseline of information comparing other similar selected places and regions to the targeted area for development and then regularly assessing the status among these areas relative to identified shared development goals and objectives. Best practices involve identification of the best-in-class cases elsewhere that have proven performance records according to the particular metrics that have been selected for the determination of success in tracking intended planned development futures. By taking such comparative measures, one is positioned better to make midcourse corrections in strategies and tactics that have been chosen to move development understandings to development actions.

Prioritized Investments

This criterion mandates that informed choices must be made in the new economy; "informed" means that the explicit processes of rationality and the politics of impacted interests both must be engaged. Inherent here is the practical reality that ranking and sequencing of differential actions and investments are essential to wise and prudent decision making for the realization of intended planned futures. The actors here should include, both formally and informally, affected stakeholders in addition to the planning practitioners and their scholarly support actors in a translational relationship.

Drawing on a policy example in U.S. economic development to illustrate this criterion, the federal government's Economic Development Administration (EDA) has specified seven investment policy guidelines for local regional strategies to be successful in attracting financial support from EDA.[17] Such strategies should be

- market based;
- proactive in nature and scope;
- focused beyond the immediate economic horizon, anticipating economic changes and diversifying the local and regional economy;
- set to maximize the attraction of private-sector investment that would not otherwise come to fruition absent EDA's investment;
- seen as having a high probability of success;
- conducive to an environment where higher-skill, higher-wage jobs are created; and
- capable of maximizing return on taxpayer investment.

Given the diverse mix of factors driving the global information society, these strategic development criteria are representative of the kind of expectations and intentions that socially responsible public institutional investors would want to be met in providing financial and other support for intelligent development locally and regionally.

Expertise of Local Experience and Local Knowledge

This criterion recognizes that expertise in intelligent development needs to include both external and abstract theoretical expertise and city-region knowledge that is concrete and acquired through local experience. The core message of this criterion is that these generic and unique local blends of expertise working interdependently tend to support and advance intelligent development. Further, we recognize that local regional "expertise" and "knowledge" may come from formal education, and it also may be earned experientially. A rich mix of both practical and educational preparation and local immersion is an ideal blend for addressing the development challenges and opportunities of today's global information society.

A potentially transformative benefit of increasingly ubiquitous information and digital infrastructure is the ability of more individuals to impact and contribute to group goals and efforts. For example, in rural areas and small towns, it is common for development planning to be executed by understaffed and even one-person organizations. In today's environment of more widespread ICTs and diverse digital platforms, some of the work traditionally done by overextended professionals can be shared and supplemented by volunteer citizen planners. Members of boards and commissions and other volunteer individuals might use information technologies to explore best practices and to identify locally appropriate baselines and benchmarks against which to measure progress on planned policy implementation. Such sharing of research and planning tasks can be challenging to steer toward common ends, but they also can enhance understanding, promote ownership of new directions in development, and bring new imagination and creativity to planned policies and actions. By experimenting and piloting such small-scale efforts, one can extend needed community learning, and in the process strengthen local civil society. This process could be seen as the power of organizing without organizations.[18]

Participation and Organization

In order to be effective in planning and implementing intelligent development, it is critical that regional and local stakeholders have full and active involvement in the processes of strategy creation, the purpose of which is to ensure the engagement of the local city-region in the competitive external environment of the global knowledge economy. Additionally, effective stakeholder participation requires organization, mandated purpose, and the allocation of time and effort to that purpose.

Thoughtful delegation of strategic planning should promote various degrees of interest and engagement in local development policy planning processes by citizen, business, and institutional stakeholders. This range of involvement might include partnerships, consultation, informing for awareness, and education in general.[19] The objective here is to ensure that *ownership* among the policy-impacted stakeholders gets developed and embedded across the locality's development culture. Such participation and civil society enhancement are meant to contribute to the nurturing of mindset change and enterprise culture development of the city-region's various actors. This criterion is a reinforcement of the principle that involvement and transparency matter even in situations where formal representatives of the public interest are in place. Such broader involvement better ensures acceptance of and sustained support for investments that include public assets. Widespread and active participation across a range of stakeholders can serve to stimulate elected and other formal representatives to be more aware of local demands and needs and to thereby be more responsive in their strategizing and decision making.

The principle to be followed here is that if particular development goals are determined to be responsive to regional and local requirements, then it is important to organize to pursue and realize those goals. Without such organization, there is less chance of being successful in development goal attainment. Organization may be permanent or statutory, that is, codified in law or formal protocol, or organization may be temporary and quite task specific. The latter, more time-bound organization routinely might take the form of a task force, for example. Ideally, interdependent organized and participatory activities as described here should function to support, supplement, and extend the impact and capacity of the regional planning unit or citizen group of the city-region. Such complementary relationships both deepen and add substance to the overall intelligent development strategy creation effort.

Alignment of Politics and Policy

Politics is a process by which groups of people make decisions—usually within the context of civic and public affairs. Often, politics has been characterized as the art and science of government. However, political behavior is not limited to government. Rather, politics is practiced across a range of human groupings, for example, from business enterprises to churches and temples to universities and various other institutions such as political parties, civic and neighborhood organizations, families, and relationships between individuals. Political agreements and contested positions may be resolved and disputed by means of procedures, some of which are formal and codified, while others are ad hoc and informal in their execution. All of these activities are subject to the methods and tactics of politics and the managing of decisions in order to gain control or power. Excessively partisan politics often impedes governance, whereas the give-and-take of compromise may enable a wider range of interests to benefit from a decision.

The planning of policy outcomes may be seen as intelligent when the intended development benefits are widely perceived to be informed, thoughtful, and not narrowly self-serving. Thereby, the politics inherent in high-impact, expensive mega-engineering and infrastructure projects can be supported and shared by a broad base of indirect stakeholders as well as direct beneficiaries. This is the case when such projects are perceived as benefitting common regional and local interests—in addition to those interests that confer private gain—as in the case of a public–private partnership, say to build a new performing arts center in the central area of a city. In addition to practicing openness, the core message of this criterion is for the planning practitioners, their stakeholders, and the planning scholars in research support roles to seek to minimize fragmented and nonaligned decisions, policies, and programs. Instead, careful continuous attention needs to be given to the reinforcement, connection, and coordination of planning and implementation actions both vertically and horizontally. In other words, effective alignment of politics and policy should be sought at all relevant policy levels, from local to state to national and across jurisdictions, so as to achieve the intended policy results. Simply stated, when the politics and the policy are well aligned, then the intended results in the form of programs and projects are more likely to be realized, thereby benefitting the locality and the broader society.

Forward-Leaning and Strategic Planning

This criterion calls for us to shift our attention from means to ends, from analysis to action, and from the descriptive to the prescriptive. In order to move effectively from *understanding* to *creating* intelligent development regional strategies in the context of global information society, *forward-leaning* thinking and resulting behavior are required. Strategic planning envisions sustained development in seeking future states that are normative. That is, the focus is on what *should be* in contrast to what *is*. These normative futures are social constructs. They should be pursued by means of informed short-term, medium-term, and long-term stages of economic sectoral and cross-sectoral development, the functions of which are enabled by selected information that increasingly is more accessible to more people and more organizations owing to more pervasive, affordable, and routinely modernized digital development or ICT infrastructure and consumer information platforms.

Intelligent Development Defined

In today's global information society, when one reflects on defining *intelligent*, various characteristics apply. Principal among these is creativity and imaginative capacity; these resources can be invaluable in a global economy and society that increasingly are driven and advanced by information, knowledge, and pervasive digital and other technologies. Additional behavioral characteristics that confer "intelligent" on effective development include evidence-based *understanding*, as measured by sound judgment based on rational thought, flexibility, swift response, and alertness in assessing new conditions, solving resulting problems, capitalizing on opportunities, and creating strategies, tactics, and actions for future prosperity and happiness.

Such development and digital development planning, therefore, is "intelligent" when these global knowledge economy behaviors and best practices are influenced by appropriate theory and the latest research, based on innovative science and technologies that are utilized fully to develop systematically for the future a community and region holistically, equitably, and multifunctionally, including attention to amenity factors and quality-of-life functions so as to grow, retain, and attract knowledge workers. These social and cultural functions are in addition to the economic production and consumption factors of the new and old economies.

The tenth criterion is synthetic in nature. The big ten criteria above have been identified to enable the measurement and evaluation of the degree to which policies of intelligent development planning may be realized. The practice of development based on these behaviors represents a guiding and integrative profile for the would-be intelligent development planner both to follow and to perfect.

Three Criteria for Continuous Improvement of Intelligent Development Practice

Mind-Set Change

In order to ensure a deepening and continuity of ongoing learning in the city-region across a range of stakeholders with interests in the area's communities, factors are instrumental in affecting the transformation of regional and local cultures from old-economy thinking and behavior to embracing more fully the opportunities that are inherent in the new global knowledge economy and information and network society. These three continuous improvement criteria are (1) mind-set change, (2) translational research and translational practice, and (3) relational thinking and behavior.

The widespread practice of these intelligent development behaviors includes the goal of forming the *mind-set change* needed to realize desired futures for understanding, planning, implementing, evaluating, and creating competitive city-regions. Importantly, the process of transforming one's old path-dependent development practice behaviors entails *doing it*. As in the mastery of any new behavior, constant practice, more practice, and commitment to perfecting that practice are the core principles for success. These, then, are the behavioral practice criteria for creating a comprehensive intelligent development strategy.

Translational Research and Translational Practice

Some of the main intellectual domains for this work include the professions of development planning, economic development, and other related academic fields such as geography and urban and regional planning. See the preceding section of this chapter on research and theory for the disciplinary and practice fields that are sources for some of the selected applicable theory and research traditions. The two principal subdomains of translational behavior are academic research and city-region development practice. Functionally,

> both planning practice and the academic field are more experimental and responsive to new opportunities than the tenets of the formal profession, testing new ways in which planning can be effective.[20]

Planners Myers and Banerjee advocate further that academia should participate more within the subdomain of practice, and those practitioners should embrace newer emerging and more exploratory views of planning. By more joint work, the profession of development planning practice may be positioned to forge an agile forward-looking mind-set that prepares itself and its client city-regions for the future opportunities and challenges of the global information society. "Indeed, the time is ripe for achieving greater heights for all of planning. The town and gown divide has to be bridged to reach that goal."[21] A practical vision for advancing both intelligent development research and practice is to establish translational relationships that will enable localities and their research and educational institutions to benefit each other's missions and mandates by means of a reciprocal and ongoing bridging process.

A working definition of translational research and practice that has informed research and practice has been drawn from the book *Urban and Regional Technology Planning: Planning Practice in the Global Knowledge Economy*.[22] In this context, translational research is driven by an explicit objective of advancing and learning from the application of relational planning theory and practice.[23] Borrowing the translational concept from clinical and basic medical research and practice, there is a need for more academic planners and professional practitioner-planners to focus their respective effort *together* on the intersection of theoretical and basic city-region planning research, empirical exploratory planning research, and operational planning practice. Bidirectional feedback and exchange should be the rule at this interface. It is by means of reciprocal, reflexive interaction that the development planning profession and it stakeholders might more readily incorporate and internalize relational understanding and relational planning behavior, resulting in the realization of new relational mind-sets and relational approaches by all development planning practitioners.

The reflective practitioner concepts of Schön have also influenced translational research.[24] These behaviors are compatible with the new-economy dynamics that are impacting the world's regions and communities (see textbox 11.1).

Just as health care is informed by the biological sciences, the psychological sciences, and their clinical applications and practice, so has the profession of urban and regional development planning been informed by the social and behavioral sciences and the policy sciences and their empirical applications and practice. The establishment of an ongoing working translational relationship between local development practitioners and researcher counterparts has at least two contributions to make: one is to take a small partial step toward the ultimate *transformation of the practice and scholarship of regional development planning professions*. The regional development professions badly need to break free of their old-economy, path-dependent practice and reposition these fields to provide intellectual and practical leadership for regions and communities to prosper in the new economy—the global knowledge economy and the networked information society.

The second contribution of significance for advancing intelligent development is to demonstrate preliminarily how individual practicing planners and planning scholars working together in reciprocal beneficial relationships can make their client regions more competitive and thereby begin the transformation process of individual regional development planners' practice being empowered to shape local development in the context of today's highly

---

TEXTBOX 11.1
Translational Practice and Translational Research (TP and TR)
for Sustained Intelligent Development

- Using medical research and practice as the general model, TP and TR should be established, practiced, and perfected at the scale of the city-region. That is, by means of systematic learning from clinical practice, basic research is advanced, and from basic research findings, clinical practice is advanced.
- To be ongoing and sustainable, intelligent development therefore needs to be a function of joint, reciprocal, and mutually beneficial working partnerships between *development practitioners* and *scholars of development*. This is known as *translational research and translational practice*. Specifically, it is analogous to the kind of work that is conducted between medical clinicians and medical researchers that is encouraged and funded especially by the U.S. National Institutes of Health.
- Working relationships between local development practitioners and development researchers and academics need to be institutionalized in the region by means of engaging research universities, four-year universities, community colleges (junior colleges or polytechnics), research institutes, and individual scholars.
- These relationships are intended also to contribute to the advancement of mindset change and the formation of a culture of intelligent development throughout the local region.
- Routinely, external experts and expertise need to be drawn into intelligent development planning. This ensures the regular infusion of fresh outside and global perspectives in an effort to maintain deep and rich development pathways that are not dependent completely on local ways of thinking and doing. Both bringing outsiders in and sending insiders out are effective tactics here.

---

interconnected society and economy. Beyond the intellectual significance that may be associated with the two contributions just noted here, there may be an additional contribution to be made to demonstrate that the substantive issues of the global information society and new economy and their technology and globalization influences can be planned and implemented intelligently and effectively—not only in the often poor policy environments of city-regions but also in the policy-neglected environments of *rural and small-town regions.*

Relational Thinking and Behavior

The theoretical perspective that best encompasses the complexities of today's globalized and technological uncertainties is *relational theory*, including especially spatial organizational and locational concepts and models. Stephen Graham and Patsy Healey early on introduced relational thinking to the practice of spatial and temporal planning.[25] In her book *Urban Complexity and Spatial Strategies: Towards a Relational Planning for Our Times*, Patsy Healey offered her perspectives on the multidimensionality of relational thinking. Such perceptions involve a

> double shift, to a more complex appreciation of the multiplicity of relational dynamics to be found in urban areas, and to a perception of strategies as fluid, revisable frames of reference, [which] unsettles many of the established conceptions of the planning policy community, and of the wider governance cultures.[26]

In addition to the Healey book, Henry Yeung clarifies a highly abstract topic and makes relational thinking more concrete and subject to being made operational for development planning practice and pragmatic policy creation. Yeung identified the essence of the core spatial and economic relationships as (1) actor-structure relationality, including the roles that various principal stakeholders need to play locally to ensure a representative regional policy planning process; (2) scalar relationality, that is, global, national, regional, and local; and (3) sociospatial relationality, that is, economic, social, political, and spatial.[27] These relationalities are embedded in the range of information age socio-technical-economic functions and their linkages that drive local and regional economies. These features are summarized in textbox 11.2.

The Preconditions for Policy Planning

The foundation for activating the above policy concepts and understandings has been laid. In all, thirteen criteria have been identified as critical to a policy framework that may be used to engage local stakeholders in strategic development planning for the future. The big ten criteria of intelligent development behavior can be used to compile the information and develop the understanding needed to know most of what is required to change old-economy behaviors to behaviors that are compatible with the complex and dynamic forces of the new economy, the global knowledge economy, the network society, and the global information society. In order to set in motion a continuous improvement process for sustaining long-term culture change locally, three additional criteria have been identified. These were framed as the "three continuous improvement criteria." In chapter 12, these thirteen criteria, in concert with seven investment criteria and the ALERT model, are offered as the means to create a successful city-region for the global information society.

TEXTBOX 11.2
Illustrations of Relational Theoretical Thinking

- Relational thinking is characterized by ascribing meaning relative to other objects, movements, linkages, and flows of physical and intangible phenomena.
- It does not put sharp edges on objects and concepts.
- It explains relationships in terms that reflect well the empirical complexities of today's networked world.
- It captures today's often-blurred, frequently asymmetric realities and overlapping, often fluid processes.
- It is a nonlinear and nonsequential way of understanding "different opportunities" that may be prioritized within an open and dynamic planning framework.
- It avoids one-size-fits-all solutions.
- It is skeptical of reductionist, overly simplistic responses to complex issues, for example, the often dominant preference for yes-no, black-white, binary-type answers to diverse and complicated questions.
- Waiting and being prepared for an appropriate moment is part of anticipatory planning and action implementation.
- It recognizes the complex interrelationships among constituents and stakeholders.
- It acknowledges that there are many geographies, not just one administrative map or a one-dimensional hierarchy of scales (Healey 2007); other selected spatial organizational and location models that were noted in the text above and have been used in practice are

  - Growth poles and polycentricity
  - Industry life-cycle and product life-cycle models
  - Flexible production and flexible specialization
  - Learning regions and innovative milieus
  - Competitive advantage, comparative advantage, and regional advantage
  - Enterprise segmentation and unequal power
  - Innovation systems and regional innovation systems (Corey and Wilson 2006).

- Life-cycle thinking deserves special attention here especially as next-generation intelligent development strategizing is engaged. Analogous to the human life cycle of infancy, childhood, adolescence, adulthood, and aging, theories also mature and change. Early theoretical, modeling, and conceptual framework formulations typically evolve from less well-developed or qualitative measures; however, as they mature, they can lend themselves to measurement based on increased quantification, thereby permitting mathematical analyses. Higgins has offered a useful related metaphor—theorizing as parenting (Higgins 2004: 143–144). An important takeaway lesson is that practitioners and scholars should ensure that useful theories grow, are nurtured, and can be improved. Simply "give a theory a chance to develop and mature" (Higgins 2004: 144). Through concrete pragmatic application, relational theory will mature in the execution and it will support more effective and complex analyses and actions.

Some Good Practices in Policy Making to Explore

From a practical perspective, one should become familiar with policy exemplars and models to learn about the policy processes being used and to understand their use for strategic planning. Especially useful for mastering the practice of intelligent development planning is to have knowledge of *places* and *policy-organization practices*. Places are helpful because they are locations where diverse policies come together. Consequently, they must be planned and implemented in ways that are coordinated effectively while practicing policy-making processes that have been tested and proven. Since policies are developed in organizational context, knowledge of the cultures and behaviors of the policy actors and their linkages can be important in informing one's policy analysis, planning, and execution practices. Places from which policy lessons may be derived include Singapore, while an exemplary organization is the Public Policy Institute of California.

The government of Singapore's web portal is worth exploring because the city-state is a benchmark for intelligent development. It has even branded itself as an "Intelligent Island."[28] It was one of the earliest political economies in the global information society to adopt ICTs and digital development as one of the principal pillars for its development future. Since its digital development matured, it has been an early innovator in inventing policy planning processes and pursuing policy content goals that are intended to embrace and steer future development to capitalize on the forces of globalization and knowledge economy–based and networked society–connected behavior externally and internally. The government's web portal is both a comprehensive and practical window into the operational and working details of the policies that, having been planned and implemented, have resulted in an intelligent development place. In 2009, Singapore was ranked in the top ten nation-branding cases globally.[29] Singapore is a useful benchmark for place branding from tourism promotion, to opening its territory to new forms of educational knowledge, to Internet marketing strategies of business-to-consumer (B2C) firms.[30]

The Public Policy Institute of California (PPIC) is introduced here as an exemplar policy support organization for at least two reasons. First, it illustrates the kinds of translational research and translational practice services that can be established subnationally to inform effective public policy making. Second, and probably more important, is the role that PPIC can play as a benchmark and even as a best practice. The institute does particularly well researching policy issues associated with the new economy and global information society. For example, PPIC's research generates findings on the future and planning for future conditions, such as climate change; information technology infrastructure; the digital divide; other infrastructure, including transportation, water, the education system, energy, and seaports; regional cooperation and local alliances across borders; immigration; demographic change; civil society; and much more.

The institute conducts and publishes policy research on regions of the state as well as the statewide policy themes just listed. The PPIC website is quite useful and user friendly for policy education. The site can be searched by publication type, publication date, title, author, and policy area. The other PPIC searchable policy areas not already listed here include economic development, employment and income, government, health, housing, political participation, public finance, and social policy. Most useful are regular and periodic surveys that take public opinion on policy issues. The PPIC's home page, from a policy organization perspective, is a best-practice case that offers insight into the operational and working details of both policy analysis and policy planning.[31]

What other good-practices policy places and policy organizations can you uncover by your own intelligent development browsing, exploration, and research? The more good practice cases in policy making available, the richer the base of information from which policy performance might be analyzed, enhanced, and improved.

Conclusion

This chapter built on earlier policy and governance discussions and recommends the adoption of intelligent development as a mind-set and practice to advance information societies. Central to advocating policy directions is the recognition of information society as something socially constructed and created and not a form dictated by technology in isolation. The information societies we live in and experience do not emerge by accident but are the result of decision making that results in both intended and sometimes unintended consequences. There are examples of both admirable and poor policy decision making that shape information society, but most important is understanding that the ICT-based changes we see need to be understood and vetted.

Notes

1. Lakoff (2004: xv)
2. Rogers (1976: 225)
3. Brown (2005)
4. Ooi and Stöber (2008); Northwest Minnesota Foundation (n.d.)
5. Corey (2000)
6. Scott (2001: 813)

7. Scott (2001: 813)
8. Communities and Local Government (2006)
9. Ohmae (1996: 143)
10. Ohmae (2005: 94)
11. Ohmae (2005: 95)
12. Ohmae (2005: 111–115)
13. de Roo and Porter (2007: ix)
14. Plummer and Taylor (2001a; 2001b; 2003)
15. Graham and Healey (1999)
16. Healey (2007: 266)
17. U.S. Economic Development Administration (2002: 17–18)
18. Shirky (2008)
19. Arnstein (1969)
20. Myers and Banerjee (2005: 127)
21. Myers and Banerjee (2005: 128–129)
22. Corey and Wilson (2006)
23. Graham and Healey (1999); Healey (2006; 2007)
24. Schön (1983)
25. Graham and Healey (1999)
26. Healey (2007: 267)
27. Yeung (2005: 43)
28. Chun (1997)
29. *Straits Times* (February 15, 2009)
30. Ooi and Stöber (2008); Henderson (2007); Olds (2007); Teo and Tan, 2002)
31. Public Policy Institute of California (n.d.)

12

The Global Information Society

Moving from What *Is* to What *Should Be*

I N THIS ERA OF globalized information, where are we headed technologically and socially? Based on the preceding discussion, the future as influenced by the diverse forces of the global information society can be expected to see technology-based information and knowledge continue to become more widespread and ubiquitous. While the already diverse range of information technologies may be expected to become even more diverse, a principal result will be to increase the amount, flow, and access of information. As a consequence, strategic planning for near ubiquity of information and communications technologies (ICTs) and digital technologies should be factored into development policies at regional and local levels.

As cities and regions approach ubiquity of various ICTs for much of their businesses, institutions, and populations, one of the most important strategic questions for development is, now that our area has much of the digital infrastructure needed for processing information in today's global information society, what information content should be used and applied? How should we proceed to mobilize these assets for the future intelligent development of our city and region? This chapter offers a strategic-level planned change process to assist local-area stakeholders in responding to these kinds of questions for future development.

From Understanding Intelligent Development to the Creation of Intelligent Development

In chapter 11, we provided an understanding of the role of policy in the context of intelligent development. The factors for understanding intelligent development were presented as two sets of criteria:

Big Ten Criteria

1. Definitions and their derivation
2. Globalization and digital development
3. Research and theory
4. Comparative methods
5. Prioritized investments
6. Expertise of local experience and local knowledge
7. Participation and organization
8. Alignment of politics and policy
9. Forward-leaning and strategic planning
10. Intelligent development defined

Three Continuous Improvement Criteria

1. Mind-set change
2. Translational research and translational practice
3. Relational thinking and behavior

The focus now shifts from discussion of the criteria for *understanding* intelligent development to the *creation* of intelligent development. Of course, what is needed is to blend both understanding and creation in order to realize intelligent development. The criteria that are offered to facilitate and enable action and the creation of intelligent development include the ALERT model and policy investment criteria.

The ALERT Model 3.0

The ALERT model is a planning practice process for knowledge-based urban and regional development. It was constructed in order to provide to interested local stakeholders a means, in the global information society/knowledge economy/network society, to steer and shape future development—that is, intelligent development. It can be used to steer development toward directions that result in a competitive and prosperous city-region. The inputs for the model were derived from the global and long-term observations, discussions, and reflections by the book's authors.

The first generation of the ALERT model was presented initially in the book *Urban and Regional Technology Planning: Planning Practice in the Global Knowledge Economy*.[1] Since that time, the model has been developed further and perfected. A second-generation version was published in 2008[2] and was used to inform the development of this book and the way the subject of information society was approached. The third generation of the model offered here represents the latest, most focused version.

The ALERT model is composed of six principal elements. Critically, the model's execution is the responsibility of *stakeholders* in the target city-region. Stakeholders are the first element of the model that should be considered. The remaining five elements of the ALERT model are part of a continuous, strategic, and progressive planned-change process, the principal intent of which ultimately is to result in a region that is prepared and positioned to cope better with and advance in the context of the uncertainties, the complexities, and the relationalities of the global information society.

Stakeholders

In order to ensure that the strategies that are created from the work of the ALERT model are representative of, and owned by, the principal interests and the common interests of the city-region, these stakeholders have to be part of the discussion throughout the process. Depending on the unique characteristics of the region, careful attention must be given to the selection and involvement of representative stakeholders. Diversity is the name of the game here. Various locations in the region should be involved. Generational diversity increasingly is important. Partly this is a function of younger representatives of society often being more facile and innovative with information technologies, including mastering their rapid changes and new platforms.

Another important representative component of a society's diversity is gender. In many societies around the globe, women need to be welcomed into the strategic planning and implementation forums. In addition to age and gender heterogeneity, other representations should include ethnicities; vulnerable and traditionally excluded and marginalized castes and classes; the poor and other income groups beyond, but including, the wealthy; and so on. The key principle is to ensure that those members of local society who will be impacted by, and will be expected to contribute to, the execution of the planned policies, programs, projects, and actions will be participating from the beginning of the ALERT model process.

Around the world, many regions are planned by regional planning organizations or authorities. So becoming a part of such official organizations may be possible, for example, as a volunteer citizen planner. Otherwise, in regions where such voluntary involvement is not possible, via community organizing it may be feasible to initiate new or to join existing grassroots efforts to participate in development planning activities. Such situations may offer opportunities to have input into development planning processes. Active nonofficial groups may influence elected officials, as well as the priorities of local regional planning organizations. These activities are important for mobilizing or resurrecting a civil society at the local level. Organizations engaged in active civil society can seek to get citizen and other specific interests represented in the development priorities that are planned by local regional planning authorities.

The organizational contexts for involvement probably should assume multiple and diverse forms—from formal to informal, from permanent to temporary or term-limited groupings, and from professional to volunteer actors. Organized, coordinated, and locationally representative systems can generate policy outcomes that reflect the cultural variations of the communities and areas of the target city-region. Direct and indirect linkages to the city-region's regional planning organization are likely to be welcomed to contribute to the official feedback functions for planning the area's development futures. Refer to chapter 13 for exercises that might be used by citizens and regional interests for such involvement.

Awareness

Awareness of the city-region's resources and assets should come from analysis of *evidence*. In order to develop the knowledge of what the region's mix of principal development functions and assets is, the first stage of the ALERT model process begins with ongoing activities of compiling *evidence* on the basic facts and state of the region. This information is needed to acquire the understanding and initial awareness of what makes the target region function now and ultimately into the future. This phase of the model sets the initial stage for inculcating a culture locally for the continuous function of information collection to have a local data base from which to inform policy analysis and policy planning. This phase of the ALERT model process therefore involves evidence gathering, especially for the purpose of becoming operationally aware of the city-region's development-driving economic and social functions that are primarily internal to the target region. The outcome of this phase of the model is initial general awareness of the region's development potential and challenges.

Layers

In order to understand the city-region's *context* and identity globally, it is essential to continue to compile evidence. However, in contrast to the ALERT model's awareness element, this phase requires comparative information gathering about the region's external relationalities. Framing this evidence gathering as engaging in benchmarking and identifying best practices and good practices is a useful way to generate informed understandings for inputs to policy planning for intelligent development.

> Best and good practices are structured information (ranging from analytical reports to narratives) about successful experiences in local contexts, concerning issues generally acknowledged as relevant, evaluated according to a set of criteria. They aim to spread knowledge and information and are selected, codified, diffused and used in many ways depending on the institutional, economic, cultural and political situations.[3]

The primary outcome of this stage of the model is additional awareness. In this case, the awareness is of the context of the city-region; its present relationships to the world external to the local area are part of the understanding needed for initial comprehensive strategic-level knowledge of the target region.

E-Business

In order for the region's stakeholders to understand what drives the local economy and society, it is important to identify its principal economic sectors along with their functions and contributions to the prosperity, well-being, and livability of the regional community. It is critical to acquire a working knowledge of the region's development assets. There are two basic factors about which information needs to be gathered and analyzed. A detailed understanding is needed of the city-region's *infrastructure* (both material and digital) and the sources of *financing* that comprise the region's principal investment patterns. This evidence is essential. Without detailed knowledge of the infrastructural systems and funding capacities (public and private sources) of the region, the feasibility of executing future development strategies will remain nonoperational.

Further, specific answers must be found to the question of what is the fundamental set of economic driving forces of the region in content or substantive terms. From the perspective of the region's interests, this learning process might proceed best from the macro to the micro level of understanding. For example, at the macro level, it is useful to classify the local regional economy by three macroeconomic sets of economic drivers in the context of the global information society: (1) production functions, (2) consumption functions, and (3) quality-of-life and amenity functions. One is reminded that in the dynamic environment of the new economy, as facilitated by ICTs and driven by the various forces of globalization, it is the *production functions* that merit particular attention and understanding. These functions can include advanced services that result in higher-skilled talent and higher-income jobs.[4] These assets require detailed inventorying at the scale of the city-region so that they can be built on and leveraged in future intelligent development strategy planning and policy making.

Next, the *consumption functions* include those retail and wholesale activities that provide the basic needs for people, families, and enterprises of the target region. Among other activities, these consumption functions include commerce (i.e., the exchange, buying, and selling of services and goods, both electronic and nonelectronic) as well as business-to-business and business-to-consumer transactions.[5] Consumption functions are interdependent in the local regional economy with the jobs created and multiplied in the sectors of the production functions (economic base theory applies here). The *quality-of-life and amenity factors* are critical to the local city-regional economy, particularly because they can operate to retain and attract knowledge and information workers. The quality of these factors is instrumental in the new economy locally. Places and areas with high-quality assets of the regional natural environment and a high quality of local educational institutions, housing, and health care, among other amenities, are complementary and supportive of those engaged in the production and consumption sectors. The result needed from this phase of the model is detailed knowledge and understanding of the city-region's principal economic drivers and the quality of local society. Such understanding may be used to consider the creation and formulation of exporting and inward investment strategies that bring external assets into the local region.

Note the use here of "e-" that precedes the word "business." The choice of this wording is intentional. It seeks to convey the permeation of electronic facilitation, ICTs, automation, and other technological process improvements throughout all aspects of doing contemporary business, that is, working and living in today's and tomorrow's modern global information society. So *business* is used in its generic sense, that is, in the sense of conducting a task or pursuing an objective. As used here, it should not be interpreted *only* in the sense of conducting commerce, trade, and industry, but definitely including profit-generating activities.

Responsiveness

Development priorities for the future of the region need to be determined here. Therefore, this stage of the model's process should identify, select, and prioritize those greatest economic demand and greatest social need policies, programs, projects, and actions for investment in the future. In this phase of the ALERT model, there is a noteworthy shift from the three earlier elements of awareness, layers, and e-business to the last two elements of the model, responsiveness and talk. The shift is from a primary concern for *understanding* the city-region toward the *creation* of a more competitive and effective one by means of intelligent development strategic planning. This shift is from what *is* the region's current state or condition toward what *should be* the region's future condition and state. It is a shift from analysis to action.

Having accumulated the knowledge and understanding of the city-region by means of earlier evidence gathering, the core function of this stage of the model is to determine the degree to which (1) the marketplace is responsive to *economic demand* and the degree to which (2) local society is responsive to the *societal and social welfare needs* of the region and its communities. For example, South Korea, in the late 1990s leapfrogged from being a minor player in digital development to becoming one of the most connected economies in the world.

South Korea's transformation was accomplished by the partnering of key actors in the private sector and government. By responding to demand for computers for video games and household and family applications, and by encouraging competition among ICT service providers, prices for broadband services were made affordable. There was recognition among South Korea's private-sector and public-sector interests that the spatially dense, often high-rise building patterns and locations greatly facilitated networking connections. Additionally, the provision of widespread training and education in computer usage and computer literacy served to raise the scale of demand for computer applications generally throughout the society. This is the kind of comprehensive perspective and coordination leading to the intelligent development of planned interventions among interdependent relationships that can serve as a model of good practice for stimulating creative strategic behavior in one's target region.

The principal outcomes of this responsiveness element of the ALERT model are investment priorities. As noted above, *investment policy criteria* are routinely used by decision makers and policy planners to assign evidence-based priorities to particular policies and their related programs and projects. The U.S. Economic Development Administration, for example, applies evaluative guidelines when making funding allocations to localities. These *policy investment criteria* include

- being market based and results driven;
- demonstrating strong organizational leadership;
- advancing productivity, innovation, and entrepreneurship;
- looking beyond the immediate economic horizon to anticipate economic changes and diversify the local regional economy;
- demonstrating a high degree of local commitment by exhibiting high levels of local-government or nonprofit *matching funds* and private-sector leverage;
- demonstrating a high degree of local commitment by clear and *unified leadership* and support by local elected officials; and
- demonstrating a high degree of local commitment by *strong cooperation* between the business sector, relevant regional partners, and local, state, and federal governments.[6]

When the intentions of these criteria are substantially met, they may be determined to be *responsive* to many of the diverse forces and relationships of the global information age. Refer to the support section at the end of this book for exercises that might be used by citizens and regional interests for developing such a working understanding of the demands, needs, gaps, and disparities that should be used to inform policies, programs, projects, and actions.

Determining responsive policies and their priorities may be stimulated in many different ways. For the purpose of fastening one's mind around this issue, three approaches are introduced briefly: (1) approaches from elsewhere, (2) anticipation strategies, and (3) remembering the basics.

Approaches from Elsewhere

From our observations and research of information society policies around the world, five noteworthy *strategic-level lessons* were found to be critical in intelligent development planning. These included (1) human capital development, (2) enterprise culture development, (3) alternative governance development, (4) equity development, and (5) mind-set change in support of achieving and sustaining new-economy and network society competitive advantage.[7] Since mind-set change was discussed in chapter 5, four of these lessons are noted here.

The fundamental nature of the new economy and the globalized information society demands a talented workforce. A workforce is needed that is well educated substantively, especially in those production sectors discussed above in the section on e-business. A workforce is needed that also brings inventiveness and creativity to the local regional economy and society. Again, one is reminded that the trend increasingly is for mind power to strengthen and grow at the expense of muscle power locally as well as globally. This trend consequently requires policies and programs in support of the *interdependent development of human capital and enterprise culture—* both in the short term and through long-term continuous investment. Those places that do not give sustained high priority of investment in local human capital and the evolution of a local culture of entrepreneurship and innovation are doomed to have to rely too heavily on importing such talent in contrast to nurturing the potentialities of talent already in the region. In times of tight economic and fiscal constraints, the worst policy stance to be taken in the context of the global knowledge economy and network society is to cut investments and budgets that are funding human capital and enterprise culture development. This is analogous to the farmer eating the seed corn that is needed to grow future crops.

In an era when old economy–organized governments and institutions continue too often to demonstrate unresponsiveness and or incompetence, the need for innovation in governance has become a topic of strategic concern and importance. The need for more effective collective decision making—or *governance*—has received a great deal of attention. There is a rich and informative literature on the need for new governance responses that are better suited to the complexities and complicated relationalities of the new global information society and new economy.[8]

Unfortunately, while the academic discussion of the need for responsible and responsive governance is rich, the actual practice and implementation of successful governance that is more befitting of the new-economy development realities is quite thin. With the primary focus being on the common good, both territorial and organizational changes require systematic study and reflection. Transformational alliances and more jurisdictional boundary fluidity might be more responsive to the new global information society realities. The European Union is exemplary for its creativity and innovation with both regional and continental governance experimentation. The EU's experience in governance merits our ongoing monitoring and assessment.

Disparities and gaps across regional economies and societies demand special collective attention. With today's localities being so highly connected and networked, the regions of states and countries can ill afford to have significant areas and segments of their communities be a drag on their collective prosperity and happiness. Vicious cycles of outmigration and hyperurbanization often result in small towns and rural areas losing their younger generation, the most highly valued asset for future development. Consequently, issues of *equity* and social justice must drive priority setting for policy investments. This is one of those seed corn metaphors that were referenced above. The development requirements in this context demand important and continuous high-priority investments. Over time, such priorities are likely to demonstrate the prescience and wisdom of intelligent development planning.[9]

Anticipatory Strategies

Intelligent development planners practice informed forward-leaning responses to economic demand and social need for the target region. For example, advanced industrial economies have lost many jobs to lower-wage locations through offshoring. By understanding those occupations that are offshorable and those that are less likely to be sent overseas, smarter strategies may be formulated and planned that better anticipate the future, especially in situations where job creation strategies break away from legacy occupations and move to new jobs dependent on knowledge and creative talent, in contrast to more routine and less innovative production activities. Japanese and U.S. Rust Belt regions are cases in point. In Europe, eastern Germany recently has been debating how best to respond to investment priorities for future development—manufacturing or research.[10] By creating strategies for job growth, retention, and attraction that are informed by the Blinder index, regional intelligent development planners might more effectively shape local prosperity. For example, if debating local jobs creation for computer programmers and telemarketers versus a range of technicians (in engineering, information, and environmental sciences) and legal and human resources support occupations, one would lean toward investing in the latter sectors over the former. Simply put, informed decisions in setting priorities and encouraging policies and investments based on solid research findings are likely to produce more successful futures for a region. Such research-based strategic planning can be put in place by investing in the establishment of ongoing translational relationships between local practicing development planners and accessible researchers, both local and distant. What additional anticipations might be used locally—in your city-region—to inform and enhance responsiveness (of the ALERT model) for more intelligent development?

Remember the Basics—They Matter

Before directly addressing issues of planning the region's future, it is useful to be reminded that part of wise responsiveness is to continue to make investment priorities that require updating and modernization. The core theme of this book is the globalization of information—which is possible only by means of information and communications technologies. As a consequence, it is imperative that city-regions, and especially rural small-town regions, pay close attention to the area's *digital development*. The equity lesson needs attention when considering access to ICTs, especially the pattern of uneven spatial distribution of broadband service and digital infrastructure. Such connectivity is critical both to individual consumers and to firms and institutions for doing business and thereby contributing to local development. Increasingly, without affordable access to such technology, intelligent development is largely out of reach for the locality. Such isolation dooms places to stunted competitive potential in comparison to other places that have a modern digital development advantage.

In addition to the critical electronic infrastructure just noted, the region's *physical infrastructure* represents another of the fundamental building blocks and investment targets for the future intelligent development of local communities. Roads, utilities, water, sanitation, rail lines, airports, and many other contemporary facilities are essential. In the electrified global information society, electricity generation and the electrical grid are particularly strategic necessities.[11] As governments worldwide have sought to stimulate their economies in response to the recent economic crisis, modernization and extension of such infrastructure has often received the highest priority for investment. Immediate local job creation that results from such investment, beyond the recent worldwide financial crisis investments in infrastructure, needs to be routinized as one of the basic ongoing responses for competitive intelligent development in the globalized network society by way of sustainable modernization practices.

The other basic building block in responding to ongoing intelligent development priorities and investments is *financing*. This means obtaining and providing the funding and the resources needed for high-priority investments. Depending on the particular priority, the financing may be a function of actors from the public sector, or the for-profit sector, or individuals, or some combination of partners. Given the large expenditures often associated with regional development, having the creditworthiness necessary to borrow into the future is essential. Responsible financing, however, means staying within the means available such that future generations are not overly burdened with too heavy a debt load. The strategic balancing of priorities over future planning periods and in light of the ability to pay and or pay off credit-based debt requires skill, honesty, and openness.

As noted in chapter 11, Singapore is a benchmark for intelligent development policy. The financing and infrastructure investment culture of Singapore, for example, is a good practice and a model for emulation in bringing together the intelligent development basics of digital development or electronic infrastructure; material and physical infrastructure; and transparent, noncorruptible financing. Indeed, after initial financing, Singapore's practice of self-financing for ongoing strategic priority investments is the kind of good practice to which other places should aspire.

Talk

The culmination of the ALERT modeling process is the sixth element, labeled "talk." This label is adopted to convey the core activity of this stage— the importance of *continuous active engagement* among the stakeholders of the city-region. In order to create strategic scenarios to guide and steer future intelligent development, the stakeholders in the target region need to imagine end-state futures. These scenarios are creations that are normative and prescriptive in nature. They are driven by what *should* be developed in the future. They should be both aspirational and pragmatic. Critically, the activities and outcomes from the prior elements of the ALERT model should be drawn on, selected, and integrated creatively. This strategic bringing together represents the required preconditions needed in order to shape and construct new futures that respond to the economic demand and social need that have been revealed via the analytic and action activities implemented in the ALERT model.

Importantly, the nearly unlimited planning possibilities of the future should be made more manageable by organizing the future into workable phases. For example, short-term, medium-term, and long-term future periods spanning a human generation have been found to be useful for the purposes of planning intelligent development. To illustrate, in real time, the short-term phase might be framed as an annual one- to two-year period or in the one- to eight-year range; the medium term might be set at nine to eighteen years; and the long-term period might cover the nineteen- to twenty-five-year time frame. These periods may be varied of course to suit the needs of the area; however, the long-term period should be set out a human generation into the future. Once the future development end states have been constructed and are under implementation, it is essential to generate the information and metrics needed to make necessary midcourse corrections. This necessitates conducting periodic surveys and assessments; consequently, monitoring and evaluation designs need to be planned and executed.

Conceptually, a practical technique that can be used to engage those stakeholders and actors with active interests in the region's future intelligent development planning is the open-systems planning approach.[12] This approach enables one to frame policy planning as follows:

- what *is*, or creation of the present scenario;
- what *will be*, or creation of a realistic future scenario—anticipate, project, forecast, and identify trends; and
- what *should be*, or creation of an idealistic future scenario—dream, imagine, and practice creativity.

For the highest-order mind-set advocated here for future planning, programs, and projects responsive to the region's demands and needs, the action priority should be in planning for feasible future scenarios that are phased in realistically over the short term, medium term, and long term. For more on operational details involved in actively constructing futures scenarios, see the book *Engaging the Future: Forecasts, Scenarios, Plans and Projects*.[13] For a future perspective, consider *Mind Set! Reset Your Thinking and See the Future*.[14] Refer to the support section at the end of this book for exercises that might be used by citizens and regional stakeholders to develop intelligent development strategies using the charrette approach.

The Kind of Talk That Stimulates Engagement and Informed Action

Operationally, the heart of the talk element of the ALERT model was defined above as continuous active engagement among the target region's representative stakeholders. Dialogue, debate, and synergistic outcomes are central to the intended ongoing engagement. In the context of stimulus-response, such engagement are the means, and the intended ends are informed planned policies and supportive actions that generate equitable and prosperous city-regions that are prepared to compete in an increasingly information-overloaded world. While the framework and mind-set of intelligent development planning, including the ALERT model, can assist in engaging the globalized information economy, it is the quality and effectiveness of policy that will largely determine the development performance of the target region. With so many places around the global economy approaching ubiquity of ICTs and digital development, imagination and creativity are at the core of a region's comparative advantage.

The ALERT Model as a Whole

Once the stakeholders have completed an initial round of the ALERT model process, then the intelligent development planner should feel free to behave nonlinearly and crossruff the phases and elements of the model. Since intelligent development planning is ongoing and continuous, the accumulation of information and knowledge enables one to improve and dig deeper into the model's subsystems. The ALERT model functions on evidence-based and criteria-measured benchmarks and from information and locally tailored bases. This enables more effective decision making, greater accountability, and transparency. These characteristics represent good practice and in particular are supportive of a responsible and healthy local civil society.

Measuring the Progress of Planned Comprehensive Intelligent Development Strategies

In all, twenty-six criteria and elements have been suggested in chapters 11 and 12. These criteria can and should be used to monitor and evaluate a city-region's status toward achieving the intelligent development strategies that have been planned. These include

- the big ten criteria of intelligent development behavior,
- the three criteria for continuous improvement of intelligent development practice, and
- the seven policy investment criteria.

These twenty criteria, in turn, are framed by the process and six elements of the ALERT Model 3.0. These include

1. stakeholders and the region's planners;
2. *A*wareness based on evidence internal to the region;
3. *L*ayers placing the region in external context;
4. *E*-business assessment of the regional economy's production, consumption, and amenities quality of life as facilitated by infrastructure and financing;
5. *R*esponsiveness of the region's economic marketplace and social welfare institutions to stakeholder demands and needs; prioritized investment goals are the principal outcomes of this element of the ALERT model; and
6. *T*alk, which involves continuous engagement of the region's stakeholders; the principal outcomes are planned future scenarios that are staged over the short term, the medium term, and the long term. Surveying and monitoring for the assessment of progress and midcourse corrections are part of the ongoing engagement and evaluation of the ALERT strategic planning.

By using the twenty criteria and the six ALERT elements, one may monitor and evaluate the status and progress being made on the planned futures that have been created using the overall comprehensive intelligent development strategy approach.

The entire system of comprehensive intelligent development strategy creation as designed and intended will produce *actionable knowledge*. In turn, as the ALERT model system and the processes embedded among its various components are implemented and activated, the stakeholders and planners will need to take their strategies deeper into the tactical action levels. As deepening progresses, the general intentions or *policies* need to be translated into increasingly more operational and concrete *programs, projects, and actions*.

From this continuous activation, the practice of relational behavior, and the support of local planning by means of institutionalized translational relationships, one may expect the mind-set change needed to transform the region's economy and society into an enterprise culture that behaves more competitively and effectively. This future vision can be realized fully by embracing the twenty-six criteria, and in the process of making them real empirically and locally, it is imperative to add one's particular improvements and unique creativity to the mix. This is not unlike learning and practicing the fundamentals of making music. Once the basics have been learned, then one might be positioned to perfect and improvise such that simple information has been transformed into strategic and actionable knowledge.

Beyond Talk: Place Promotion, Branding, and Organization for Planning Implementation

Once stakeholders and planners have completed an initial cycle of executing the ALERT model, it is critical to follow through. It is important to avoid the situation in which a strategy gets generated but remains unused or unaddressed. In addition to the monitoring and evaluation activities that have been noted elsewhere in this book, planned strategy realization requires ongoing attention and nurturing, or elimination if no longer relevant.

With the world-class place promotion event of the Shanghai Expo 2010 fresh in our mind, it is an excellent case from which to derive marketing and promotional lessons. The place promotion mind set of Shanghai has been in continuous development and evolution for some time.[15] Similar long-term place promotion will be needed for any city-region that has gone through an ALERT modeling process. This applies to large city-regions such as Shanghai as well as small-town and rural regions and other intermediate-sized places.

A good practice case[16] in rural place branding is Ingenuity Frontier.[17] It is a collaborative project of the Northwest Minnesota Foundation, Bemidji State University, the Headwaters Regional Development Commission, Northland College, and the Minnesota Department of Employment and Economic Development. These partners have strategized (1) to increase the local region's talent pool in manufacturing and applied engineering, (2) to promote a culture locally of innovation in manufacturing and applied engineering, and (3) to brand rural Northwest Minnesota as a hub of manufacturing and applied engineering talent and innovation.

To implement these goals, the partners are executing "a targeted marketing campaign to attract high-skill workers and businesses to Northwest Minnesota." They framed their branding strategy around the organizing concept of ingenuity as "an imaginative and clever design or construction."[18] Promotion in cyberspace is an essential ingredient in today's global information society.[19] Thus the regional planning organization needs to ensure that new-economy capacity-building initiatives are well marketed and disseminated through national and global networks.

As has been noted elsewhere in this book, organization is essential for planning. The same is true for implementation. There needs to be an organized effort, ideally mobilized by a local regional organization staffed by professional planners mandated to implement strategies and with mind-sets and experience in the practice of intelligent development. Such mobilization is often most effective when executed in collaboration with the active involvement of the business and nongovernmental communities of the region. Without these capacities, it may be necessary to organize stakeholder volunteers to do the job or to collaborate with local planning organizations to complement their planning practice. Refer to chapter 13 for some analogous suggestions on how such resources and volunteer capacity might be mobilized.

It should be noted that audiences and participants both internal and external to the target planning region need to be addressed by these ongoing planning approaches of place promotion, branding, and organization for implementation of the region's planned strategies. Campaigns of information and communication for the education of both insiders and outsiders are central in today's highly globalized and interdependent environments.

Coming Full Circle

The ALERT model was derived from our empirical translational research and our engagement with the global knowledge economy and network society. Thereby, we were positioned to integrate our long-standing empirical practice work with directly relevant theoretical and conceptual statements from a wide range of disciplinary and practice fields.

This integration of the empirical and the theoretical was framed in the book *Urban and Regional Technology Planning: Planning Practice in the Global Knowledge Economy.*[20] One of the principal subthemes of that book was to ensure that development practitioners, both professionals and citizen volunteers, had their particular development interests introduced and addressed.

Indirectly, the writings of Patsy Healey, especially on governance and collaboration, have been supportive of our conceptualization of intelligent development behavior. Patsy Healey is a pioneering thinker and interpreter at the seam of development planning theory and practice.[21] Early in the life cycle of the influence of Habermas' theory of communicative action[22] in planning, Healey's article "Planning through Debate: The Communicative Turn in Planning Theory" was instrumental in stimulating fresh and progressive thinking among development and planning academics and practitioners.[23] The early ideas for this article were sketched out in 1990.[24] Judith Innes captured this significant shift in dominant thinking in her article "Planning Theory's Emerging Paradigm: Communicative Action and Interactive Practice."[25] During this early stage in the evolution of communicative action theory, Innes in 1994 wrote a particularly prescient and concise statement:

> A new paradigm of planning is taking shape in which planning is increasingly seen as primarily an interactive, communicative and discursive process. The ideas which frame this view are drawn from Habermas, Giddens, Forester, Healey and Sager, among others. The research on practice shows that increasingly, plans, policies and implementation strategies are developed through group processes, often involving stakeholders, or through networks of interconnected participants in constant communication. In this type of process, information is produced and used differently than in the conventional approach where experts advise policy officials, or planners act as information providers and plan makers. Knowledge of more kinds from more sources is used, including the knowledge of citizens and other stakeholders. Often a conscious effort is made to negotiate over knowledge and socially construct a shared view of the "facts" and the problem. In this context, it is less appropriate to seek knowledge to serve instrumental rationality, and more to serve the goal of communicative rationality. For planning processes to be communicatively rational, they must attempt to meet conditions of ideal speech and discourse. These differ significantly from the criteria of scientific method.[26]

So, going on two decades later, Innes' statement is reflected significantly in our intelligent development formulation. Additionally, in the applied public policy realm of national economic development, including at the substate scale, the administration of President Barack Obama has embraced key communicative planning and action criteria for investment priorities for federal funds in collaborative regional innovation and to help economically distressed and underserved communities.[27] It should be noted further that these communicative planning concepts entered the literature just *before* the Internet began to diffuse throughout the global knowledge economy and well before social media reached the current stage of near ubiquity that we experience today.[28] Again, the intended readership of this book should range across the generations and the many interests that comprise our local and global societies. The actors and roles, in general, should include representative early-stage through mature-stage businesses, all levels of government, relevant development institutions, workers and unions, community organizations, and individuals. Particular stakeholders are

- large, small, and medium-sized business enterprises as well as organized labor;
- public-sector actors and organizations from various levels/layers of government, such as local, multijurisdictional, and regional, including executive office and elective office holders (e.g., local legislative representatives);
- nongovernmental and not-for-profit institutions, especially human capital representatives of primary/preschool to tertiary school levels; social welfare organizations; and other place-specific governance actors not noted above; and
- selected individuals and students, ensuring that cross-generational representatives and cultural/ethnic diversity are in the mix.[29]

All of these roles and actors that should influence regional and local development futures need to be at the table in order for intelligent development to have an opportunity to be realized.

We believe that the stage has been set, theoretically, translationally, and in preparation for practice, for the empowerment of our reader-stakeholders to engage in influencing the intelligent development of their city-regions. From this engagement and informed decision making, one can expect an elevation in the quality of public as well as corporate policy planning and implementation. One should also expect more voices—indeed, more informed voices—to be at the local tables of development strategizing. Institutionalized and elected actors across global and local society need to have all interests at the table to ensure that growth and equity are represented in future development.

Looking to the Future

Drawing inspiration from Nietzsche's "New Barbarian" spirit, Angell and Ezer have observed that "while the West struggles to *understand* the information age using its outmoded ways of thinking, a sub-class in India is *defining* this new era."[30] They state further that

> ICTs herald a new age—an age that marks the end of development as we know it. Technology becomes our means of interpretation, and influences our explanations of the world. ICTs give a different explanation as technology is absorbed into the background of our interpretation. Those most free from the shackles of ritualized myth are the most able to take advantage of new interpretations. And it is those on the periphery that are the least constrained by conventional wisdom.[31]

As suggested by Angell and Ezer, being on the periphery of the globalized new economy may represent a comparative opportunity for emergent economies. Being relatively less burdened by prior and conventional approaches (i.e., path dependency), developing economies and developing regions may have greater freedom for innovation, if only because their producers and consumers have relied less on old-economy thinking and behavior as compared to the more developed industrialized economies and regions.

However, if the people and institutions of any region can motivate themselves to use the new realities of the new global information society, the new knowledge economy, and the new networked society to set themselves on a new pathway of practicing and perfecting intelligent development, then they should be able to compete more effectively. Thereby, such places can be positioned to invent and create new development content and strategies that use digital development and are more liberated from old thinking and behavior. Fresh imaginative content directions are likely to result.

Such behavioral transformation is analogous to mastering music by means of perfection through practice and performance. It involves initiating and establishing the new intelligent development mind-set. Even more critical, once that mind-set begins to be imprinted, it is the continuous perfection via practice that enables the intelligent development practitioner to use relational thinking and behavior to demonstrate mind-set change on a routine basis. Ideally, such practice behavior would be developed and strengthened in *translational* interdependence with researcher-scholars. From these mutually supportive relationships, then, one is positioned to advance, extend, and practice value-added development. By being informed by the intelligent development criteria presented earlier and by benchmarking a city-region's new development performance against good practices elsewhere, one has the comparative indicators that can be used systematically to initiate planning and assess the new development outcomes, and in the process improve competitiveness, attractiveness, and investment opportunities.

The overarching goal for this book has been to suggest that in the new world of excessive information and hypercomplexities, some sense can be made through analysis, and some useful actions can be taken to influence local future development. The book's various frameworks and their use have pointed to pathways for taking interdependent informed actions. These frameworks can be used to evaluate and make judgments about the quality of planning done by others, especially by unresponsive or incompetent politicians who rely on seat-of-the-pants decision making rather than informed and thoughtful decisions. And these frameworks can be used to inform one's own planning strategies and efforts. Imagination and creativity, when applied intelligently and strategically, are offered here as key ingredients for the empowerment and mobilization needed to influence successful development in the future.

Notes

1. Corey and Wilson (2006)
2. Wilson and Corey (2008)
3. Vettoretto (2009: 1069)
4. Blinder (2007)
5. Corey and Wilson (2009)
6. U.S. Economic Development Administration (n.d.)
7. Corey and Wilson (2006: 178–179)
8. Healey (2007); de Roo and Porter (2007)
9. Rawls (2001); Cramme and Diamond (2009)
10. Dougherty (2009)
11. Schewe (2007)
12. Jayaram (1976)
13. Hopkins and Zapata (2007)
14. Naisbitt (2006)
15. Wu (2000)
16. Vettoretto (2009)
17. Northwest Minnesota Foundation (n.d.)
18. Northwest Minnesota Foundation (n.d.: 1)
19. Aurigi (2005)
20. Corey and Wilson (2006)
21. Innes and Booher (2010: 25)
22. Habermas (1984)
23. Healey (1992)
24. Healey (1992)
25. Innes (1995a)
26. Innes (1995b)
27. U.S. Economic Development Administration (n.d); U.S. Economic Development Administration (2011)
28. Wilson and Corey (2011)
29. Yeung and Lin (2003); Lim (2003)
30. Angell and Ezer (2006: 165)
31. Angell and Ezer (2006: 175)

IV

SUPPORT SECTION

13

Intelligent Development Planning Charrette

Understanding the processes and impacts associated with the evolution of information society is just a start. For social scientists there is also the desire to harness changes in society to gain benefits and minimize harm. The goal of this learning exercise is to apply what we have learned so far and to practice the process of establishing an intelligent development strategy for a local community, although other scales of application will also work. This strategy is intended (1) to identify and prioritize local strategic investment opportunities in the context of the global knowledge economy and network society and (2) to plan the priority investments into the future. The charrette is a learning exercise intended to prepare one, in concert with others, to engage in *co-learning* in order to be able to practice the *co-creation* of planned strategies for better future states for one's city-region.

What is the ultimate end state of this learning? The exercise involves learning and practicing (1) the planning of *behavioral process activities* and (2) the creation of *knowledge economy and network society content outcomes*. Both of these functions are interdependent and are needed to practice intelligent development planning and implementation effectively and on a continuous-improvement basis.

The Need

Citizens, businesspersons, government officials, and other stakeholders should be positioned to understand, practice, and routinely utilize the processes of intelligent development. In order to accomplish this, a method is needed that works—especially for overcommitted and busy participants. Ideally, what is needed is a method that can also be used within a relatively short period of time to demonstrate and motivate participants to implement intelligent development planning for their locality. The charrette may be the method that best addresses most of these capacity challenges.

What Is a Charrette and Why Use It?

Traditionally, a charrette is an intensive effort to complete a project quickly. In the context of this book, a charrette is an intensive planning task by multiple persons to seek a shared regional development vision, and in the process to develop a working understanding of the factors that comprise the vision. Also, the charrette offers a context and opportunity to collaborate with others in the design of the actions needed to attain the vision.

For the purposes of mastering the content and processes of intelligent development planning, a charrette has the following attributes and benefits:

- It takes place within a compressed, limited time period.
- It enables an awareness of cause-and-effect relationships that can be derived from analysis of the region's principal economic drivers and their national and global context.
- This awareness can be used to inform actions that might be taken to address the gaps and disparities between the region's current state of development and its desired development. These actions are framed in the form of planned scenarios for various future states of development.
- Especially at the beginning of a group learning process, a charrette can be used to produce an early synoptic agreement on a planned comprehensive strategy that encompasses and aligns the means and ends relationships needed to attain the desired states of development in the future.
- The charrette method aids in laying out general options for informed choice. By debating priorities for investment and alternatives among planned futures, the space is provided to bring evidence, ideas, politics, and policy options to bear systematically and by means of thoughtful group dialogue and debate.
- Joint ownership of solutions is promoted by moving through the charrette method.
- The charrette facilitates the collaboration of diverse stakeholders with multiple interests in the development of the region. These interests and stakeholders should include businesspersons, workers, residents, vol-

unteer citizen planners and professional planners, youngsters such as students and young adults, representatives of nonprofit organizations, and so on.

Importantly, in order to diffuse and broaden involvement in and to produce the desired impacts of intelligent development planning and implementation throughout the planning region, the charrette technique may be used by planners to train for needed mind-set change and to help operationalize the working criteria of intelligent development among the region's representative stakeholders. The desired and intended result is the establishment of a mind-set and culture in which imagination, creativity, enterprise, equity, and the routine nurturing of successful development performance and happiness become the norm among the region's stakeholders.

Intelligent Development Planning Criteria

For your community, envision having professional planners, citizens, and the range of other local stakeholders needed to produce useful evidence. This evidence needs to be in the form of documented actionable knowledge that has been informed and influenced by means of the intelligent development planning practice behaviors that are embedded in the twenty-six criteria discussed in chapters 11 and 12.

The twenty-six criteria and factors of intelligent development planning that have been introduced and elaborated in the preceding two chapters are available for selection and relational nonlinear application during the charrette activities. By way of reminder and summary, these criteria and factors include the following:

- the big ten criteria of intelligent development behavior,
- the three criteria for continuous improvement of intelligent development,
- the seven policy investment criteria, and
- the six factors that comprise the ALERT model.

Regional stakeholder individuals and groups should use the charrette to engage in practicing and experimenting with the application of appropriate combinations of these criteria and factors over various stages and planned time frames. These kinds of phases are suggested by the initial sequencing of the ALERT model, and these activities are important means for learning by doing and for thereby being positioned to perfect effective planned strategies for intelligently developing one's local region. The charrette activities can empower local regional stakeholders to be prepared to move collectively and systematically from understanding local assets to mobilizing them to be positioned to take the planned actions necessary to realize a more globally and economically competitive city-region or rural and small-town region.

Strategically and pragmatically, the work of these regional local stakeholders must produce prioritized investments that attract funds initially for infrastructure and encourage investments for development that ranges beyond physical and digital infrastructure. Operationally, this means working toward accomplishing the intentions and characteristics that are represented in the seven "responsiveness" policy investment criteria discussed in chapter 12 as part of the *R* of the ALERT model. This is feasible when being guided by and executed in conjunction with the other nineteen intelligent development criteria. As a reminder, a brief listing of all twenty-six criteria is offered next.

Big Ten Criteria of Intelligent Development Behavior

Derive and define the core of each critical idea, regional issue, and selected method that is encountered in the strategic planning (e.g., do this for "the new economy locally").

Operate from the mind-set that the various *globalization forces and digital development* technologies drive intelligent development, and these drivers need to be harnessed and steered in service of local and regional aspirations and goals. In order to improve our understanding of these new forces and drivers, the critical digital, physical, and quality educational infrastructures and support systems need to become more responsive to the new development demands of the global knowledge economy. Both in rural and urban regions, greater attention needs to be paid to such technology-based economic factors and indicators as

1. unique local and regional assets;
2. talent development, retention, and attraction;
3. capacity for creativity and entrepreneurship;
4. embracing of economic dynamism;
5. a pervasive digital economy;
6. knowledge-sector jobs; and
7. sensitivity to globalization development potentialities.[1]

Draw on contemporary *research and theory* and work at practicing relational theory with a steadfast focus on the analysis-to-action relationship.

Contextualize the strategic planning via *comparative methods*—that is, utilize external knowledge and measures by means of benchmarking and best practices.

Utilize the *expertise of local experience and local knowledge* in concert with external knowledge.

Encourage *participation and organization for involvement* to enhance an engaged regional civil society by means of informed and organized engagement.

Align politics and policy by ensuring that the priority interests of the city-region's principal stakeholders are included, informed, debated, and rationalized.

Knowledge economy and network society *investments should be prioritized* rationally in response to the economic demand and social need of the target region.

Be *forward leaning and strategic* in which alternative future scenarios are framed as short term, medium term, and long term.

This multidimensional summative and synthesized criterion may be framed as a profile for the intelligent development planner. In sum, development planning is *defined as intelligent* when

- good and best practices are influenced by appropriate framing concepts, theory, and the latest relevant research findings;
- innovative science and technology are utilized fully to develop a region competently, holistically, equitably, multifunctionally, and sustainably;
- the planning includes analysis and action attention to selected economic production, consumption, and amenity factors and quality-of-life functions so as to retain, grow, and attract knowledge workers and to stimulate inward revenues and investments; and
- co-learning action plans of development practitioners and development scholars enable them to engage empirically with the various subsystems of the intelligent development system and its applicable frameworks; it is by such translational practice and research that changed mind-sets and relational behavior will be perfected and rendered sustainable.

Continuous Improvement of Intelligent Development Practice

- Mind-set change
- Translational research and translational practice
- Relational thinking and behavior

ALERT Model Elements and Criteria

- Stakeholders
- Awareness—evidence
- Layers—context
- E-business—infrastructure, finance, production, consumption, amenities
- Responsiveness—economic demand, social need, prioritized investments
- Talk—scenarios, surveys, monitoring, evaluation

Policy Investment Criteria

- Are market oriented.
- Are proactive in nature and scope.
- Look beyond the immediate economic horizon, anticipate economic changes, and diversify the local and regional economy.
- Maximize the attraction of private-sector investment that would not otherwise come to fruition absent the leveraging of targeted, often external government investment.
- Have a high probability of success.
- Should result in an environment where higher-skill, higher-wage jobs are created.
- Should maximize return on taxpayer investment and other co-investor partners.

Proposed Actions

An intelligent development planning charrette allows regional stakeholders to practice co-learning, action research, and action planning activities to produce effective policy investments. The process for the charrette is detailed below.

There should be coach tutors in support of the learning and practice of intelligent development planning. The coach tutor role might be played by volunteers solicited from local educational institutions or by charrette participant stakeholders themselves. The coach tutor will need some self-study on the processes and content issues in advance of the other charrette participants. This role may also be performed by teams to share the advance learning tasks. Especially for charrette exercises taking place in rural and small-town environments, another option might be to initiate and develop a working relationship remotely with an expert coach tutor at a research university. The expert might also be able to mobilize students to assist in the review and comment roles on the work outcomes of the charrette group.

The goal of local charrette events is to get on with the business of learning and practicing intelligent development—by engaging it. Local stakeholders wanting to improve their regions in the context of the new economy need to "just do it!" And in the process of doing, one will have begun to seed the required mind-set change and sustainable learning-by-doing and reinvention of regional-scaled local new economies—both urban and rural environments.

In places and regions where there is professional regional planning capacity, they should be encouraged to begin the development of an emerging culture of intelligent development. This can be achieved by playing the role of trainers and mobilizing the stakeholder/citizen planners of their local regions to share in the planning and implementation of intelligent development planning strategies. Working groups, task forces, and would-be local leaders of representative interests across an area's key institutions and organizations will be positioned better to work with the regional planners and their regional planning organizations to produce intelligent development–informed policies and programs in the years ahead.

Planning for Intelligent Development

Translating the above knowledge from the work of the charrette into creating more informed development policies is at the heart of this book. This translation is likely to be more effective if the task is engaged and shared by the professional planner and the volunteer citizen planner alike. This is the relational relationship that was discussed in chapter 11. In democratic situations, buttressed by today's wealth of more accessible information, the time has never been better for citizens and other information consumers to motivate local providers to supply the services and goods needed and demanded by the regional marketplace of ideas and by the local economy and society.

Working with the Local Regional Planning Organization

One can translate this book's knowledge most effectively by engaging actively and strategically with the subject matter and the development processes discussed above. In real-world terms, this might be accomplished in several ways. If the city-region has a regional planning organization that is mandated to initiate and oversee the future development of the area and its localities, then one might seek a voluntary association to assist informally or formally in the work of that organization. This might be done individually or in collective ways. For example, if stakeholders from a particular district of the region have organized into groupings of common interests, then the planning organization might be approached for the development of a working affiliation. Ideally, the regional planning organization might be solicited to establish mutually beneficial relationships for co-learning and the advancement of the local future development function.

Creating Your Own Working Group for Intelligent Development Planning

In situations where there is not a local regional planning governance organization, it may be necessary for individuals and organizations to come together around common concerns and similar development interests. In either case, the collective expression of interest may be sufficient, if only informally, to mobilize around similar concerns and aspirations for the future development of a region and its communities. In both of these cases—that is, an area with or without a formal regional planning organization—an early need is to form a source of fresh perspectives intended to infuse new energy into the local discourse about improving the region's future development. Armed with the analysis and action framework of the twenty-six intelligent development criteria, a grassroots effort can catalyze movement toward the planning of policies and programs to enable the region to compete more successfully in the global knowledge economy and network society. Creative tensions and co-responsibilities between a region's various providers and a range of consumers are more likely to stimulate greater responsiveness toward the goal, producing better, happier, and more prosperous local communities.

Sample Charrette Script

To aid the reader in making the linkages between the twenty-six intelligent development criteria and the charrette learning exercise, each criterion is emphasized below. The three continuous improvement criteria introduced in chapter 11 are not only important to, but are embedded in the concept and practice of these intelligent development behaviors: *mind-set change, translational research and translational practice*, and *relational thinking and behavior*. To begin to influence local development planning, these practices should be initiated, established, and sustained for the planning region. Such practical and working tactics as framing (refer to the "Framing" section in chapter 11) and branding support comprehensive intelligent development strategy creation because they are *forward leaning and strategic* (refer to the big ten criteria in chapter 11), they help to *align politics and policy* (refer to the big ten criteria in chapter 11), and they provide a shared vision and planning mandate which is vital to the talk phase of the ALERT model. These activities help in conveying coherent and pragmatic worldviews that are so critical in stimulating widespread interest across the planning region and ownership in and the development of a working consensus for effective future and continuous intelligent development.

The initial practice and ongoing perfection of intelligent development behaviors and processes will enable and empower learning participants to embrace *mind-set change* and shift their old-economy perspectives and actions more to incorporate the global knowledge economy and network society *research and theory* (refer to the big ten criteria in chapter 11), content, and contexts into their new intelligent development behaviors, actions, and *prioritization of investments* (refer to the responsiveness element criterion in chapter 12).

For the stakeholders engaged in these charrette learning activities, some of the value-added spin-offs from practicing *comparative methods* (refer to the big ten criteria in chapter 11) include developing a common ground of understanding for *participation and organization* (refer to the big ten criteria in chapter 11) activities that are vital to the implementation of the talk phase (refer to the talk element criterion in chapter 12); a common set of working concepts; and a shared shorthand language. This aids networking, team building, collaboration, and coordination across organizational and institutional boundaries during the execution of the ALERT model.

As intelligent development requires continuous monitoring and refinement, the learning pathways are intended to be staged and progressive, with later learning drawing on earlier understandings and developed insights. This learning is also intended to be relational, such that once the entire ALERT model process has been completed initially and sequentially for the planning region, one should feel free to crossruff in a nonlinear and fuzzy planning[2] fashion among the phases of the ALERT model's strategic planning processes. One need not be constrained by fixed linear-only conceptualizations; use the frameworks creatively! The fluidity and blending of the new economy's various content and process factors need to be planned and implemented in flexible, dynamic, and overlapping ways so as to reflect better the relational, unbounded, nuanced, and highly interconnected nature of today's globalized local economy and information society.

To best enable a proper introduction to intelligent development behaviors and their foundational interdependencies amongst the twenty-six criteria, these initial learning activities should not be performed in a rush. In addition to the research work that goes into this learning, gestation and reflection are critical particularly to mastering these new mind-set change processes (refer to the three criteria in chapter 11). Given that these learning activities typically are to be performed in the context of other, often full-time daily routine duties and responsibilities, several weeks are needed to prepare each of the tasks described below, and at least a week should be available for review and feedback by a coach or tutor in comprehensive intelligent development strategic planning. This charrette learning exercise covers a ten-week time frame and uses the ALERT model (as outlined in chapter 12). This exercise permits the internalization and practice of the full set of twenty-six intelligent development criteria that include the ALERT model.

Stage 1 (weeks 1 and 2). First ALERT model paper on the elements of awareness (evidence) and layers (context).

A critical precondition of the charrette exercise is to identify the region's principal *stakeholders.*[3] In addition to members of an existing governing and policy board or commission for the local planning region, list the names of the current formal and informal organizations or groups that are impacted by, and that influence or impinge upon, the work of the planning organization for the region's development. Initially, brainstorm outside the box by considering nontraditional participation. These may consist of interests that have not historically been a part of local strategic planning involvement for the target region. Draw upon relational concepts (refer to the three criteria in chapter 11); in considering stakeholders (refer to chapter 12), they may encompass representatives that are temporary or permanent, and those likely to be influenced directly or indirectly by resulting strategies. Consider individuals and organizations, and consider stakeholders that are sectoral and content based and those that are process and functionally based in their particular stakes and interests in the region. A selection process needs to be designed and used to select a number and mix of participants that seems feasible. In accordance with the ultimate implementation of the talk phase, after the initial documentation of the ALERT model's process has been put in place, then it is important to periodically and routinely update and refresh the range of stakeholders as priorities and issues demonstrate their natural dynamics of participatory ebb and flow of varying involvement. Over time, this will mean revising the current stakeholder configuration to one that better reflects changing regional demands and needs.

Stage 1 will require stakeholder participants to perform initial *awareness* and *layers* exploration of the planning region. Awareness[4] and layers[5] are the basic informational elements of the ALERT model. These two sets of activities provide the initial compilation of information. This is the evidence-based context and factual foundation for the three following elements (refer to chapter 12 for e-business, responsiveness, and talk) of the ALERT model. The principal outcome from the two phases of awareness and layers as analyzed together is actionable knowledge. Additionally, the layers element of the ALERT model needs some focused discussion situating the planning region within a relational and geographic context, that is, substate neighbor regions, statewide, subnationally, nationally, and globally.[6] Also, since the awareness element of the ALERT model in particular needs to be refined continuously during the planning period, one constantly should elaborate, update, and document the region's development aspirations, problems, demands, needs, and priorities.

Both the awareness element and the layers element findings for the target planning region should be documented in a brief double-spaced, three-page (maximum) paper of narrative that will be submitted to the outside tutor coach by a time to be set later. Note that tables and figures (e.g., maps, graphs, charts) must be used. These are the actionable knowledge building blocks of evidence upon which planned actions will be based.

In organizing the awareness and layers paper, the composition of the parts of each paper and the positioning of those parts should be as follows: (1) body of the paper—three pages of text beyond the narrative, and unlimited supports may be attached in the form of (2) references, (3) tables, (4) figures, and (5) endnotes, but only if needed. Be sure to cite in the text, in parentheses, the author and date of publication of each reference in support of the analyses and interpretations of the evidence.

As to the figures and tables, each should be numbered and titled individually. So that there is a linkage made between the interpretive text and the tables and figures, each table and figure should be referenced explicitly, in parentheses, in the text. Remember, tables and figures are the structure, the skeletal framework or foundation, from which the text or narrative of analysis and interpretation are derived and supported. The source of each table or figure is to be cited on its respective page, as well as by means of a full bibliographic entry that is to be included and positioned alphabetically by author in the references section of the paper. Adopt a common writing style and format usage for all reports that are generated for all phases of the ALERT model learning exercises.

Note: This continuous process of evidence gathering for awareness and contextual layers identification for the locality should include, but not be limited to, daily (if possible) monitoring of the Worldwide Web, selected local and global principal newspaper(s), and other periodical local news and information sources influencing public opinion for the planning region. Both online and offline sources should be considered to inform such initial ongoing monitoring for trends and shifts in popular would-be policy planning discourse. This information is useful especially for identifying the popular economic demands and societal needs of the planning region. Also, for the wider continental level and global level context, one should be reviewing daily the hardcopy or Web-based versions of such quality popular international periodicals as the *Financial Times*, the *Wall Street Journal*, and the *Economist*, among others. Social media and networking information sources increasingly are important to today's local and global society; using these diverse information sources and technology platforms requires close attention and special care in order to stay current.

As evidence is accumulated, one should seek to engage and pay explicit attention to the interests of the principal stakeholders[7] of the planning region and the roles that these respective actors play in the development of the area. Remember that stakeholders may be actors in formal roles or informal roles.

In order for each participant stakeholder to learn and experience the parts and the whole of intelligent development understanding and creation, it is recommended that the papers for each stage of the charrette process be implemented individually or in two-person teams. Then, upon the completion of each phase, the range of principal findings, interpretations, and actionable knowledge should be aggregated into an integrated report of whatever length and detail is needed to capture both the essence and the scope of core findings that will inform and influence the next stage of the charrette process. The outcome is an "Awareness and Layers Stage 1 Report" that has been derived from each of the individual papers. This division of labor that first generates individual papers and then these synthesized collective reports should be followed again in stages 2 and 3. These stages are elaborated below. Post these reports regularly for access by participants.

Week 3. Feedback should be provided by the coach tutor on the first ALERT model stage 1 paper on the elements of awareness and layers from the perspectives of intelligent development. The critical outcome is that this first paper should inform in an overarching way and make the reader aware of the many factors that go into the functioning of the local regional economy. By way of brief and early understanding, the region's principal economic drivers should be identified and briefly elaborated.

Stage 2 (weeks 4 and 5). Second ALERT model paper on elements e-business (content) and responsiveness (demand, need, and prioritized investments).

Stakeholder learner-participants should continue to drill down further into operationalizing the ALERT model by focusing and elaborating on the sectors/functions of the *e-business*[8] element. Each function of electronic business should be considered, and then selected e-business functions should be explicated briefly to convey the planning region's current major economic drivers, its principal development assets, and the respective strengths, weaknesses, opportunities, threats, and priorities (e.g., employ a kind of triage process). Additionally, learning participants will continue to drill down into the ALERT model by focusing on the *responsiveness*[9] element.

Two principal questions should be addressed and answered for responsiveness: how are for-profit market forces responding to the economic demands of the planning region, and how are nonprofit institutions such as governments and nongovernmental organizations at all levels responding to the social needs of the region? Societal needs, for example, include education; housing; health care; quality-of-life amenities; access to transportation and, importantly, affordable access to information technologies and their networked connections; clean water; quality environment; and so on, and should reflect the kinds of youth-through-maturity life-cycle changes that most regional ecosystems undergo. In addition to researching the literature, business and government documents, local data sources, and newspapers, other information sources also need to be searched, reviewed, and monitored regularly in order to assess these various dimensions and the degrees of responsiveness in the region. This three-page, double-spaced paper of narrative is due at a deadline to be set. Be sure to continue to provide, use, and refer to tables and figures (i.e., maps, graphs, and charts). Again, cite and refer to this evidence in support of the analyses and interpretations; the references section of the paper is in addition to the three pages of narrative. Continue to collect evidence and deepen your fundamental grasp of the region's economy and society by means of deepening awareness and layers understanding.

The composition and positioning of the parts of the stage 2 ALERT model paper should be as follows: (1) body of the paper—three pages of text, (2) references, (3) tables, (4) figures, and (5) endnotes, but only if needed.

Week 6. Feedback should be provided by the coach tutor on the second ALERT model paper on the elements of e-business and responsiveness from the perspectives of intelligent development. The critical outcome of this stage 2 paper should be a preliminary set of investment priorities that may be used initially to guide the reduction of the principal gaps and disparities among the region's perceived economic demands and its social needs. In turn, these priorities initially should inform the future strategic planning of the next phase of the ALERT model; this is the *talk* element, or stage 3, of the ALERT model charrette process.

Stage 3 (weeks 7 to 9). Final practice paper on talk (continuous engagement and planned futures scenarios).

The last paper of the charrette practice exercise is to focus on the *talk*[10] element of the ALERT model. For the talk element, thinking should shift from the exploration and generation of actionable knowledge toward how to take action on that knowledge—that is, imagining and constructing ideal desired future scenarios for the planning of intelligent development for the local region. Among other actions to be determined by the working group are surveys and the identification of specific what *should be* operational futures. These future states are informed from the knowledge obtained during the implementation of the previous ALERT model phases. The desired future states should be articulated explicitly and then operationally planned and documented in the stage 3 paper.

This means detailing selected and unique intelligent development assets for the local planning region from the present state or condition of what *is* (as derived from the awareness, layers, e-business, and responsiveness elements) to create and articulate what *should be* future scenarios, that is, idealistic and intended futures that can be used for the implementation of policies, programs, projects, and actions. Preliminary branding strategies and evaluation planning also need to be formulated in this paper as a means of articulating how the region and its stakeholders can use intelligent development planning to achieve the what *should be* future scenarios. Simply, one must articulate the initial means of getting to the what *should be* ends. For the operational details of staging futures planned scenarios, consider the open systems planning (OSP) approach.[11]

Since the talk element is ongoing and continuous, intelligent development needs to have built into it ways to routinely survey local development conditions and to regularly monitor and evaluate the impact of planned policies, programs, and projects so as to be able to make midcourse corrections. These continuous functions may be conceived as going beyond the principal talk activities of scenario construction. The majority of the final stage 3 paper should outline futures planning scenarios for the short term, the medium term, and the long term for the planning region. For the next generation, these scenarios are intended to ensure that the region's businesses and institutions reduce the economic demand and societal need that have been researched and assessed on an increasingly deeper and systematic basis. Remember, throughout the ALERT model planning period, it is important to continue to collect and update evidence and thereby deepen one's own, and the collective understanding of the region's awareness, layers, e-business, and responsiveness in order to represent effectively the current on-the-ground condition of the planning region.

The final stage 3 paper's text or narrative should not exceed five double-spaced pages. The support material of references, tables, and figures are in addition to the five pages of narrative or text. Again, in the text, be sure to cite and refer explicitly to the cumulative and updated evidence in support of the interpretations and strategic planning scenarios. Tables and figures (e.g., maps, graphs, photos, charts) should be positioned after the text and references.

Realistic and feasible innovation, while applying and practicing creativity, is key to the talk element of the ALERT model. As noted by Albert Einstein, "Imagination is more important than knowledge."[12] As more places, people, and enterprises around the world produce their digital development and networking capacities, imaginative and intelligent development planning and implementation represent the pathway toward competitive advantage and niche positioning for a region in today's and tomorrow's reality of increasingly widespread distribution, access, diversity of platforms, and use of information and communications technologies.

Note: The principal and ultimate assessment criterion for the final stage 3 paper is focused on the quality of the creativity, innovative, and imaginative treatment of the discussion for the idealistic future scenarios, or what *should be* the intelligent development futures for the assigned planning region. Again, these scenarios should be staged by short-term, medium-term, and long-term phases—and they should be rooted explicitly in evidence that supports the planned future scenarios. Such evidence should be rooted in, revised, and updated by means of ongoing surveys and findings that go beyond the earlier research and analyses of the ALERT model stages of awareness, layers, e-business, and responsiveness.

The composition and positioning of the parts of the final paper should be as follows: (1) body of the paper—five pages of text, (2) references, (3) tables, (4) figures, and (5) endnotes, but only if needed.

Week 10. PowerPoint presentations by the stakeholder learner-participants. In order to learn from each other across the localities of the planning region and to generate synergies of relational imagination and creativity, presentations of the core messages from the final stage 3 charrette practice papers need to be made. By thematic, sectoral, and subareas of the planning region, these presentations should be limited to fifteen minutes each. Initially, ten minutes immediately following each presentation should be set aside for group discussion, questions, and answers. The tutor coach should also comment briefly during each postpresentation session. Lastly, an additional unlimited amount of time should be devoted to transregional and synoptic discussion. Such give-and-take engagement sessions often generate fresh ideas and innovative value-added outcomes that can be useful in informing alternative futures scenarios.

The presentations of the final charrette practice paper findings and planned futures should be made via PowerPoint presentations. Fifteen to twenty slides per presentation is a reasonable working number of slides for the size and timing of each presentation.

Conclusion

At the end of this charrette learning exercise in operationalizing the ALERT model and the intelligent development translational process, the stakeholder participants should be prepared to engage in the preparation of comprehensive intelligent development strategic planning, the outcomes of which are documented so that they can be assessed systematically by matching them against the ideals and standards of the twenty-six intelligent development planning behavior criteria. These behaviors can be expected to produce strategic investment opportunities that over time can improve the development of the planning region to compete more effectively in the global knowledge economy and network society. Finally, after completing the initial learning process of the charrette exercise, it will be necessary to shift stakeholder collective attention to the more operational and tactical planning preparation level. The planned policies need to be translated into actions, especially in the forms of programs and projects.

Notes

1. LaMore et al. (2009)
2. de Roo and Porter (2007)
3. Corey and Wilson (2006: 218, 104–107)
4. Corey and Wilson (2006: 112–114, 228–229)
5. Corey and Wilson (2006: 114–126, 229–230)
6. Corey and Wilson (2006: 114–126, 229–230)
7. Corey and Wilson (2006: 104–107)
8. Corey and Wilson (2006: 126–128, 230–233)
9. Corey and Wilson (2006: 128–131, 231–233)
10. Corey and Wilson (2006: 131–133, 233–234)
11. Corey and Wilson (2006: 212–213); Jayaram (1976)
12. Einstein (1931: 97)

References

Abler, R., Adams, J. S., and Gould, P. 1977. *Spatial Organization: The Geographer's View of the World*. Englewood Cliffs, NJ: Prentice Hall.

Adams, J. 1999. The social implications of hypermobility. In *Proceedings of the Workshop on the Economic and Social Implications of Sustainable Transportation* (OECD), pp. 95–134. http://john-adams.co.uk/wp-content/uploads/2006/00071363.PDF#page=95.

Adams, P. C. 1995. A reconsideration of personal boundaries in space-time. *Annals of the Association of American Geographers* 85:267–285.

———. 2009. *Geographies of Media and Communication: A Critical Introduction*. Chichester: Wiley-Blackwell.

Adams, P. C., and Ghose, R. 2003. India.com: The construction of a space between. *Progress in Human Geography* 27:414–437.

Agar, J. 2003. *Constant Touch: A Global History of the Mobile Phone*. Cambridge: Revolutions in Science.

Ahmed, A. M., Zairi, M., and Alwabel, S. A. 2006. Global benchmarking for Internet and e-commerce applications. *Benchmarking: An International Journal* 13(1–2): 68–80.

Al-Fakhri, M. O., Cropf, R. A., Higgs, G., and Kelly, P. 2008. E-government in Saudi Arabia: Between promise and reality. *International Journal of Electronic Government Research* 4(2): 59–82.

Al-Nuaim, H. A. 2009. How "E" are Arab municipalities? An evaluation of Arab capital municipal web sites. *International Journal of Electronic Government Research* 5(1): 50–63.

Alemneh, D. G., and Hastings, S. K. 2006. Developing the ICT infrastructure for Africa: Overview of barriers to harnessing the full power of the Internet. *Journal of Education for Library and Information Science* 47(1): 4–16.

Amin, H. 2008. E-business from Islamic perspectives: Prospects and challenges. *Journal of Internet Banking and Commerce* 13(3). http://www.arraydev.com/commerce/jibc/2008-12/Hanudin_Final__JIBC.pdf.

Angell, I. O., and Ezer, J. 2006. New barbarians at the gate: The new spirit emerging in India. *Information Society* 22:165–176.

Antonelli, C. 2000a. Collective knowledge communication and innovation: The evidence of technological districts. *Regional Studies* 34:535–547.

———. 2000b. Restructuring and innovation in long-term regional change. In G. L. Clark, M. P. Feldman, and M. S. Gertler (eds.), *The Oxford Handbook of Economic Geography*. New York: Oxford University Press, pp. 395–410.

Appadurai, A. 1990. Disjuncture and difference in the global cultural economy. *Theory, Culture and Society* 7:295–310.

Apulu, I., and Ige, E. O. 2011. Are Nigeria SMEs effectively utilizing ICT? *International Journal of Business and Management* 6(6): 207–214.

Arab Media. 2011. *Cyber Activism Changing the World? Bloggers convene in Denmark to discuss.* http://www.radsch.info/2011/05/cyber-activism-changing-world-bloggers.html.

Armbrust, W. 2007. New media and old agendas: The Internet in the Middle East and Middle Eastern studies. *International Journal of Middle East Studies* 39:531–533.

Arminen, I. 2006. Social functions of location in mobile telephony. *Perspectives of Ubiquitous Computing* 10:319–323.

Arnstein, S. R. 1969, July. A ladder of citizen participation. *Journal of the American Institute of Planners* 35(4): 216–224.

Arrow, K. J. 1985. Economic history: A necessary though not sufficient condition for an economist *American Economic Review* 75(2): 320–323.

Atkinson, R. D., and Gottlieb, P. D. 2001. *The Metropolitan New Economy Index: Benchmarking Economic Transformation in the Nation's Metropolitan Areas*. Cleveland: Progressive Policy Institute.

Audretsch, D. 2000. Knowledge, globalization, and regions: An economist's perspective. In J. H. Dunning (ed.), *Regions, Globalization, and the Knowledge-Based Economy*. New York: Oxford University Press, pp. 63–81.

Audretsch, D., and Feldman, M. P. 1996. R&D spillovers and the geography of innovation and production. *American Economic Review* 86:630–640.

Augé, M. 2000. *Non-Places: Introduction to an Anthropology of Supermodernity* (J. Howe, trans.). London: Verso.

Aurigi, A. 2005. *Making the Digital City: The Early Shaping of Urban Internet Space*. Aldershot: Ashgate.

Auster, E. R. 1990. The interorganizational environment: Network theory, tools, and applications. In Frederick Williams and David V. Gibson (eds.), *Technology Transfer: A Communication Perspective*. Newbury Park, CA: Sage, pp. 63–89.

Avidan, I., and Kellerman, A. 2004. Distance in the Internet by time and route: An empirical examination. *Contemporary Israeli Geography: Horizons* 60–61:77–88.

Avila, A. 2009. Underdeveloped ICT areas in Sub-Saharan Africa. *Informatica Economica* 13(2): 136–146.

Barlow, J. P. 1994. The economy of ideas. *Wired* 2.03:1–17. http://www.wired.com/wired/archive/2.03.

Batty, M. 1997. Virtual geography. *Futures* 29:337–352.

Bell, D. 1976. *The Coming of Post-industrial Society: A Venture in Social Forecasting.* 2nd ed. New York: Basic Books.

Belton, K. A. 2010. From cyberspace to offline communities: Indigenous peoples and global connectivity. *Alternatives* 35(3): 193–215.

Ben-David, D., and Loewy, M. B. 1998. Free trade, growth and convergence. *Journal of Economic Growth* 3:143–170.

Ben-Ze'ev, A. 2004. *Love Online: Emotions on the Internet.* Cambridge: Cambridge University Press.

Benedikt, M. 1991. Cyberspace: Some proposals. In M. Benedikt (ed.), *Cyberspace: First Steps.* Cambridge, MA: MIT Press, pp. 119–224.

Beniger, J. R. 1986. *The Control Revolution: Technological and Economic Origins of the Information Society.* Cambridge, MA: Harvard University Press.

Bennis, W. G., Benne, K. D., Chin, R., and Corey, K. E. (eds.). 1976. *The Planning of Change.* 3rd ed. New York: Holt, Rinehart and Winston.

Blainey, A. 1966. *Tyranny of Distance: How Distance Shaped Australia's History.* Melbourne: Macmillan.

Blinder, A. S. 2007. *How Many U.S. Jobs Might Be Offshorable?* CEPS Working Paper No. 142. Princeton, NJ: Princeton University Press.

Blumen, O., and Kellerman, A. 1990. Gender differences in commuting distance, residence and employment location: Metropolitan Haifa 1972–1983. *Professional Geographer* 42:54–71.

Boisot, M. H. 1998. *Knowledge Assets: Securing Competitive Advantage in the Information Economy.* Oxford: Oxford University Press.

Bolter, J. D., and Grusin, R. 1999. *Remediation: Understanding New Media.* Cambridge, MA: MIT Press.

Bolton, R. 2005. *Habermas's Theory of Communicative Action and the Theory of Social Capital.* Paper read at the Annual Conference of the Association of American Geographers, Denver, Colorado. http://web.williams.edu/Economics/papers/Habermas.pdf.

Boneva, B., and Kraut, R. 2002. Email, gender, and personal relationships. In B. Wellman and C. Haythornthwaite (eds.), *The Internet in Everyday Life.* Malden, MA: Blackwell, pp. 372–403.

Bonss, W. 2004. *Introduction.* The Mobility and the Cosmopolitan Perspective Workshop, Munich Reflexive Modernization Research Centre.

Bonss, W., and Kesselring, S. 2001. Mobilität am Übergang von der Ersten zur Zweiten Moderne. In U. Beck and W. Bonss (eds.), *Die Modernisierung der Moderne.* Frankfurt am Main: Suhrkamp, pp. 177–190.

———. 2004. *Mobility and the Cosmopolitan Perspective.* Paper presented at the Mobility and the Cosmopolitan Perspective Workshop, Munich Reflexive Modernization Research Centre.

Borgmann, A. 1999. *Holding on to Reality: The Nature of Information at the Turn of the Millennium.* Chicago: University of Chicago Press.

Bouty, I. 2000. Interpersonal and interaction influences on informal resource exchanges between R&D researchers across organizational boundaries. *Academy of Management Journal* 43(1): 50–65.

Braman, S. 1989. Defining information: An approach for policymakers. *Telecommunications Policy* 13:233–242.

Breton, G., and Lambert, M. (eds.). 2003. *Universities and Globalization: Private Linkages, Public Trust.* Paris: UNESCO and Université Laval.

Brooker-Gross, S. R. 1980. Usages of communication technology and urban growth. In S. D. Brunn and J. O. Wheeler (eds.), *The American Metropolitan System: Present and Future.* New York: Wiley, pp. 145–159.

Brown, J. 2005. A plan to brand this city. Theage.com.au. http://www.theage.com.au/news/business/a-plan-to-brand-this-city/2005/07/03/1120329323933.html.

Bruszt, L., Vedres, B., and Stark, D. 2005. Shaping the web of civic participation: Civil society websites in Eastern Europe. *Journal of Public Policy* 25(1): 149–163.

Bryson, J. R., Daniels, P. W., Henry, N., and Pollard, J. (eds.). 2000. *Knowledge, Space, Economy.* London: Routledge.

Budhwar, P., Varma, A., Malhotra, N., and Mukherjee, A. 2009. Insights into the Indian call centre industry: Can internal marketing help tackle high employee turnover? *Journal of Services Marketing* 23(5): 351–362.

Butcher, N., Latchem, C., Mawoyo, M., and Levey, L. 2011. Distance education for empowerment and development in Africa. *Distance Education* 32(2): 149–158.

Cairncross, F. 1997. *The Death of Distance. How the Communications Revolution Will Change Our Lives.* Boston: Harvard Business School Press.

Camagni, R. 1991. Introduction: From the local "milieu" to innovation through cooperation networks. In R. Camagni (ed.), *Innovation Networks: Spatial Perspectives.* London: Belhaven, pp. 1–11.

Cameron, M. A. 2010. Text, media, and constituent power: Latin America from ancient to modern times. *Canadian Journal of Latin American & Caribbean Studies* 35(70): 29–50.

Carey, J., and Moss, M. L. 1985. The diffusion of new telecommunication technologies. *Telecommunications Policy* 9:145–158.

Carter, A. P. 1989. Knowhow trading as economic exchange. *Research Policy* 18:155–163.

Castells, M. 1985. High technology, economic restructuring and the urban-regional process in the United States. In M. Castells (ed.), *High Technology, Space and Society.* Beverly Hills: Sage, pp. 11–40.

———. 1989. *The Informational City: Information, Technology, Economic Restructuring and the Urban-Regional Process.* Oxford: Blackwell.

———. 1996. *The Rise of the Network Society.* Oxford: Blackwell.

———. 1998. *End of Millennium.* Oxford: Blackwell.

———. 2000. *The Rise of the Network Society.* 2nd ed. Oxford: Blackwell.

———. 2001. *The Internet Galaxy: Reflections on the Internet, Business, and Society.* New York: Oxford University Press.

Castells, M., Fernánddez-Ardèvol, M., Qiu, J. L., and Sey, A. 2007. *Mobile Communication and Society: A Global Perspective.* Cambridge, MA: MIT Press.

Castells, M., and Hall, P. 1994. *Technopoles of the World: The Making of Twenty-First-Century Industrial Complexes.* London: Routledge.

Chacko, E. 2007. From brain grain to brain gain: Reverse migration to Bangalore and Hyderabad, India's globalizing high tech cities. *GeoJournal* 68(2–3): 131–140.

Chan, S., Vogel, D., and Ma, L. C. K. 2007. Mobile phone communication innovation in multiple time and space zones: The case of Hong Kong culture. *Journal of Global Information Management* 15(4): 79–85.

Chandler, A. D., Jr., and Cortada, J. W. (eds.). 2000. *A Nation Transformed by Information: How Information Has Shaped the United States from Colonial Times to the Present.* New York: Oxford University Press.

Chun, W. C. 1997. IT2000: Singapore's vision of an intelligent island. In P. Droege (ed.), *Intelligent Environments: Spatial Aspects of the Information Revolution.* Amsterdam: Elsevier Science, pp. 49–65.

Chung, J. 2008. Comparing online activities in China and South Korea: The Internet and the political regime. *Asian Survey* 48(5): 727–751.

CIA. 2003. *World Factbook.* https://www.cia.gov/library/publications/the-world-factbook.

Clark, G. L., Feldman, M. P., and Gertler, M. S. (eds.). 2000. *The Oxford Handbook of Economic Geography.* New York: Oxford University Press.

Cohen, L., and El-Sawad, A. 2007. Lived experiences of offshoring: An examination of UK and Indian financial service employees' accounts of themselves and one another. *Human Relations* 60(8): 1235–1262.

Collato, F. 2010. Is Bangalore the Silicon Valley of Asia? *Journal of Indian Business Research* 2(1): 52–65.

Comer, J. C., and Wikle, T. A. 2008. Worldwide diffusion of the cellular telephone, 1995–2005. *Professional Geographer* 60:252–269.

Communities and Local Government. 2006, February. *A Framework for City-Regions.* http://www.eukn.org/E_library/Economy_Knowledge_Employment/Urban_Economy/Urban_Economy/A_framework_for_city_regions_UK.

Cooke, P., Uranga, M. G., and Etxebarria, G. 1998. Regional systems of innovation: An evolutionary perspective. *Environment and Planning A* 30:1563–1584.

Cooper, G. 2001. The mutable mobile: Social theory in the wireless world. In B. Brown, N. Green, and R. Harper (eds.), *Wireless World: Social and Interactional Aspects of the Mobile Age.* London: Springer, pp. 19–31.

Cordoba-Pachon, R. C., and Orr, K. 2009. Three patterns to understand e-government: The case of Colombia. *International Journal of Public Sector Management* 22(6): 532–554.

Corey, K. E. 2000. Intelligent corridors: Outcomes of electronic space policies. *Journal of Urban Technology* 7(2): 1–22.

Corey, K. E., and Wilson, M. I. 2006 *Urban and Regional Technology Planning: Planning Practice in the Global Knowledge Economy.* London: Routledge.

———. 2009. E-business and e-commerce. In R. Kitchin and N. Thrift (eds.), *International Encyclopedia of Human Geography,* vol. 3. Oxford: Elsevier, pp. 285–290.

Couclelis, H. 1998. Worlds of Information: The Geographic Metaphor in the Visualization of Complex Information. *Cartography and Geographic Information Systems* 25:209–220.

———. 2009. Rethinking time geography in the information age. *Environment and Planning A* 41:1556–1575.

Couclelis, H., and Gale, N. 1986. Space and spaces. *Geografiska Annaler* 68B: 1–12.

Cowan, R., David, P., and Foray, D. 2000. The explicit economics of knowledge codification and tacitness. *Industrial and Corporate Change* 9:211–253.

Cox, J. 2006. Is there a first-mover advantage in the market for Japanese video game systems? *Asia Pacific Journal of Economics & Business* 10(1): 18–33.

Cramme, O., and Diamond, P. (eds.). 2009. *Social Justice in the Global Age*. Oxford: Polity.

Crang, M., Crang, P., and May, J. (eds.). 1999. *Virtual Geographies: Bodies, Space and Relations*. London: Routledge.

Cruz, P., Muñoz-Gallego, P., and Laukkanen, T. 2010. Mobile banking rollout in emerging markets: Evidence from Brazil. *International Journal of Bank Marketing* 28(5): 342–371.

Crystal, D. 2006. *Language and the Internet*. Cambridge: Cambridge University Press.

Cullen, R. 2009. Culture, identity and information privacy in the age of digital government. *Online Information Review* 33(3): 405–421.

de Roo, G., and Porter, G. (eds.). 2007. *Fuzzy Planning Role of Actors in a Fuzzy Governance Environment*. Aldershot: Ashgate.

Deleuze, G., and Guattari, F. 1986. *Nomadology*. New York: Semiotext(e).

DeVol, R. C. 1999. *America's High-Tech Economy: Growth, Development, and Risks for Metropolitan Areas*. Santa Monica, CA: Milken Institute.

Dhakal, D., Pradhan, G., and Upadhyaya, K. 2009. Nepal and Bhutan: Economic growth in two Shangri-Las. *International Journal of Social Economics* 36(1): 124–137.

Dicken, P. 2007. *Global Shift: Mapping the Changing Contours of the World Economy*. 5th ed. New York: Guilford.

Diki-Kidiri, M. 2008. *Securing a Place for a Language in Cyberspace*. Paris: UNESCO.

Dodge, M. 2001. Guest editorial. *Environment and Planning B: Planning and Design* 28:1–2.

Dodge, M., and Kitchin, R. 2001. *Mapping Cyberspace*. London: Routledge.

Dougherty, C. 2009. Debate in Germany: Research or manufacturing? *New York Times*. http://www.nytimes.com/2009/08/12/business/global/12silicon.html?page wanted=all&_r=0.

Drori, G. S. 2007. Information society as a global policy agenda: What does it tell us about the age of globalization? *International Journal of Comparative Sociology* 48:297–316.

Dunning, J. H. 2000a. *Regions, Globalization, and the Knowledge-Based Economy*. New York: Oxford University Press.

———. 2000b. Regions, globalization, and the knowledge economy: The issues stated. In J. H. Dunning (ed.), *Regions, Globalization, and the Knowledge-Based Economy*. New York: Oxford University Press, pp. 7–41.

Dupagne, M. 1997. A theoretical and methodological critique of the principle of relative constancy. *Communication Theory* 7:53–76.

Duranton, G. 1999. Distance, land, and proximity: Economic analysis and the evolution of cities. *Environment and Planning A* 31:2169–2188.

Edosomwan, S., Prakasan, S., Kouame, D., Watson, J., and Seymour, T. 2011. The history of social media and its impact on business. *Journal of Applied Management and Entrepreneurship* 16(3): 79–91.

Ein-Dor, P. 2008. The Internet in Israel: 1999–2007 with international comparisons. *Journal of Global Information Technology Management* 11(3): 65–93.

Einstein, A. 1931. *Cosmic Religion: With Other Opinions and Aphorisms.* New York: Covici-Freide.

Eldon, E. 2009. Facebook grows across the Middle East. *Inside Facebook.* http://www.insidefacebook.com/2009/10/16/facebook-grows-across-the-middle-east.

Eriksson, K., Kerem, K., and Nilsson, D. 2008. The adoption of commercial innovations in the former Central and Eastern European markets. *International Journal of Bank Marketing* 26(3): 154–169.

EU (European Union). 2006. eUSER Population Survey 2005. http://www.idnfocus.com/directory/internet_statistics.html.

European Commission. 1996. *The Information Society.* Luxembourg: Office for Official Publications of the European Communities.

———. 2002. Qualitative study on cross border shopping in 28 European countries. http://ec.europa.eu/consumers/topics/cross_border_shopping_en_pdf.

———. 2006. Consumer protection in the Internet market. Special *Eurobarometer* 252. http://ec.europa.eu/public_opinion/archives/ebs/ebs252_en.pdf.

Evans, P. B., and Wurster, T. S. 1997. Strategy and the new economics of information. *Harvard Business Review* 75(5): 71–82.

Eyerman, R., and Löfgren, O. 1995. Romancing the road: Road movies and images of mobility. *Theory, Culture and Society* 12:53–79.

Fabrikant, S. I., and Buttenfield, B. P. 2001. Formalizing semantic spaces for information access. *Annals of the Association of American Geographers* 91:263–280.

Falk, T., and Abler, R. 1980. Intercommunications, distance and geographical theory. *Geografiska Annaler* 62:59–67.

Feather, J. 1994. *The Information Society: A Study of Continuity and Change.* London: Library Association Publishing.

Feldman, M. P. 1994. *The Geography of Innovation.* Dordrecht: Kluwer.

———. 2000. Location and innovation: The new economic geography of innovation, spillovers, and agglomeration. In G. L. Clark, M. P. Feldman, and M. S. Gertler (eds.), *The Oxford Handbook of Economic Geography.* New York: Oxford University Press, pp. 373–394.

Feldman, M. P., and Audretsch, D. 1999. Innovation in cities: Science-based diversity, specialization and localized competition. *European Economic Review* 43:409–429.

Feldman, M. P., and Florida, R. 1994. The geographic sources of innovation: Technological infrastructure and product innovation in the United States. *Annals of the Association of American Geographers* 84:210–229.

Felsenstein, D. 1993. *Processes of Growth and Spatial Concentration in Israel's High Technology Industries* (Hebrew). PhD dissertation, Hebrew University, Jerusalem.

Fidelie, L. H. 2009. "Internet gambling: Innocent activity or cybercrime." *International Journal of Cyber Criminology* 3(1): 476–491. http://www.cybercrimejournal.com/lauraijcc2009.pdf.

Fischer, C. S. 1992. *America Calling: A Social History of the Telephone to 1940.* Berkeley: University of California Press.

Florida, R. 1995. Toward the learning region. *Futures* 27:527–536.

Forrester Research. 2008. *Worldwide PC Adoption Forecast, 2007 to 2015*. http://www. forrester.com/Worldwide+PC+Adoption+Forecast+2007+To+2015/fulltext/-/E -RES42496.

Forsyth, A., and Crewe, A. 2010. Suburban technopoles as places: The international campus-garden-suburb style. *Urban Design International* 15(3): 165–183.

Fowler, H. 1965. *Curiosity and Exploratory Behavior*. New York: Macmillan.

Freedom House. 2011a. *Freedom on the Net*. http://www.freedomhouse.org/report/ freedom-net/freedom-net-2011.

———. 2011b. *Freedom of the Press*. http://www.freedomhouse.org/report/freedom -press/freedom-press-2011.

Freund, P., and Martin, G. 1993. *The Ecology of the Automobile*. Montreal: Black Rose Books.

Friedman, E. J. 2005. The reality of virtual reality: The Internet and gender equality advocacy in Latin America. *Latin American Politics and Society* 47(3): 1–34.

Friedman, T. L. 2005. *The World Is Flat: A Brief History of the Twenty-First Century*. New York: Farrar, Strauss and Giroux.

Friedmann, J., and Wolff, G. 1982. World city formation: An agenda for research and action. *International Journal for Urban and Regional Research* 6:309–344.

Gabriele, A. 2010. "Cuba: The surge of export-oriented services." *Economics, Management and Financial Markets* 5(4): 151–175.

Ganne, B., and Lecler, Y. 2009. From industrial districts to poles of competitiveness. In B. Ganne and Y. Lecler (eds.), *Asian Industrial Clusters, Global Competitiveness and New Policy Initiatives*. Singapore: World Scientific.

Garnsey, E. 1998. The genesis of the high technology milieu: A study of complexity. *International Journal of Urban and Regional Research* 22:361–377.

Gharbia, S. B. 2011. The Internet freedom fallacy and Arab digital activism. http:// nawaat.org/portail/2010/09/17/the-internet-freedom-fallacy-and-the-arab-digital -activism/.

Gibson, W. 1984. *Neuromancer*. London: Gollancz.

Giddens, A. 1990. *The Consequences of Modernity*. Cambridge: Polity Press.

Global Reach. 2004. Global Internet statistics (by languages). http://www.glreach .com/globstats/index.php3 (Inactive).

Goddard, J. 1990. Editor's preface. In M. E. Hepworth, *Geography of the Information Economy*. New York: Guilford, pp. xiv–xvii.

———. 1992. New technology and the geography of the UK information economy. In K. Robins (ed.), *Understanding Information Business, Technology and Geography*. London: Belhaven, pp. 178–201.

Golledge, R. G. 1995. Primitives of spatial knowledge. In T. L. Nyerges, D. M. Mark, R. Laurini, and M. J. Egehofer (eds.), *Cognitive Aspects of Human-Computer Interaction for Geographic Information Systems*. Boston: Kluwer.

———. 1999. Human wayfinding and cognitive maps. In R. G. Golledge (ed.), *Wayfinding Behavior: Cognitive Mapping and Other Spatial Processes*. Baltimore, MD: Johns Hopkins University Press.

Golob, T. F., and Regan, A. 2001. Impacts of information technology on personal travel and commercial vehicle operations: Research challenges and opportunities. *Transportation Research C* 9:87–121.

Gong, W. 2009. National culture and global diffusion of business-to-consumer e-commerce. *Cross Cultural Management: An International Journal* 16(1): 83–101.

Gottmann, J. 1961. *Megalopolis*. New York: Twentieth Century Fund.

GPS Magazine. 2011. http://www.gpsmagazine.com/2009/10/gps_us_household_penetration.php.

GPS World. 2007. http://www.gpsworld.com.

Graham, S. 1998. The end of geography or the explosion of place? Conceptualizing space, place and information technology. *Progress in Human Geography* 22:165–185.

Graham, S., and Healey, P. 1999. Relational concepts of space and place: Issues for planning theory and practice. *European Planning Studies* 7(5): 623–646.

Grantham, A., and Tsekouras, G. 2004. Information society: Wireless ICTs' transformative potential. *Futures* 36:359–377.

Habermas, J. 1984. *The Theory of Communicative Action: Vol. 1. Reason and the Rationalization of Society* (T. McCarthy, trans.). Boston: Beacon Press (originally published in German in 1981).

Hackler, D. 2000. Industrial location in the information age: An analysis of information-technology-intensive industry. In J. O. Wheeler, Y. Aoyama, and B. Warf (eds.), *Cities in the Telecommunications Age: The Fracturing of Geographies*. New York: Routledge, pp. 200–218.

Haddon, L. 2000. Social exclusion and information and communications technologies. *New Media and Society* 2:387–406.

———. 2004. *Information and Communication Technologies in Everyday Life: A Concise Introduction and Research Guide*. Oxford: Berg.

Hägerstrand, T. 1970. What about people in regional science? *Papers of the Regional Science Association* 24:7–21.

———. 1992. Mobility and transportation—are economics and technology the only limits? *Facta and Futura* 2:35–38.

Halal, W. E. 1993. The information technology revolution: Computer hardware, software, and services into the 21st century. *Technological Forecasting and Social Change* 44:69–86.

Halbwachs, M. 1980. *The Collective Memory* (F. J. Dulles and V. Y. Ditter, trans.). New York: Harper and Row.

Hall, P. (ed.). 1986. *Technology, Innovation and Economic Policy*. New York: St. Martin's.

Hampton, K. N., and Wellman, B. 2002. The not so global village at Netville. In B. Wellman and C. Haythornthwaite (eds.), *The Internet in Everyday Life*. Malden, MA: Blackwell, pp. 345–371.

Hans, v. Z. 2005. The variety of information society development paths in central Europe. *AI & Society* 19(3): 309–326.

Hanson, S. 1998. Off the road? Reflections on transportation geography in the information age. *Journal of Transport Geography* 6:241–249.

Harasim, L. M. 1993. Networlds: Networks as social space. In L. M. Harasim (ed.), *Global Networks: Computers and International Communication*. Cambridge, MA: MIT Press, pp. 16–34.

Hargittai, E. 1999. Weaving the Western web: Explaining differences in Internet connectivity among OECD countries. *Telecommunications Policy* 23:701–718.

Harris, R. 1998. The Internet as a GPT: Factor market implications. In E. Helpman (ed.), *General Purpose Technologies and Economic Growth*. Cambridge, MA: MIT Press, pp. 140–165.

Hartley, J., Green, L., and Lumby, C. 2010. Refused classification and the proposed Australian Internet filter: An assault on the Open Society. *Australian Journal of Communication* 37(3): 1–14.

Harvey, D. 1989. *The Condition of Postmodernity*. Oxford: Blackwell.

Healey, P. 1992, April. Planning through debate: The communicative turn in planning theory. *Town Planning Review* 63(2): 143–162.

———. 2006. Place development in a relational world. *Town & Country Planning* 75(11): 1–4.

———. 2007. *Urban Complexity and Spatial Strategies: Towards a Relational Planning for Our Times*. London: Routledge.

Henderson, J. C. 2007. Uniquely Singapore? A case study in destination branding. *Journal of Vacation Marketing* 13(3): 261–274.

Hepworth, M. E. 1990. *Geography of the Information Economy*. New York: Guilford.

Higgins, E. T. 2004. Making a theory useful: Lessons handed down. *Personality and Social Psychological Review* 8(2): 138–145.

Hochmair, H., and Frank, A. U. 2001. A semantic map as basis for the decision process in the WWW navigation. In D. R. Montello (ed.), *Conference on Spatial Information Theory*. Morrow Bay, CA: Springer.

Hodgson, G. 1999. *Economics and Utopia: Why the Learning Economy Is Not the End of History*. London: Routledge.

Hopkins, L. D., and Zapata, M. A. (eds.). 2007. *Engaging the Future: Forecasts, Scenarios, Plans and Projects*. Cambridge, MA: Lincoln Institute of Land Policy.

Hot Telecom. 2009. *Country Profile Saudi Arabia*. Hot Telecom.

Hotz-Hart, B. 2000. Innovation networks, regions, and globalization. In G. L. Clark, M. P. Feldman, and M. S. Gertler (eds.), *The Oxford Handbook of Economic Geography*. New York: Oxford University Press, pp. 432–450.

Howard, P. E. N., Busch, L., and Sheets, P. 2010. Comparing digital divides: Internet access and social inequality in Canada and the United States. *Canadian Journal of Communication* 35(1): 109–128.

Howard, P. E. N., Rainie, L., and Jones, S. 2002. Days and nights on the Internet. In B. Wellman and C. Haythornthwaite (eds.), *The Internet in Everyday Life*. Malden, MA: Blackwell, pp. 45–73.

Howells, J. 2000. Knowledge, innovation and location. In J. R. Bryson, P. W. Daniels, N. Henry, and J. Pollard (eds.), *Knowledge, Space, Economy*. London: Routledge, pp. 50–62.

Høyer, K. G. 2000. Sustainable tourism or sustainable mobility? The Norwegian case. *Journal of Sustainable Tourism* 8:147–160.

Hubbard, P., Kitchin, R., Bartley, B., and Fuller, D. 2002. *Thinking Geographically: Space, Theory and Contemporary Human Geography*. London: Continuum.

Hudson, D. 2009. Undesirable bodies and desirable labor: Documenting the globalization and digitization of transnational American dreams in Indian call centers. *Cinema Journal* 49(1): 82–102.

Hupkes, G. 1982. The law of constant travel time and trip-rates. *Futures* 14:38–46.

Hwang, W., Jung, H.-S., and Salvendy, G. 2006. Internationalisation of e-commerce: A comparison of online shopping preferences among Korean, Turkish and US populations. *Behaviour and Information Technology* 25:3–18.

IASP (International Association of Science Parks). 2007. *Facts and Figures of Science and Technology Parks in the World.* IASP.

Imrie, R. 2000. Disability and discourses of mobility and movement. *Environment and Planning A* 32:1641–1656.

Innes, J. E. 1995a. Planning theory's emerging paradigm: Communicative action and interactive practice. *Journal of Planning Education and Research* 14(3): 183–189.

———. 1995b. *Toward a Theory of Knowledge for Communicative Planning.* Abstract submitted for presentation at the ninth AESOP (Association of European Schools of Planning) Congress, Glasgow, August 17–19.

Innes, J. E., and Booher, D. E. 2010. *Planning with Complexity: An Introduction to Collaborative Rationality for Public Policy.* London: Routledge.

InsideFacebook. 2010. *The Facebook Global Monitor.* http://www.insidefacebook.com/facebook-global-market-monitor.

Internet World Stats. 2009. *Internet World Users by Language.* http://www.internetworldstats.com/stats7.htm.

———. 2011. *Usage and Population Statistics.* http://www.internetworldstats.com.

ITU (International Telecommunication Union). 2004. *Information technology.* http://www.itu.int/ITU-D/ict/statistics.

———. 2008. *World Information Society Report.* http://www.itu.int/ITU-D/ict/doi/material/WISR07-chapter3.pdf.

———. 2011. *Measuring the Information Society.* Geneva: ITU.

———. 2012. *Statistics.* http://www.itu.int/ITU-D/ict/statistics.

Iyer, P. 2001. *The Global Soul: Jet Lag, Shopping Malls, and the Search for Home.* New York: Random House.

Jaffe, A. B., Trajtenberg, M., and Henderson, R. 1993. Geographic localization of knowledge spillover as evidenced by patent citations. *Quarterly Journal of Economics* 108:577–598.

James, W., Torres-Baumgarten, G., Petkovic, G., and Havrylenko, T. 2008. Exploring web language orientation in emerging markets: The case of Serbia and the Ukraine. *Journal of Targeting, Measurement and Analysis for Marketing* 16(3): 189–202.

Jamtsho, S., and Bullen, M. 2007. Distance education in Bhutan: Improving access and quality through ICT use. *Distance Education* 28(2): 149–161.

Janelle, D. G. 1968. Central place development in a time-space framework. *Professional Geographer* 20:5–10.

———. 1991. Global interdependence and its consequences. In S. D. Brunn and T. R. Leinbach (eds.), *Collapsing Space and Time: Geographic Aspects of Communication and Information.* London: Harper Collins Academic, pp. 49–81.

———. 2004. Impact of information technologies. In G. Hanson and G. Giuliano (eds.), *The Geography of Urban Transportation*, 3rd ed. New York: Guilford, pp. 86–112.

Jansen, E. 2006. *NetLingo: The Internet Dictionary*. http://www.netlingo.com.

Jayaram, G. K. 1976. Open systems planning. In W. G. Bennis, K. D. Benne, R. Chin, and K. E. Corey (eds.), *The Planning of Change*, 3rd ed. New York: Holt, Rinehart and Winston, pp. 275–283.

Jin, D. J., and Stough, R. R. 1998. Learning and learning capability in the Fordist and post-Fordist age: An integrative framework. *Environment and Planning A* 30:1255–1278.

Johnson, B., and Lundvall, B. 2001. *Why All This Fuss about Codified and Tacit Knowledge?* Paper presented at DRUID Winter Conference.

Jordan Ministry of Information and Communications Technology. 2006. *Jordan e-Government Program*. http://www.thieswittig.eu/docs/MPC_Strategies/Jordan/Jordan_e-GovernmenStrategy.pdf.

Kapow. 2005. *Top-Ten Business Users of SMS Text Messaging*. http://www.kapow.co.uk.

Katz, P. L. 1988. *The Information Society: An International Perspective*. New York: Praeger.

Kauffman, R., and Techatassanasoontorn, A. A. 2009. Understanding early diffusion of digital wireless phones. *Telecommunications Policy* 33:432–450.

Kaufmann, V. 2002. *Re-thinking Mobility: Contemporary Sociology*. Aldershot: Ashgate.

Keane, J. 2003. *Global Civil Society?* Cambridge: Cambridge University Press.

Kellerman, A. 1984. Telecommunications and the geography of metropolitan areas. *Progress in Human Geography* 8:222–246.

———. 1985. The evolution of service economies: A geographical perspective. *Professional Geographer* 37:133–143.

———. 1986. The diffusion of BITNET: A communications system for universities. *Telecommunications Policy* 10:88–92.

———. 1989. *Time, Space and Society: Geographical-Societal Perspectives*. Dordrecht: Kluwer.

———. 1993. *Telecommunications and Geography*. London: Belhaven.

———. 1994. Commuting as experience and its ramifications for telecommuting. *NETCOM* 8:225–234.

———. 1997. Fusions of information types, media, and operators, and continued American leadership in telecommunications. *Telecommunications Policy* 21:553–564.

———. 1999. Leading nations in the adoption of communications media 1975–1995. *Urban Geography* 20:377–389.

———. 2000. Phases in the rise of information society. *Info* 2:537–541.

———. 2002a. Conditions for the development of high-tech industry: The case of Israel. *Tijdschrift voor Economische en Sociale Geografie* 93:270–286.

———. 2002b. *The Internet on Earth: A Geography of Information*. London: Wiley.

———. 2006a. Broadband penetration and its implications: The case of France. *Netcom* 20:237–246.

———. 2006b. *Personal Mobilities*. London: Routledge.

———. 2007. Cyberspace classification and cognition: Information and communications cyberspaces. *Journal of Urban Technology* 14:5–32.

———. 2008. International airports: Passengers in an environment of "authorities." *Mobilities* 3:161–178.

———. 2009. End of spatial reorganization? Urban landscapes of personal mobilities in the information age. *Journal of Urban Technology* 16:47–61.

———. 2010. Mobile broadband services and the availability of instant access to cyberspace. *Environment and Planning A* 42:2990–3005.

———. 2012. *Daily Spatial Mobilities: Corporeal and Virtual.* Aldershot: Ashgate.

Kellerman, A., and Paradiso, M. 2007. Geographical location in the information age: From destiny to opportunity? *GeoJournal* 70:195–211.

Kenyon, S., Lyons, G., and Rafferty, J. 2002. Transport and social exclusion: Investigating the possibility of promoting inclusion through virtual mobility. *Journal of Transport Geography* 10:207–219.

Kern, S. 1983. *The Culture of Time and Space, 1880–1918.* Cambridge, MA: Harvard University Press.

Kesselring, S., and Vogl, G. 2004. *Mobility Pioneers: Networks, Scapes and Flows between First and Second Modernity.* Paper presented at the Mobility and the Cosmopolitan Perspective Workshop, Munich Reflexive Modernization Research Centre.

Kirsch, S. 1995. The incredible shrinking world? Technology and the production of space. *Environment and Planning D: Society and Space* 13:529–555.

Kitchin, R. 1998. *Cyberspace: The World in the Wires.* Chichester: Wiley.

Knight, J. 2006. *Higher Education Crossing Borders: A Guide to the Implications of the General Agreement on Trade in Services (GATS) for Cross-border Education.* Paris: Commonwealth of Learning, Vancouver, and UNESCO.

Knights, D., and Jones, B. 2007. Outsourcing the economy to India: Utopian and dystopian discourses of offshoring. *The International Journal of Sociology and Social Policy* 27(11/12): 433–446.

Knox, P. L. 1995. World cities and the organization of global space. In R. J. Johnston, P. J. Taylor, and M. J. Watts (eds.), *Geographies of Global Change: Remapping the World in the Late Twentieth Century.* Oxford: Blackwell, pp. 232–247.

Kopomaa, T. 2000. *The City in Your Pocket: Birth of the Mobile Information Society.* Helsinki: Gaudeamus.

Kshetri, N. B. 2001. Determinants of the locus of global e-commerce. *Electronic Markets* 11:251–257.

———. 2009. The evolution of the Chinese online gaming industry. *Journal of Technology Management in China* 4(2): 158–179.

Kwan, M. P. 2001a. Cyberspatial cognition and individual access to information: The behavioral foundation of cybergeography. *Environment and Planning B* 28:21–37.

———. 2001b. *Time, Space, Information Technologies and Urban Geographies.* Paper presented at the Digital Communities conference, Chicago.

Lacohée, H., Wakeford, N., and Pearson, I. 2003. A social history of the mobile telephone with a view of its future. *BT Technology Journal* 21:203–211.

Laffey, K., and Laffey, D. 2010. Risky business: London's listed firms and their American gamble. *Journal of Strategic Management Education* 6(4): 265–282.

Lakoff, G. 2004. *Don't Think of an Elephant! Know Your Values and Frame the De-bate*. White River Junction, VT: Chelsea Green Publishing.

LaMore, R., et al. 2009. *An Assessment of the Knowledge Economy in Northern Michigan and the Eastern Upper Peninsula*. http://www.reicenter.org/upload/documents/kea -report.pdf.

Lash, S., and Urry, J. 1994. *Economies of Signs and Space*. London: Sage.

Latour, B. 1987. *Science in Action: How to Follow Scientists and Engineers through Society*. Cambridge, MA: Harvard University Press.

———. 1997. *On actor network theory: A few clarifications*. Mimeo (unpublished).

Laurier, E. 2001. The region as a socio-technical accomplishment of mobile workers. In B. Brown, N. Green, and R. Harper (eds.), *Wireless World: Social and Inter-actional Aspects of the Mobile Age*. London: Springer, pp. 46–61.

Law, R. 1999. Beyond "women and transport": Towards new geographies of gender and daily mobility. *Progress in Human Geography* 23:567–588.

Lechner, F. J. 2009. *Globalization: The Making of World Society*. Chichester: Wiley-Blackwell.

Lee, R. S., and Wu, T. 2009. Subsidizing creativity through network design: Zero-pricing and net neutrality. *Journal of Economic Perspectives* 23(3): 61–76.

Lefebvre, H. 1991. *The Production of Space*. Oxford: Blackwell.

Leiss, W. 1976. *The Limits to Satisfaction: An Essay on the Problem of Needs and Com-modities*. Toronto: University of Toronto Press.

Lessig, L. 2001. *The Future of Ideas: The Fate of the Commons in a Connected World*. New York: Random House.

Levinson, S. C. 2003. *Space in Language and Cognition: Explorations in Cognitive Diversity*. Cambridge: Cambridge University Press.

Levy, P. 1998. *Becoming Virtual: Reality in the Digital Age* (R. Bononno, trans.). New York: Platinum.

Lewis, W. 1948. *America and Cosmic Man*. London: Nicholson and Watson.

Li, F., Whalley, J., and Williams, H. 2001. Between physical and electronic spaces: The implications for organizations in the networked economy. *Environment and Planning A* 33:699–716.

Liang, B., and Mackey, T. 2009. Searching for safety: Addressing search engine, web-site, and provider accountability for illicit online drug sales. *American Journal of Law and Medicine* 35(1): 125–184.

Lim, G. C. 2003, December 19. Asian thoughts for good governance. In *Life-Culture and Regional Development Planning: Making Gyeonggi a Livable Place*. World Life-Culture Forum 2003. Suwon, South Korea: Kyonggi Research Institute, pp. 3–31.

Loewenstein, G. 2002. Psychology of curiosity. *International Encyclopedia of the So-cial and Behavioral Sciences*. http://www.sciencedirect.com.

Longan, M. W. 2002. Building a global sense of place: The community networking movement in the United States. *Urban Geography* 23:213–236.

Lundvall, B. A., and Maskell, P. 2000. Nation states and economic development: From national systems of production to national systems of knowledge creation and learning. In G. L. Clark, M. P. Feldman, and M. S. Gertler (eds.), *The Oxford Hand-book of Economic Geography*. New York: Oxford University Press, pp. 353–372.

Lyman, P., and Varian, H. R. 2000. *How Much Information?* School of Information Management and Systems, University of California, Berkeley. http://www.sims .berkeley.edu/research/projects/how-much-info.

———. 2003. *How Much Information? 2003.* School of Information Management and Systems, University of California, Berkeley. http://www.sims.berkeley.edu/ research/projects/how-much-info-2003.

Lyon, D. 1988. *The Information Society: Issues and Illusions.* Cambridge: Polity Press.

———. 1995. The roots of the information society idea. In N. Heap, R. Thomas, G. Einon, R. Mason, and H. Mackay (eds.), *Information Technology and Society: A Reader,* pp. 54–73.

Lyons, G. 2002. Internet: Investigating new technology's evolving role, nature and effects on transport. *Transport Policy* 9:335–346.

Machlup, F. 1962. *The Production and Distribution of Knowledge in the United States.* Princeton, NJ: Princeton University Press.

———. 1980. *Knowledge and Knowledge Production.* Princeton, NJ: Princeton University Press.

———. 1983. Semiotic quirks in studies of information. In F. Machlup and U. Mansfield (eds.), *The Study of Information: Interdisciplinary Messages.* New York: Wiley, pp. 641–671.

Maciel, M., Whalley, J., and van der Meer, R. 2006. Foreign investment and consolidation in the Brazilian mobile telecommunications market. *Info: The Journal of Policy, Regulation and Strategy for Telecommunications, Information and Media* 8(3): 60–77.

Malecki, E. J. 2000. Creating and sustaining competitiveness: Local knowledge and economic geography. In J. R. Bryson, P. W. Daniels, N. Henry, and J. Pollard (eds.), *Knowledge, Space, Economy.* London: Routledge, pp. 103–119.

Malecki, E. J., and Gorman, S. P. 2001. Maybe the death of distance, but not the end of geography: The Internet as a network. In T. R. Leinbach and S. D. Brunn (eds.), *Worlds of E-Commerce: Economic, Geographical and Social Dimensions.* Chichester: Wiley, pp. 87–105.

Malecki, E. J., and Moriset, B. 2008. *The Digital Economy: Business Organization, Production Processes, and Regional Developments.* London: Routledge.

Mamaghani, F. 2010. The social and economic impact of information and communication technology on developing countries: An analysis. *International Journal of Management* 27(3): 607–615.

Mansfield, E. J. 1991. Academic research and industrial innovation. *Research Policy* 20:1–12.

Markusen, A. 1996. Sticky places in a slippery space: A typology of industrial districts. *Economic Geography* 72:293–313.

Martin, W. J. 1988. *The Information Society.* London: Aslib.

Martin, W. J. 1995. *The Global Information Society.* Aldershot: Aslib Gower.

Marvin, C. 1988. *When Old Technologies Were New: Thinking about Electric Communication in the Late Nineteenth Century.* New York: Oxford University Press.

Maskell, P. 2000. Social capital, innovation and competitiveness. In S. Baron, J. Field, and T. Schuller (eds.), *Social Capital: Critical Perspectives*. Oxford: Oxford University Press, pp. 111–123.

Maskell, P., and Malmberg, H. 1999a. The competitiveness of firms and regions: "Ubiquitification" and the importance of localized learning. *European Urban and Regional Studies* 6:9–25.

———. 1999b. Localized learning and industrial competitiveness. *Cambridge Journal of Economics* 23:167–185.

Massey, D. 1993. Power-geometry and a progressive sense of place. In J. Bird, B. Curtis, T. Putnam, G. Robertson, and L. Tickner (eds.), *Mapping the Futures: Local Cultures, Global Change*. London: Routledge, pp. 59–69.

———. 1994. *Space, Place and Gender*. Cambridge: Polity Press, 1994.

———. 2005. *For Space*. London: Sage.

Masuda, Y. 1980. *The Information Society as Post-Industrial Society*. Washington, DC: World Future Society.

Matthiessen, C. W., Schwarz, A. W., and Find, S. 2006. World cities of knowledge: Research strength, networks and nodality. *Journal of Knowledge Management* 10(5): 14–25.

McLuhan, M. 1964. *Understanding Media*. New York: McGraw-Hill.

Merrifield, A. 1993. Place and space: A Lefebvrian reconciliation. *Transactions of the British Institute of Geographers* 18:516–531.

Merton, R. K. 1968. *Social Theory and Social Structure*. New York: Free Press.

Metters, R. 2008. A case study of national culture and offshoring services. *International Journal of Operations & Production Management* 28(8): 727–747.

Miles, I., and Robins, K. 1992. Making sense of information. In K. Robins (ed.), *Understanding Information Business, Technology and Geography*. London: Belhaven, pp. 1–26.

Mitchell, W. J. 1995. *City of Bits: Space, Place, and the Infobahn*. Cambridge, MA: MIT Press.

Mohr, L. 2007. State control of the Internet reins in Cuba's future. *SAIS Review* 27(2): 151–152.

Mokhtarian, P. L. 1997. Now that travel can be virtual, will congestion virtually disappear? *Scientific American* 277(4): 61.

———. 2000. Telecommunications and travel. In *Transportation in the New Millennium*. Washington, DC: Transportation Research Board. http://onlinepubs.trb.org/onlinepubs/millennium/00115.pdf.

Mokhtarian, P. L., and Chen, C. 2004. TTB or not TTB, that is the question: A review and analysis of the empirical literature on travel time (and money) budgets. *Transportation Research A* 38:643–675.

Mokyr, J. 2002. *The Gifts of Athena: Historical Origins of the Knowledge Economy*. Princeton, NJ: Princeton University Press.

Monck, C., Porter, D., Quintas, P., Storey, D., and Wynarczyk, P. 1988. *Science Parks and the Growth of High Technology Firms*. London: Routledge.

Mosco, V. 1996. *The Political Economy of Communication: Rethinking and Renewal*. London: Sage.

Mutula, S. M., and van Brakel, P. 2006. E-readiness of SMEs in the ICT sector in Botswana with respect to information access. *Electronic Library* 24(3): 402–417.

Myers, D., and Banerjee, T. 2005, Spring. Toward greater heights for planning: Reconciling the differences between profession, practice and academic field. *Journal of the American Planning Association* 71(2): 121–129.

Naisbitt, J. 2006. *Mind Set! Reset Your Thinking and See the Future.* New York: HarperCollins Publishers.

Nationmaster. 2009. *Internet Statistics.* http://www.nationmaster.com/cat/int-internet.

Nobis, C., and Lenz, B. 2004. *Changes in Transport Behavior by the Fragmentation of Activities.* Paper presented at the Thirtieth Congress of the International Geographical Union (IGU), Glasgow.

Nolan, R. L. 2000. Information technology management since 1960. In A. D. Chandler Jr. and J. W. Cortada (eds.), *A Nation Transformed by Information: How Information Has Shaped the United States from Colonial Times to the Present.* New York: Oxford University Press, pp. 217–256.

Northwest Minnesota Foundation. n.d. *Ingenuity Frontier: Engineering at Work in Northwest Minnesota.* Bemidji, MN: Northwest Minnesota Foundation.

NTIA (National Telecommunications and Information Administration). 1999. *Falling through the Net: Defining the Digital Divide.* http://www.ntia.doc.gov/ntia home/fallingthru.html.

———. 2002. *A Nation Online: How Americans Are Expanding Their Use of the Internet.* http://www.ntia.doc.gov/ntiahome/dn/anationonline2.pdf.

Nunes, M. 2006. *Cyberspaces of Everyday Life.* Minneapolis: University of Minnesota Press.

Nye, J. S., Jr., and Owens, W. A. 1996. America's information edge. *Foreign Affairs* 75:20–36.

Ó hUallacháin, B. 1999. Patent places: Size matters. *Journal of Regional Science* 39:613–636.

OECD (Organisation for Economic Co-operation and Development). 2000. *Knowledge Management in the Learning Society.* Paris: Center for Educational and Research and Innovation.

———. 2009. *Communications Outlook.* http://www.oecd.org/general/mobilephone callslowestinfinlandnetherlandsandswedensaysoecdreport.htm.

———. 2011a. *The Future of the Internet Economy.* Paris: OECD. http://www.oecd.org/dataoecd/24/5/48255770.pdf.

———. 2011b. *OECD Broadband Statistics to December 2010.* http://www.oecd.org/do cument/54/0,3746,en_2649_34225_38690102_1_1_1_1,00.html.

Ogden, M. R. 1994. Politics in a parallel universe. *Futures* 26:713–729.

Ohmae, K. 1996. *The End of the Nation State: The Rise of Regional Economies.* New York: Free Press Paperbacks.

———. 2005. *The Next Global Stage: Challenges and Opportunities in Our Borderless World.* Upper Saddle River, NJ: Wharton School Publishing.

Okoli, C., Mbarika, V. W. A., and McCoy, S. 2010. The effects of infrastructure and policy on e-business in Latin America and sub-Saharan Africa. *European Journal of Information Systems* 19(1): 5–20.

Olds, K. 2007. Global assemblage: Singapore, foreign universities, and the construction of a global education hub. *World Development* 35(6): 959–975.

Ooi, C. S., and Stöber, B. 2008, January. *Authenticity-in-Context: Embedding the Arts and Culture in Branding Berlin and Singapore. Creative Encounters.* Working paper no. 6. Copenhagen: Copenhagen Business School. http://www.cbs.dk/creative encounters.

OpenNet Initiative. 2009. *Internet Filtering in the Middle East and North Africa.* http://opennet.net/sites/opennet.net/files/ONI_MENA_2009.pdf.

Otsuka, Y. 2007. Making a case for Tongan as an endangered language. *Contemporary Pacific* 19(2): 446–473, 664.

Palfrey, J. 2010. Four Phases of Internet Regulation. *Social Research* 77(3): 981–996.

Paradiso, M. 2009. Google and the Internet: A megaproject nesting within another megaproject. In S. Brunn (ed.), *Engineering Earth: The Impacts of Megaengineering Projects.* Dordrecht: Kluwer.

Patterson, K. D. W., Washington, M., Cavazos, D., and Brigham, K. 2010. Process and emergence in contested terrain. *International Journal of Organizational Analysis* 18(1): 105–128.

Pearson, R. 1993. Gender and new technology in the Caribbean. In J. Momsen (ed.), *Women and Change in the Caribbean.* Bloomington: Indiana University Press.

Peatling, S., and O'Rourke, J. 2012. IT Giants in Price Probe. *The Age,* April 29, 2012. http://www.theage.com.au/technology/technology-news/it-giants-in-price-probe-20120428-1xs16.html#ixzz1tUob3366.

Pena-Sanchez, R. 2010. Fixed, mobile and internetal teledensity estimates in Latin American countries. *Advances in Competitiveness Research* 18(1): 121–128.

Péruch, P., Gaunet, F., Thinus-Blanc, C., and Loomis, J. 2000. Understanding and learning virtual spaces. In R. Kitchin and S. Freundschuh (eds.), *Cognitive Mapping: Past, Present, and Future.* London: Routledge, pp. 108–115.

Pew Internet and American Life Project. 2012. *Digital Differences.* http://pewinternet .org/~/media//Files/Reports/2012/PIP_Digital_differences_041312.pdf.

Plummer, P., and Taylor, M. 2001a. Theories of local economic growth (part 1): Concepts, models and measurement. *Environment and Planning A* 33:219–236.

———. 2001b. Theories of local economic growth (part 2): Model specification and empirical validation. *Environment and Planning A* 33:385–398.

———. 2003. Theory and praxis in economic geography: "Enterprising" and local growth in a global economy. *Environment and Planning C* 21:633–649.

Poon, J. P. H., Hsu, J. Y., and Jeongwook, S. 2006. The geography of learning and knowledge acquisition among Asian latecomers. *Journal of Economic Geography* 6:541–559.

Porat, M. 1977. *The Information Economy: Definition and Measurement.* Publication 77-12(1). Washington, DC: U.S. Department of Commerce, Office of Telecommunications.

Postman, N. 1999. *Building a Bridge to the Eighteenth Century.* New York: Knopf.

Powell, W. 1990. Neither market nor hierarchy: Network forms of organizing. In B. Staw (ed.), *Research in Organizational Behavior.* Greenwich, CT: JAI, 295–336.

Powell, W., and Brantley, P. 1992. Competitive cooperation in biotechnology: Learning through networks? In N. Nohria and R. Eccles (eds.), *Networks and Organizations*. Boston: Harvard Business School Press, 366-394.

Pred, A. 1977. *City Systems in Advanced Economies*. London: Hutchinson.

Prensky, M. 2001. Digital natives, digital Immigrants. *On the Horizon* 9(5): 1–10.

Public Policy Institute of California. n.d. *Home Page of the Public Policy Institute of California*. http://www.ppic.org/main/home.asp.

Quail, C., and Larabie, C. 2010. Net neutrality: Media discourses and public perception. *Global Media Journal* 3(1): 31–n/a.

Rahimi, S., and Bowman, D. 2007. Social network site banned in UAE. *Arabian Business*. http://www.arabianbusiness.com/social-network-site-banned-in-uae-124819.html.

Ramos, F., Tajú, G., and Canuto, L. 2011. Promoting distance education in higher education in Cape Verde and Mozambique. *Distance Education* 32(2): 159–175.

Rai, S., Pedersen, M., and Kazakeviciute, A. 2010. A framework for the co-creation of ICT innovation: Empirical results from India. *Journal of Information Technology Case and Application Research* 12(4): 13–36.

Raubal, M., Miller, H. J., and Bridwell, S. 2004. User-centred time geography for location-based services. *Geografiska Annaler* 86B: 245–265.

Rawls, J. 2001. *Justice as Fairness: A Restatement*. 2nd ed. Cambridge, MA: Belknap Press of Harvard University Press.

Reuters. 2007. Syria blocks Facebook in Internet crackdown. http://www.reuters.com/article/2007/11/23/us-syria-facebook-idUSOWE37285020071123.

Rheingold, H. 1993. A slice of life in my virtual community. In L. M. Harasim (ed.), *Global Networks: Computers and International Communication*. Cambridge, MA: MIT Press, pp. 57–82.

Rice, R. E., and Katz, J. E. 2003. Comparing Internet and mobile phone usage: Digital divides of usage, adoption, and dropouts. *Telecommunications Policy* 27:597–623.

Roberts, J. 2000. *The Drive to Codify: Implications for the Knowledge-Based Economy*. Paper presented at the Eighth International Joseph A. Schumpeter Society Conference, University of Manchester.

Rogers, E. M. 1976. Communication and development: The passing of the dominant paradigm. *Communication Research* 3:213–240.

———. 1995. *Diffusion of Innovations*. 4th ed. New York: Free Press.

Rose, I. N., and Owens, Martin D. 2005 *Internet Gaming Law* Larchmont, NY: Mary Anne Liebert.

Roszak, T. 1991. *The Cult of Information: A Neo-Luddite Treatise on High-Tech, Artificial Intelligence and the True Art of Thinking*. 2nd ed. Berkeley: University of California Press.

Sakamura, K. 2003. *Ubiquitous Computing: Making It a Reality*. Presentation. ITU Telecom World, Geneva.

Salaff, J. W. 2002. Where home is the office: The new form of flexible work. In B. Wellman and C. Haythornthwaite (eds.), *The Internet in Everyday Life*. Malden, MA: Blackwell, pp. 464–495.

Salomon, I. 1986. Telecommunications and travel relationships: A review. *Transportation Research A* 20:223–238.

Salter, M. B. 2003. *Rights of Passage: The Passport in International Relations.* Boulder, CO: Lynne Rienner.

——. 2004. Passports, mobility, and security: How smart can the border be? *International Studies Perspectives* 5:71–91.

——. 2007. Governmentalities of an airport: Heterotopia and confession. *International Political Sociology* 1:49–66.

Sassen, S. 1991. *The Global City: New York, London, Tokyo.* Princeton, NJ: Princeton University Press.

——. 2001. Cities in the global economy. In R. Paddison (ed.), *Handbook of Urban Studies.* London: Sage, pp. 256–272.

Saxenian, A. 1994. *Regional Advantage: Culture and Competition in Silicon Valley and Route 128.* Cambridge, MA: Harvard University Press.

Schement, J. R. 1989. The origins of the information society in the United States: Competing visions. In J. L. Salvaggio (ed.), *The Information Society: Economic, Social, and Structural Issues.* Hillsdale, NJ: Erlbaum, pp. 29–50.

Schewe, P. F. 2007. *The Grid: A Journey through the Heart of Our Electrified World.* Washington, DC: Joseph Henry Press.

Schiller, H. I. 1981. *Who Knows: Information in the Age of the Fortune 500.* Norwood, NJ: Ablex.

Schivelbusch, W. 1978. Railroad space and railroad time. *New German Critique* 14:31–40.

Schön, D. A. 1983. *The Reflective Practitioner: How Professionals Think in Action.* New York: Basic Books.

Schrag, Z. M. 1994. Navigating cyberspace—maps and agents: Different uses of computer networks call for different interfaces. In G. C. Staple (ed.), *Telegeography 1994: Global Telecommunications Traffic.* Washington, DC: Telegeography, pp. 44–52.

Scott, A. J. 1993. *Technopoles: High-Technology Industry and Regional Development in Southern California.* Los Angeles: University of California Press.

——. 2001. Globalization and the rise of city-regions. *European Planning Studies* 9(7): 813–826.

Selwyn, L., and Golding, H. 2010. Revisiting the regulatory status of broadband Internet access: A policy framework for net neutrality and an open competitive Internet. *Federal Communications Law Journal* 63(1): 91–139.

Shefer, A., and Frenkel, A. 1998. Local milieu and innovations: Some empirical results. *Annals of Regional Science* 32:185–200.

Sheller, M. 2004. Mobile publics: Beyond the network perspective. *Environment and Planning D: Society and Space* 22:39–52.

Sheller, M., and Urry, J. 2000. The city and the car. *International Journal of Urban and Regional Research* 24:737–757.

Sheth, J. 2009. The call center couple: India's new middle class. *Journal of Indian Business Research* 1(1): 10–13.

Shields, R. 1996. Introduction: Virtual spaces, real histories and living bodies. In R. Shields, (ed.), *Cultures of Internet: Virtual Spaces, Real Histories, Living Bodies.* London: Sage, pp. 1–10.

———. 1997. Flows as a new paradigm. *Space and Culture* 1:1–7.

———. 2003. *The Virtual*. London: Routledge.

Shirky, C. 2008. *Here Comes Everybody: The Power of Organizing without Organizations*. New York: Penguin.

Short, J. R., and Kim, Y. H. 1999. *Globalization and the City*. Essex: Addison Wesley Longman.

Shrum, W. 1985. *Organized Technology: Networks and Innovation in Technical Systems*. West Lafayette, IN: Purdue University Press.

Simonsen, K. 2004. Networks, flows, and fluids—reimagining spatial analysis? *Environment and Planning A* 36:1333–1340.

Software and Information Industry Association. 2008. http://www.siia.net.

SocialBakers. 2011. *Facebook Statistics*. http://www.socialbakers.com.

Solnit, R. 2000. *Wanderlust: A History of Walking*. New York: Viking.

Sölvell, Ö., and Birkinshaw, J. 2000. Multinational enterprises and the knowledge economy: Leveraging global practices. In J. H. Dunning (ed.), *Regions, Globalization, and the Knowledge-Based Economy*. New York: Oxford University Press, pp. 82–106.

Sroka, M. 1998. Commercial development of the Internet and WWW in Eastern Europe. *Online Information Review* 22(6): 367–376.

Stalder, F. 2006. *Manuel Castells: The Theory of the Network Society*. Cambridge, UK: Polity.

Standage, T. 1998. *The Victorian Internet: The Remarkable Story of the Telegraph and Nineteenth Century's On-line Pioneers*. New York: Walker.

Statistics Canada. 2004. *E-Commerce: Household Shopping on the Internet (The Daily)*. http://www.statcan.gc.ca/daily-quotidien/040923/dq040923a-eng.htm.

Steinfeld, C., and Salvaggio, J. L. 1989. Toward a definition of information society. In J. L. Salvaggio (ed.), *The Information Society: Economic, Social, and Structural Issues*. Hillsdale, NJ: Erlbaum, pp. 1–14.

Stewart, T. A. 1997. *Intellectual Capital*. London: Nicholas Bradley.

Stivers, R. 1999. *Technology and Magic: The Triumph of the Irrational*. New York: Continuum.

Storper, M. 1993. Regional "worlds" of production: Learning and innovation in the technology districts of France, Italy and the USA. *Regional Studies* 7:433–455.

———. 2000a. Globalization and knowledge flows: An industrial geographer's perspective. In J. H. Dunning (ed.), *Regions, Globalization, and the Knowledge-Based Economy*. New York: Oxford University Press, pp. 42–62.

———. 2000b. Globalization, localization, and trade. In G. L. Clark, M. P. Feldman, and M. S. Gertler (eds.), *The Oxford Handbook of Economic Geography*. New York: Oxford University Press, pp. 146–165.

Stover, C. 2010. Network neutrality: A thematic analysis of policy perspectives across the globe. *Global Media Journal* 3(1): 75–n/a.

Straits Times. 2009, February 15. Singapore tops nation brand perception. *Straits Times*. https://home-in-singapore.sg/Default.aspx?tabid=1767.

Swivel. 2008. Number of books published per year in the U.S. http://www.swivel.com/data_columns/spreadsheet/1534590?page=1 (Inactive).

Teo, T. S. H., and Tan, J. S. 2002. Senior executives' perceptions of business-to-consumer (B2C) online marketing strategies: The case of Singapore. *Internet Research* 12(3): 258–275.

Thrift, N. 1995. A hyperactive world. In R. J. Johnston, P. J. Taylor, and M. J. Watts (eds.), *Geographies of Global Change: Remapping the World in the Late Twentieth Century*. Oxford: Blackwell, pp. 18–35.

———. 2004. Driving in the City. *Theory, Culture and Society* 21:41–59.

Thulin, E., and Vilhelmson, B. 2004. *Virtual Mobility and People's Use of Time and Place: Developments in Sweden*. Paper presented at the Thirtieth Congress of the International Geographical Union (IGU), Glasgow.

Toffler, A. 1970. *Future Shock*. New York: Bantam Books.

———. 1981. *The Third Wave*. New York: Bantam Books.

Tornatzky, L. G., and Fleischer, M. 1990. *The Processes of Technological Innovation*. Lexington, MA: Lexington.

Torrens, P. M. 2008. Wi-Fi Geographies. *Annals of the Association of American Geographers* 98:59–84.

Touraine, A. 1974. *The Postindustrial Society: Tomorrow's Social History: Classes, Conflicts and Culture in the Programmed Society* (L. F. X. Mayhew, trans.). London: Wildwood House.

Townsend, A. 2001. Mobile communications in the twenty-first century city. In B. Brown, N. Green, and R. Harper (eds.), *Wireless World: Social and Interactional Aspects of the Mobile Age*. London: Springer, pp. 62–77.

Tsotsis, A. 2011. Egypt shuts down Noor, Its last ISP. *Techcrunch*. http://techcrunch .com/2011/01/31/reports-egypt-shutting-down-noor-its-last-isp.

UNESCO. 2003. *Cultural and Linguistic Diversity in the Information Society*. Paris: UNESCO. http://unesdoc.unesco.org/images/0013/001329/132965e.pdf.

———. 2008. *International Literacy Statistics: A Review of Concepts, Methodology and Current Data*. Montreal: UNESCO Institute for Statistics.

United Nations. 2012. *Millennium Development Goals Indicators*. http://mdgs.un.org/ unsd/mdg/Data.aspx.

United Nations Development Programme. 2008. *Human Development Report*. http:// hdr.undp.org/en/reports/global/hdr2011.

Urry, J. 2000. *Sociology beyond Societies: Mobilities for the Twenty-First Century*. London: Routledge.

———. 2003. *Global Complexity*. Cambridge: Polity Press.

———. 2007. *Mobilities*. Cambridge: Polity Press.

U.S. Bureau of the Census. 2003. *Statistical Abstract of the United States 2002*. http:// archive.org/details/statisticalabst00censgoog.

———. 2006. *2006 Statistical Abstract: The National Data Book*. http://www.census. gov/compendia/statab/2006/2006edition.html.

———. 2009. *2006 American Community Survey*. http://factfinder2.census.gov.

———. 2011. *2011 Statistical Abstract: The National Data Book*. Table 1054. http:// www.census.gov/compendia/statab.

———. 2012. *Population by Country*. http://www.census.gov/population/interna tional/data/countryrank/rank.php.

U.S. Department of Commerce. 2012. *Quarterly Retail E-Commerce Sales.* http://www.census.gov/retail/mrts/www/data/pdf/ec_current.pdf.

U.S. Department of Education, National Center for Education Statistics. 2011. *The Condition of Education 2011*(NCES 2011-033). http://nces.ed.gov/fastfacts/display .asp?id=80.

U.S. Economic Development Administration. 2002, November. *Comprehensive Economic Development Strategy (CEDS) Guidelines.* Washington, D.C.: U.S. Department of Commerce. http://www.ct.gov/ecd/lib/ecd/CEDS_Flyer_Wht_ Backround%5B2%5D.pdf.

———. 2011. *FY 2011 University Center Economic Development Program Competition: Announcement of Federal Funding Opportunity.* Washington, DC: U.S. Economic Development Administration. http://www.grants.gov/search/search. do?mode=VIEW&oppId=83973.

———. N.d. *Investment Priorities.* http://www.eda.gov/investmentPriorities.htm.

Valleywag. 2007. *The World Map of Social Networks.* http://valleywag.com/273201/ the-world-mapof-social-networks?tag=techdatajunkie.

Vettoretto, L. 2009. A preliminary critique of the best and good practices approach in European spatial planning and policy-making. *European Planning Studies* 17(7): 1067–1083.

Vilhelmson, B., and Thulin, E. 2001. Is regular work at fixed places fading away? The development of ICT-based and travel-based modes of work in Sweden. *Environment and Planning A* 33:1015–1029.

Visser, E.-J., and M. Lanzendorf. 2004. Mobility and accessibility effects of B2C e-commerce: A literature review. *Tijdschrift voor Economische en Sociale Geografie* 95:189–205.

von Hippel, E. 1987. Cooperation between rivals: Informal knowhow trading. *Research Policy* 16:291–302.

Wajcman, J. 2000. Reflections on gender and technology studies: In what state is the art? *Social Studies of Science* 30:447–464.

Walcott, S. E. 2006. High technology clusters in India and China: Divergent paths. *Indian Journal of Economics and Business.* http://www.chinacenter.net/docs/ Susan%20M.%20Walcott.pdf.

Warf, B. 1997. Counterhegemonic discourses and the Internet. *Geographical Review* 87(2): 259–274.

———. 2001. Segueways into cyberspace: Multiple geographies of the digital divide. *Environment and Planning B: Planning and Design* 28:3–19.

Warf, B., and Vincent, B. 2007. Religious diversity across the globe: A geographic exploration. *Social and Cultural Geography* 8:597–613.

Warlaumont, H. 2010, Social networks and globalization: Facebook, YouTube and the impact of online communities on France's protectionist policies. *French Politics* 8(2): 204–214.

Webster, F. 1994. What information society? *Information Society* 10:1–23.

———. 2006. *Theories of the Information Society.* 3rd ed. London: Routledge.

Wellman, B. 2001a. Computer networks as social networks. *Science* 293:2031–2034.

———. 2001b. Physical place and cyberplace: The rise of personalized networking. *International Journal of Urban and Regional Research* 25:227–252.

Wertheim, M. 1999. *The Pearly Gates of Cyberspace: A History of Space from Dante to the Internet*. New York: Norton.

Wilson, M. I. 1995. The office farther back: Business services, productivity, and the offshore back office. In P. T. Harker (ed.), *The Service Productivity and Quality Challenge*. Dordrecht: Kluwer, pp. 203–224.

———. 2001. Location, location, location: The geography of the dot com problem. *Environment and Planning A* 28:59–71.

———. 2003. Chips, bits, and the law: An economic geography of Internet gambling. *Environment and Planning A* 35(7): 1245–1260.

Wilson, M. I., and Corey, K. (eds.). 2000. *Information Tectonics: Space, Place, and Technology in an Electronic Age*. Chichester, UK: Wiley.

———. 2008. The ALERT model: A planning-practice process for knowledge-based urban and regional development. In T. Yigitcanlar, K. Velibeyoglu, and S. Baum (eds.), *Knowledge-Based Urban Development: Planning and Applications in the Information Era*. Hershey, PA: Information Science Reference, pp. 82–100.

———. 2011, January. Approaching ubiquity: Global trends and issues in ICT access and use. *Journal of Urban Technology* 18(1): 7–20.

Woodward, P. 1990. Getting a start in data entry. *China Business Review*, January–February.

Woolley, R., Turpin, T., Marceau, J., and Hill, S. 2008. Mobility matters: Research training and network building in science. *Comparative Technology Transfer and Society* 6(3): 159–186.

World Bank. 2011. Gross national income. *World Development Indicators Database*. http://siteresources.worldbank.org/DATASTATISTICS/Resources/GNIPC.pdf.

Wu, F. 2000. Place promotion in Shanghai, PRC. *Cities* 17(5): 349–361.

Yeung, H. W. C. 2005. Rethinking relational economic geography. *Transactions of the Institute of British Geographers* 30:37–51.

Yeung, H. W. C., and Lin, G. C. S. 2003, April. Theorizing economic geographies of Asia. *Economic Geography* 79(2): 107–128.

Yusuf, S., and Nabeshima, K. 2006. *Postindustrial East Asian Cities: Innovation for Growth*. Washington, DC: World Bank.

Zackariasson, P., and Wilson, T. 2010. Paradigm shifts in the video game industry. *Competitiveness Review* 20(2): 139–151.

Zook, M. A. 1998. The web of consumption: The spatial organization of the Internet industry in the United States. http://socrates.berkeley.edu/~zook/pubs/acsp1998 .html (Inactive).

———. 2001. http://socrates.berkeley.edu/~zook/domain_names (Inactive).

———. 2005. *The Geography of the Internet Industry: Venture Capital, Dot-coms, and Local Knowledge*. Malden, MA: Blackwell.

Zook, M., Dodge, M., Aoyama, Y., and Townsend, A. 2004. New digital geographies: Information, communication, and place. In S. D. Brunn, S. L. Cutter, and J. W. Harrington Jr. (eds.), *Geography and Technology*. Dordrecht: Kluwer, pp. 155–176.

Zook, M. A., and Graham M. 2007. Mapping DigiPlace: Geocoded Internet data and the representation of place. *Environment and Planning B* 34:466–482.

Zuckerman, E. 2011. Civil disobedience and the Arab Spring. http://www.ethanzucker man.com/blog/2011/05/06/civic-disobedience-and-the-arab-spring.

Index

Webster, Frank, 17–18, 69
Wellman, Barry, 59
Western Europe, information society in,
    145–49, 146*t*
Wi-Fi, 56, 58
Wolff, Goetz, 33
working group, for intelligent
    development planning, 241–42
world cities, 33

World Wide Web (WWW), 50
Wu, Tim, 132

Yemen, 171
Yeung, Henry, 207

zero-price rule, 132
Zook, Matthew, 60
Zuckerman, Ethan, 178–79

About the Authors

Kenneth E. Corey is professor of geography and professor of urban and regional planning at Michigan State University, East Lansing. His research and teaching have focused on the role of information and communications technologies in subnational regional planning, especially in Asia, and the application of public policy strategic planning processes to subnational regions. Selected earlier books have included *Urban and Regional Technology Planning: Planning Practice in the Global Knowledge Economy* with Mark I. Wilson (2006) and *The Planning of Change*, 3rd ed., with Warren G. Bennis, Kenneth D. Benne, and Robert Chin (1976).

Aharon Kellerman is professor emeritus at the University of Haifa, Israel, and serves as president of Zefat Academic College, Israel. He further serves as vice president of the International Geographical Union (IGU). His interests include information geography, the Internet, and mobilities. Among his past books are *Daily Spatial Mobilities: Physical and Virtual* (2012), *Personal Mobilities* (2006), and *The Internet on Earth: A Geography of Information* (2002).

Mark I. Wilson is professor and associate director of the School of Planning, Design and Construction at Michigan State University. He also serves as chair of the International Geographical Union's Commission on the Geography of Global Information Society. Research interests include the relationships between people, places, and technology and the planning and impact of mega-events such as the Olympics and World's Fairs. Earlier books with Kenneth E. Corey include *Urban and Regional Technology Planning: Planning Practice in the Global Knowledge Economy* (2006) and the edited volume *Information Tectonics: Space, Place, and Technology in an Electronic Age* (2000).